The Complete Idiot's Guide to a Healthy Cat Reference Card

First-Year Checklist

This card will help you keep close at hand vital information on your cat and where to obtain veterinary care. Keep photos to monitor your cat's growth and development and to create a scrapbook of your kitty's life.

Cat's name: _____

Breed: _____

Sex: _____ Date of sterilization: _____

Date of birth: _____ When cat was obtained: _____

Where cat was obtained: _____

I.D. or microchip number: _____

Distinguising markings and color: _____

First FRCP (3-way) vaccine and exam: _____

Second FRCP (3-way) vaccine and exam: _____

Fecal check for worms: _____

FeLV blood test: _____

Deworming: _____

First FeLV vaccine: _____

Second FeLV vaccine: _____

Rabies vaccine: _____

Other vaccines: _____

Record of Other Vet Visits:

Date	Reason for Visit	Treatment

D1507422

alpha
books

tear here

My Cat's Medical History

Regular Veterinarian: _____

Address: _____

Phone Number: _____

Emergency Veterinary Care: _____

Address: _____

Phone Number: _____

Medications My Cat Takes: Dosage

_____

_____

_____

_____

_____

Medications My Cat Doesn't Take:

_____

_____

_____

Dates of Veterinary Visits and Reason: Treatment

_____

_____

_____

_____

_____

_____

_____

_____

_____

_____

_____

_____

Dates of Dental Cleanings:

_____

_____

_____

_____

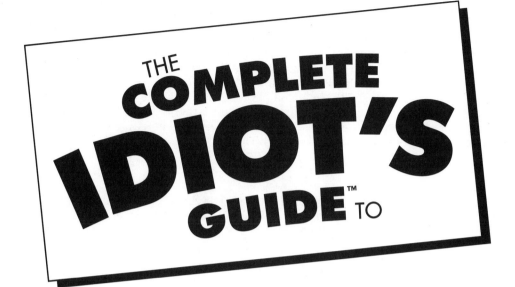

THE
COMPLETE IDIOT'S GUIDE™ TO

A Healthy Cat

by Elaine Wexler-Mitchell, D.V.M., A.B.V.P.

alpha books

A Division of Macmillan General Reference
A Pearson Education Macmillan Company
1633 Broadway, New York, NY 10019-6785

Copyright © 1999 by Elaine Wexler-Mitchell, D.V.M., A.B.V.P.

All rights reserved. No part of this book shall be reproduced, stored in a retrieval system, or transmitted by any means, electronic, mechanical, photocopying, recording, or otherwise, without written permission from the publisher. No patent liability is assumed with respect to the use of the information contained herein. Although every precaution has been taken in the preparation of this book, the publisher and author assume no responsibility for errors or omissions. Neither is any liability assumed for damages resulting from the use of information contained herein. For information, address Alpha Books, 1633 Broadway, 7th Floor, New York, NY 10019-6785.

THE COMPLETE IDIOT'S GUIDE TO & Design are registered trademarks of Macmillan, Inc.

Macmillan General Reference books may be purchased for business or sales promotional use. For information please write: Special Markets Department, Macmillan Publishing USA, 1633 Broadway, New York, NY 10019.

International Standard Book Number: 1-58245-057-9
Library of Congress Catalog Card Number: 99-29615

02 01 00 99   4 3 2 1

Interpretation of the printing code: the rightmost number of the first series of numbers is the year of the book's printing; the rightmost number of the second series of numbers is the number of the book's printing. For example, a printing code of 99-1 shows that the first printing occurred in 1999.

Printed in the United States of America

Note: This publication contains the opinions and ideas of its author. It is intended to provide helpful and informative material on the subject matter covered. It is sold with the understanding that the author and publisher are not engaged in rendering professional services in the book. If the reader requires personal assistance or advice, a competent professional should be consulted.

The author and publisher specifically disclaim any responsibility for any liability, loss or risk, personal or otherwise, which is incurred as a consequence, directly or indirectly, of the use and application of any of the contents of this book.

Alpha Development Team

Publisher
Kathy Nebenhaus

Editorial Director
Gary M. Krebs

Managing Editor
Bob Shuman

Marketing Brand Manager
Felice Primeau

Acquisitions Editors
Jessica Faust
Michelle Reed

Development Editors
Phil Kitchel
Amy Zavatto

Assistant Editor
Georgette Blau

Production Team

Development Editor
Amanda Pisani

Production Editor
Stephanie Mohler

Copy Editor
Lynn Northrup

Cover Designer
Mike Freeland

Illustrator
Kevin Spear

Book Designers
Scott Cook and Amy Adams of DesignLab

Indexer
Johnna Van Hoose Dinse

Layout/Proofreading
Marie Kristine Parial-Leonardo
Linda Quigley

Contents at a Glance

Part 1: Getting Off to a Good Start   **1**

1 Ready or Not, Here I Come!   3
Bringing a new cat into your home.

2 The Lowdown on the Essentials   13
Everyday requirements for your cat.

3 Kitty Boot Camp Begins   25
Basic training for your cat.

Part 2: Basic Health Care   **37**

4 Is Your Cat Having a Bad Hair Day?   39
Does your cat need grooming?

5 How Do You Know if Your Cat Is Sick?   49
Cats are not very good about letting us know how they feel.

6 Annual Health Care for Your Cat   63
Did your cat pass its physical exam?

7 Does Your Cat Need to Go Under the Knife?   75
Elective surgeries to consider for your cat.

8 Vaccinating Your Cat   85
Needles don't really hurt!

9 How to Choose a Veterinarian   95
Finding a veterinarian who you and your cat like.

Part 3: From Kittenhood to Old Age   **105**

10 Kitty Adolescence   107
The trials and tribulations of growing up.

11 Kitty Sex Life   117
They figure out the birds and the bees by themselves!

12 How to Care for a Feline Senior Citizen   127
Your cat's golden years.

Part 4: The Body Systems and Their Diseases   **141**

13 The Cat's Need to Breathe   143
The nose, throat, and lungs are all parts of the respiratory tract.

14 Look Out Stomach, Here It Comes   153
The mouth, stomach, intestines, and liver make up the digestive tract.

15 Is Beauty Only Skin Deep?   167
    The skin and dermatological conditions in cats.

16 Grooving to a Perfect Beat   179
    The heart and blood are part of the cardiovascular system.

17 The Musculoskeletal System   193
    The bones and muscles—and what connects them.

18 It's All Got to Do with Hormones   203
    *The endocrine system of a cat and the major diseases that
    affect it.*

19 Kitty's Got a Lot of Nerve   213
    Diseases of the neurologic system and senses of the cat.

20 It's All About Pee   223
    *The kidneys, bladder, and urethra are parts of the urinary
    tract.*

21 The Dreaded Viruses   235
    The microorganisms without cures.

Part 5: Problems with Cats   245

22 Does Your Cat Play Nicely with Its Friends?   247
    How cats get along with each other.

23 Keeping Kitty Problems from Getting Out of Hand   257
    Behaviors and hazards surrounding cats in your home.

24 Special Considerations for Your Cat   267
    Working your life around your cat.

25 Are There Risks to Cat Ownership?   279
    You should be aware of how a cat could affect your health.

Appendices

A Glossary   287

B Readings and Resources   291

   Index   294

Contents

Part 1: Getting Off to a Good Start   **1**

1 Ready or Not, Here I Come!   **3**

It's Fun to Be Young and Naïve 3
   It's Like Having a Baby 4
   Personality Testing 5
   Keep Kitty Safe 5
The Wisdom in Acquiring an Older Cat 6
   The Benefits of Owning an Adult Cat 6
   Time to Get Adjusted 7
Hey, That's Uncomfortable 7
   The Best Method 8
   Other OK Methods 8
   Methods to Avoid 9
   Skittish Kitty 9
Let's Meet Your New Friends 9
   Who Will Fit in Best 10
   Steps to Integration Success 11
   A Little Privacy Counts 11

2 The Lowdown on the Essentials   **13**

Providing Proper Nutrition to Your Cat 13
   What's in That Can? 14
   Not That Dry Cereal Again 15
   Variety Is the Spice of Life 16
   I Want to Help My Kitty Build Good Teeth and Bones 16
When Your Cat Needs a Stiff Drink 17
   Fresh Water Is a Must 18
   "Alternative" Water Sources 18
Some Time to Be Alone 19
   Timid Kitty 19
   Give Your Cat a Break 19
Using the Potty 20
   Litterbox Styles—Functional to Designer 20
   What's in the Box 21
   Litterbox Maintenance 22
The Dangers of the Great Outdoors 22

3 Kitty Boot Camp Begins   25

You Better Not Bite 26
   "Play" Biting 26
   The Hunt Continues 27
All Cats Need to Scratch Somewhere 27
Keep It in the Box 29
Restful Sleep for All 31
   Cat Naps 31
   Managing the Kitty Night Owl 32
   A Preference for Your Pillow 33
The Counters Are Off-Limits 34
   What's Cooking, Baby? 34
   What Else Can You Do? 34

Part 2: Basic Health Care   37

4 Is Your Cat Having a Bad Hair Day?   39

Start with the Claws 40
Should You Comb or Should You Brush? 41
   Start Off Young and Bribe 41
   Useful Flea Combs 41
   What About Your Longhaired Cat? 42
   Hairballs 43
Ouch, That Hurts! 43
   Matting in Longhaired Cats 43
   Matting in Shorthaired Cats 44
Bath Time!? 44
Give Up? 46
   How to Pick a Groomer 46
   Giving Your Cat a Perfect Hairdo 46

5 How Do You Know if Your Cat Is Sick?   49

Is Your Feline Anorexic? 50
   When Your Cat Won't Eat 50
   How to Make Your Cat Eat 50
   What About Water? 51
Kitty's Nose Is Warm 51
   What Causes a Fever? 52
   What You Should Do if Your Cat Has a Fever 53

When Your Cat Is Acting Funny 53
  Irritability 54
  Failure to Respond 54
Typical Signs of Illness 54
  How Bad Is It? 55
  When to Go to the Emergency Room 55
Checking Out Your Medicine Cabinet 56
  Cleaning Cuts 56
  Ointments and Creams 56
  Cleaning Around the Eyes 56
  Kitty Has an Upset Stomach 56
  Kitty Is Constipated 57
  Kitty Gets Carsick 57
  Kitty Was Just Stung by a Bee 57
  Encounters with Oil 58
A Spoonful of Sugar Helps the Medicine Go Down 58
  There Must Be an Easier Way 58
  Liquid Medication 59
  "Pilling" a Cat 59
  Doesn't It Come Another Way? 60

6 Annual Health Care for Your Cat   63

Did Your Cat Pass Its Physical? 64
  What's Involved in an Annual Exam? 64
  Does It Hurt? 65
All Those Needles! 66
  How Do Vaccines Work? 67
  Have Vaccines Been Linked to Cancer? 67
  Kitty Needs Shots 68
  Adverse Responses to Vaccines 68
A Cheshire Cat Smile 69
  Brushing Your Cat's Teeth 69
  Other Ways to Keep Teeth Clean 70
  Do You Need to Take Your Cat to a Dentist? 70
  Is Dentistry Safe? 71
  Pulling Teeth 71
Parasite Control 71
  When Your Cat Has Worms 71
  Flee, Fleas! 72
  Other Parasites That Can Make Your Cat Itch 74

7 Does Your Cat Need to Go Under the Knife? 75

The Draperies Are in Shreds! 75
   What's Involved in Declawing? 76
   Is Declawing Cruel? 77
   Declawing Alternatives 77
   Side Effects to Declawing 78
Prevent a Paternity Suit 78
   What Is Neutering? 78
   Why Neuter? 78
   Will Neutering Change Your Cat's Personality? 79
   When Should You Neuter? 79
   Cats with Only One Testicle 79
Prevent Unwanted Pregnancy 80
   Is Your Cat a Hussy? 80
   What Is Spaying? 81
   When to Spay 81
   The Benefits of Spaying 81
Hernias in Cats 82
   Types of Hernias 82
   How Serious Is a Hernia? 83
   What if It's Not Fixed? 83

8 Vaccinating Your Cat 85

What You Should Know About Vaccinating Your Cat 86
   Evaluating Risk 86
   How Diseases Are Spread 87
The Core Vaccines 87
   Feline Rhinotracheitis, Calici, and Panleukopenia 88
   Rabies 89
Non-Core Vaccines 90
   Chlamydia 91
   Feline Leukemia Virus 91
   Feline Infectious Peritonitis (FIP) 92
   Bordetella 93
   Ringworm Vaccine 93
   How to Determine if a Vaccine Is Causing a Problem 94

9 How to Choose a Veterinarian   95

Selection Basics 96
   Location 96
   Face Value 96
   Is This a Full-Service Clinic? 97
What About Referrals? 98
Feeling Comfortable 98
   Effective Communications 98
   This Was a Good Experience 99
Should You Look for a Deal? 100
   Do You Get What You Pay For? 100
   Your Cat Is Unique 101
Veterinary Specialists 101
   What Is a Cat Practice? 102
   What if Your Cat Has a Special Problem? 103
   Emergency Providers 103
   Holistic Veterinarians 103

Part 3: From Kittenhood to Old Age   105

10 Kitty Adolescence   107

You Call This Normal? 107
   Oral Personality 108
   Define a Scratching Post 108
   Kittens Just Want to Have Fun 108
Naughty Kitty! 109
   Who's the Boss? 110
   Attack Cat! 111
   Missing the Litterbox 111
   A True "Scaredy Cat" 112
Kitten Growth Stages 112
   Birth to One Month 112
   Four to Six Weeks 112
   Six to Eight Weeks 113
   Eight to Sixteen Weeks 113
   Sixteen to Twenty-Four Weeks 113
Looking for Love 113
   Male "Coming of Age" 114
   Female "Coming of Age" 114

11 Kitty Sex Life   117

The Act 117
   Kitty's in the Mood 118
   A Tomcat's Always in the Mood 118
When Your Cat Is Pregnant 119
   Signs of Pregnancy 119
   What to Look For 120
Can You Terminate Your Cat's Pregnancy? 120
   Ovariohysterectomy 121
   Medical Intervention 121
   Kitty Birth Control 121
The Birth of Kittens 122
   How Long Does Labor Last? 122
   Responding to a Difficult Labor 123
   What Occurs During Labor? 123
   Examining Newborns 124
Raising an Orphan 124
   Feed Me 125
   Potty Me 125
   Keep Me Safe and Warm 125

12 How to Care for a Feline Senior Citizen   127

How Long Will Your Cat Live? 127
   When Is Your Cat Old? 128
   Keeping Up on the Aging Process 129
   Senior Health Care Program 130
What Will Cause Your Kitty's Demise? 130
   Hyperthyroidism 130
   Chronic Renal Failure 131
   Hypertension 131
   Cancer 132
   Diabetes Mellitus 132
   Inflammatory Bowel Disease (IBD) 133
   Liver Disease 133
   Heart Disease 133
   Neurological Disease 134
   Lung Disease 134
Keeping Your Old Friend Comfortable 134
   Hydration 135
   Nutrition 136

Aching Bones *137*
A Comfy Place to Lay *137*
Keep Your Cat from Being Eaten Alive *137*
Knowing When to Let Go 138
Quality of Life *138*
Euthanasia *138*
Are You Crazy to Be This Upset? 139
It's Okay to Cry *139*
Do Others Share the Grief? *139*
Should You Get a New Pet? *139*

Part 4: The Body Systems and Their Diseases   141

13 The Cat's Need to Breathe   143

It' Snot Funny 144
How You Can Cure Your Cat's Sneezing *144*
Allergies *145*
Irritants *145*
Something Stuck Up Kitty's Nose? *145*
How You Can Help Alleviate Sneezing *146*
Your Cat Has a Cold 146
Viral Infections *147*
Bacterial Infections *148*
Fungal Infections *148*
If the URI Doesn't Go Away *149*
Could Your Cat Have Asthma? 149
Signs of Asthma *149*
Treating Asthma *150*
Pneumonia 150
Why Would a Cat Get Pneumonia? *151*
Treating Pneumonia *151*

14 Look Out Stomach, Here It Comes   153

It All Starts in the Mouth 154
Don't Call Me Tuna Breath *154*
Aching Teeth *154*
Look at Those Gums *154*
Kitty's Going to Be Sick 155
Spitting Up Hairballs *156*
Is Your Cat Bulimic? *157*

Does Your Cat Have the Flu? 157
Other Causes of Vomiting 157
What Is a Foreign Body? 158
Getting to the Box 159
Bland Is Better 159
Check Out the Litterbox 159
Inflammatory Bowel Disease (IBD) 160
Intestinal Cancer 161
When Your Kitty Is Constipated 161
Help for Kitty Constipation 161
What Has Stopped Up Your Cat? 162
If Your Cat Is Turning Yellow 162
What Is a Fatty Liver? 162
Other Causes of Liver Disease 164

15 Is Beauty Only Skin Deep?   **167**

Itchy Cat 168
Finding the Cause 168
Allergies Cause Itchiness 168
Atopy 169
Itchiness Caused by Diet 170
Flea Allergy 170
Contact Allergies 170
Zitty Kitty 171
Diagnosing Acne 171
Food Bowl Reaction 172
Clearing the Lesions 172
Ringworm Is Not a Worm 172
Diagnosing Ringworm 173
Treating Ringworm 173
Looking Mangy 173
Does Your Cat Have Ear Mites? 174
Can Your Cat Get Scabies? 175
Cheyletiella 175
Demodex 176
Insect and Spider Bites 176
Bee Stings 176
The Itsy-Bitsy-Spider Bite 176
Cats Can Get Skin Cancer 177
If You See a Lump 177
Sun Exposure and Cancer 178

16 Grooving to a Perfect Beat   179

How the Heart and Circulatory System Work 180
Blood and Bleeding 181
How to Stop Bleeding *181*
Don't Let It Bleed *182*
If Your Cat Is Anemic 182
Causes for Low Red Blood Cell Production *183*
Causes for Red Blood Cell Loss *183*
Diagnosing Anemia *184*
Born with a Bad Heart 184
Leaky Valves *185*
How the Heart Is Evaluated *186*
Treatment for Congenital Heart Disease *186*
Heart Muscle Disease 187
Dilated Cardiomyopathy *187*
Hypertrophic Cardiomyopathy *187*
Restrictive Cardiomyopathy *188*
High Blood Pressure 189
Feline Heartworm Disease 189
How Common Are Heartworms? *189*
Diagnosing Heartworms *190*
Treating Heartworms *190*

17 The Musculoskeletal System   193

It's Hard to Get Up in the Morning 193
Can You Prevent DJD? *194*
Don't Take Two Aspirin and Call in the Morning *195*
It's Broken 196
Assessing the Injury *196*
Putting the Puzzle Together *197*
Is Amputation an Option? *197*
The Healing Process *197*
Sprains and Strains 197
Assessing Soft-Tissue Injuries *198*
The Healing Process *198*
Could Your Cat Tear Its Cruciate? *198*
Born with Strange Bones 199
Beauty Is in the Eye of the Beholder *199*
Kitty Has Extra Toes *200*
Surgery for Bone Deformities *201*

18 It's All Got to Do with Hormones   203

If Your Cat Has a "Hyper" Thyroid 203
The Function of the Thyroid 204
Signs of Hyperthyroidism 204
Treating Hyperthyroidism 204
Drug Therapy 205
Take 'Em Out 205
Nuke Them Out 206
Cats Can Be Diabetics Too 207
Signs of Diabetes 207
Treating Diabetes 208
Uterine Infections 209
Signs of Pyometra 209
Treating Pyometra 209
Cats Can Get Breast Cancer 210
Prevention 210
If You Feel a Lump 210
Treating Breast Cancer 210

19 Kitty's Got a Lot of Nerve   213

Eyes See You 214
Ouch! A Scratch on the Eye 214
Kitty Pinkeye 215
Stop Crying 216
Should You Worry About Blindness? 216
Kitties and Convulsions 216
Diagnosing Seizures 217
Treating Seizures 218
Born with Neurologic Problems 219
Cats with Bad Backs 220
Tests for the Spine 220
Traumatic Experience 220
Kitties with Slipped Disks 221
Cauda Equina Syndrome 221

20 It's All About Pee   223

Lower Urinary Tract Disease 224
Theories Are Changing 224
Blood in the Urine 224
How to Make Your Cat More Comfortable 225
What About Diet? 226

Kitty Can't Pee! 226
   It's Gonna Cost How Much? 226
   Three Strikes and You're Out 227
Is This Cat Stoned? 227
   The Origin of Stones 228
   How Stones Are Diagnosed 228
   Treatment for Stones 229
   Can Stones Recur? 229
Kitty's Kidneys 229
   Signs of Dysfunctional Kidneys 230
   Kidney Infection 230
   Breed-Specific Kidney Disease 231
   Old Kidneys 231
   Specific Treatments 232
   Is the Clock Ticking? 233

21 The Dreaded Viruses   **235**

Feline Leukemia Virus 235
   Can You Test Your Cat for FeLV? 236
   What Does FeLV Do? 236
   Protection Against the Virus 236
   Coping with FeLV 237
Feline Immunodeficiency Virus 237
   How Cats Get Infected 237
   Diagnosing FIV 238
   The Impact of FIV 238
   Care for FIV-Positive Cats 239
Feline Infectious Peritonitis 239
   So What Is FIP? 239
   Building a Diagnosis of FIP 240
   Dealing with FIP 241
   What About the FIP Vaccine? 241
   Decreasing Risk 241
   Filling the Loss 242
Could Your Cat Be Rabid? 242
   Vaccinating Against Rabies 242
   Signs of Rabies 242
"Parvo" for Cats 243
   Signs of Panleukopenia 243
   Testing for Panleukopenia 243
   What's the Prognosis? 243

Part 5: Problems with Cats — 245

22 Does Your Cat Play Nicely with Its Friends? — 247

How Many Is Too Many? 248
  The Top Cat 248
  Young or Old? 249
  Male or Female? 249
  The Transition 249
  And the Answer Is… 250
The Problem with Strays 250
  Really Lost, or Just Cruisin'? 251
  All in the Family 251
  Can a Stray Fit In? 252
No Trespassing 252
  An Uninvited Guest 252
  Discouraging Trespassers 252
Kitty-to-Kitty Conflicts 253
  War Wounds and Battle Scars 253
  Dealing with Abscesses 254
  Reducing the Likelihood of Abscesses 254
  Bigger than a Cat 255

23 Keeping Kitty Problems from Getting Out of Hand — 257

When Your Good Kitty Does Bad Things 257
  Licking 258
  Kitty's Being Mean! 258
  House-soiling 259
  Turn It Down! 261
The War on Fleas 261
  Available Ammunition 262
  Getting the Best Guns 262
  Other Casualties to Consider 263
'Tis the Season 263
  Summertime 264
  Trick or Treat 264
  Christmas and Chanukah 264

24 Special Considerations for Your Cat   267

The Suitcases Are Out; You Know What That Means 267
Safe and Secure 268
Cars, Ick! 269
Flying the Friendly Skies 270
A Room with a View 271
Kitty Needs to Stay Home 271
Boarding's Not That Bad 271
Pet Sitters 272
The Big Move 273
Who Are These Strangers? 274
Getting Used to the New Digs 274
If Your Cat Is Lost 275
Call Out the Search Team 275
Could There Be Another Explanation? 275
If You Die, What Happens to Your Cat? 276
Can You Count on Your Family? 276
Check Out Your Will 277

25 Are There Risks to Cat Ownership?   279

Gesundheit! 280
How DO You Know It's the Cat? 280
Less-Allergenic Breeds 280
Making Life More Bearable 280
Honey, It's Your Turn to Scoop 281
How Cats Become Infected 282
How Humans Are Infected 282
Treatment for Toxoplasmosis 283
Cat Scratch Fever Really Exists 284
Signs of Cat Scratch Fever 284
Diagnosis and Treatment 284
The Joys of Cat Ownership 286

Appendices

A Glossary   **287**

B Readings and Resources   **291**

Index   **294**

Foreword

If cats could talk to us, they'd probably tell us that living with a complete idiot is risky business; such a person can't possibly provide the care necessary to assure the optimal health and well-being of the cats in his charge. They'd probably say that knowledgeable humans make the best companions. And if they had a list of books they wish humans would read, I suspect that *The Complete Idiot's Guide to a Healthy Cat* would rank high at the top. This outstanding volume is lighthearted and humorous, entertaining and easy-to-read, but packed with practical and important information.

Do you want to get a cat? Should you get an inexperienced kitten or a seasoned adult? This book gives you the pros and cons of each choice. Time to get a litterbox? How many and what kinds should you consider? This book lets you know. What about the intricacies of cat care? How should you choose a veterinarian, and when should you take your cat for vaccines? What kind of food should you provide, and how often should you offer it? Do you have grooming questions? What about fleas? Behavior problems? The list goes on and on; are you getting confused? This book will help clear the confusion.

Dr. Wexler-Mitchell's years of experience as a practicing feline veterinarian have given her the ability to make this book both informative and readable. She understands what cat lovers need to know, and she explains it in a way that even complete idiots can comprehend. I've had the pleasure to work closely with her in her leadership roles in the American Association of Feline Practitioners and the Academy of Feline Medicine, and I've seen how actively involved she is with feline medicine's cutting edge. She definitely has the knowledge to provide the most reliable and up-to-date information available. Even though readers might be clueless regarding cat care when they begin this book, they certainly won't be by the time they finish it. It's just what the cat ordered. So read it; your cat will be much healthier and happier if you do!

Dr. James R. Richards
Director, Cornell Feline Health Center

Introduction

There are approximately 66 million pet cats in the United States, and the number of pet cats has exceeded that of pet dogs throughout the 1990s. The fast-paced, on-the-run lifestyle that many of us lead makes a cat the perfect four-legged companion. Domestic pet cats share many traits with their wild, big-cat brothers and sisters, but they have adapted to live in our homes. A cat's ability to hunt for food, find shelter, and readily reproduce in the wild, however, has also created problems worldwide with millions of feral cats.

You have opened this book with the hopes of increasing your knowledge of cats and their care. The value of a pet cat is not in the purchase price, but in the space it occupies in your heart. Whether you have a Persian with long, flowing hair, or a domestic shorthair with tabby patches, day-to-day husbandry is generally the same. Differences in home care may depend on the number of cats that live in your home. Some of you may only share your home with one cat, while others may own more than they care to admit.

In *The Complete Idiot's Guide to a Healthy Cat,* you will find out about the different life stages of the cat and what you should expect as a cat develops from a kitten to a senior citizen. I will discuss the aspects of home cat care and training your cat to be a model roommate. You will learn about routine health care and working with a veterinarian, and you will learn about many of the common diseases and problems that can affect cats. This knowledge will allow you to make better decisions about your cat's health, because you will have a better understanding of what is normal and what is not.

Fortunately, cat ownership is easy and relatively problem-free. The information on diseases and behavior problems contained in this book are not meant to intimidate you, but merely to serve as a reference in case of need. Cat ownership is a wonderful experience!

The Extras

To enhance the presentation of materials in this book, you'll find several boxes scattered throughout the text:

Kitty Ditty

These boxes define words that may be unfamiliar to you and clarify information about cats.

Worth a Paws

In these boxes you'll find important tips on cat care.

Avoid CATastrophe

These boxes provide information that is must-have knowledge for the cat owner.

Meow Wow

Look in these boxes for trivia and interesting tidbits on cats.

Acknowledgments

I was not sure how much work would be involved with the writing of this book, but writing while continuing a full-time veterinary practice was quite a juggle and a struggle. I want to thank my husband, Howard, for his encouragement on this project and his never-ending positive attitude. He often gives me the extra nudge to excel at ventures I undertake.

The staff at The Cat Care Clinic all rallied behind this project, and Sarah Reed, one of my technicians, was instrumental in helping me get it all together. I would also like to thank Dr. Kristi Fisher who helped make sure that I stayed on track, and my friend Lynne Etkins, who helped ensure that this all made sense.

I would also like to thank my parents who supported my decision to become a veterinarian and helped me to achieve my dream.

Trademarks

All terms mentioned in this book that are known to be or are suspected of being trademarks or service marks have been appropriately capitalized. Alpha Books and Macmillan General Reference cannot attest to the accuracy of this information. Use of a term in this book should not be regarded as affecting the validity of any trademark or service mark.

Part 1
Getting Off to a Good Start

It is easy to become a cat owner, and this is one of the beauties of having cats as pets. There are some basic needs that you need to provide to your feline friend, and in return you will be supplied with love and entertainment. You may have expectations about how you want your cat to act, and believe it or not, you can have control over cat behaviors.

Just like no two people are alike, neither are any two cats. We do know that cats are creatures of habit, and you want to make sure that those habits are ones that fit harmoniously into your household. Understanding and recognizing what motivates a cat really helps in the integration process.

The next few chapters will teach you about what a cat needs from you. It will also teach you about how you can mold your cat into the perfect companion!

CUDDLES

Chapter 1

Ready or Not, Here I Come!

In This Chapter

➤ Starting with a kitten

➤ Starting with an adult

➤ How to hold your cat

➤ Introducing a new addition to your household

Over 66 million pet cats live in households in the United States. What is it about these creatures that has made them the most popular pet in the last decade? Is it their grace and beauty? Or is it their ability to be somewhat independent and fit into our busy lifestyles? Regardless of the reasons, it is cool to be a cat owner, and you don't have to be a crazy "cat person."

You have decided to become a cat owner and are about to embark on selecting your perfect companion. You would like to think that you have the upper hand in the decision to own a cat, but in reality, often it is the cat that chooses you. Each cat has a unique personality and different behavior patterns, and hopefully you will find the perfect fit for your household.

It's Fun to Be Young and Naïve

Everyone knows that kittens are adorable and fun, but they also require more work and training than older cats. When you are trying to decide between getting a kitten or an adult cat, you should think about the time and energy that you will be able to commit to the new pet.

Avoid CATastrophe

Although they love the taste of milk, cats are fairly lactose–intolerant. They lack the enzyme needed to properly digest the sugar found in cow's milk, so more than a taste or two will usually cause diarrhea. Cats, like humans, like to ingest things that are not good for them!

It's Like Having a Baby

Kittens younger than six weeks may not be fully weaned or mature enough to leave their mothers. If you are considering a kitten younger than six weeks of age, it is important to find out whether or not the animal is capable of eating solid food. You will also want to know what it will eat. I would advise against adopting a kitten younger than 6 weeks unless there are special circumstances, such as abandonment.

Kittens are born blind and do not open their eyes until they are 10 to 14 days old. If you find a kitten, and its eyes are closed, then you will have to perform the duties that the mother cat would normally perform. These duties include keeping the kitten warm and safe, bottle-feeding it with proper cat milk replacer, and "pottying" the kitten. Kittens do not know how to eliminate on their own until they are about four weeks old, and their mothers stimulate them to eliminate by licking their genitalia. This action can be replicated by using a cotton ball or tissue soaked in warm water and gently wiping the kitten's genitalia.

Four-week-old kittens can start eating soft food on their own and should be able to use a litterbox. By 6 weeks, a kitten has its baby teeth and should be able to eat dry kitten food.

Six-week-old kittens like these are always looking for things to get into.

Kittens teethe and chew on things, so you need to make your home "kitty safe." This means picking up objects that the kitten could potentially chew or swallow such as buttons, coins, rubber bands, and newspaper ties. Kittens also occasionally chew on telephone and electrical cords, so these items need to be monitored. Kittens are small enough to get into and under many things that you may want to keep them out of, so you may need to limit the areas that the kitten has access to.

Despite these considerations, it is wonderful to watch a small kitten grow up and develop into a cat. Unfortunately, this happens in a relatively short period of time, and it is over before you know it! On the other hand, acquiring an adult cat can be an equally rewarding experience.

Personality Testing

The most important quality in your cat is its personality. You can tell a lot about personality even with kittens. To test a cat's personality, hold it in your arms and see if it is relaxed or tense. Cradle it upside down in your arms like a baby, and again see how it reacts. If you are looking for an affectionate cat, and the one you are testing will not let you hold it for more than a second, you may want to reconsider your choice or plan that you will have to work on training the animal to relax.

The next test is to touch the animal's ears, open its mouth, and touch its toes. Again, the more the cat is willing to let you handle it, the more likely it is to be generally trusting of you. If you put the cat down and walk away, is it interested in you? Does it follow you? I do think that there is chemistry between certain cats and certain people. Is the kitten interested and playful? Test this by throwing a small toy, or even make one with a ball of paper. All these factors will give you some ideas about what the cat's personality is like.

Worth a Paws

Kittens are not impressed when you buy them expensive toys to play with. A kitten may get as much enjoyment batting around a wad of paper or tinfoil as it would with a large plastic ball with a bell inside. Before investing in fancy toys or accessories for your cat, buy a few reasonably priced items and see which holds the animal's interest.

Keep Kitty Safe

The kitten should always be transported inside a carrier when you bring it home. Although the animal may cry and scratch when in the carrier, it is for its own good as well as yours. You may feel like you have good control of a kitten by carrying it, but if startled, the digging of claws into your arms may cause you to release it. If this occurs outside there are many risks. There is also danger if you are driving in your car and the cat is not in a carrier. If you slam on the brakes and the cat goes flying, it could end up under your feet.

You should not leave a new kitten unattended when you first bring it home. If it is small, it could end up getting stuck or lost somewhere. When you can't supervise the kitten, confine it in a small room with a litterbox, food, and water. You want the cat to become acclimated to its new surroundings. You also want to be sure that it knows where a litterbox is and that it is eating and drinking. Be sure to take the kitten to the area of the litterbox every few hours until you feel comfortable that it will go there by itself.

The first time a kitten leaves its familiar home, mother, and littermates is a scary experience. When you get home, don't be disappointed if the kitten is not as active and friendly as it was when you first saw it. It is adjusting to its new environment and this usually lasts a day or two. It also may not eat or drink normally at first.

The Wisdom in Acquiring an Older Cat

Adult cats need good homes too. There are many reasons why adult cats are available for ownership. These include:

➤ The owners move and cannot bring them into their new homes.

➤ The owner dies.

➤ Retired purebred show cats often need homes because breeders need to make room for new cats.

➤ After acquiring a cat, some people find out that they (or their family members) are allergic to cats.

➤ If a cat is not getting along with other cats or pets in the household, it might be better off in a new home.

➤ Cat ownership is just too much trouble for some people.

The latter cause is sad but all too common. Deciding to acquire a cat should be a commitment to care for the animal for its entire life, which may last 13 or more years.

The Benefits of Owning an Adult Cat

Busy working people, Good Samaritans, senior citizens, and families with young children are all good candidates for adult cat ownership. When you get an adult cat, there is little question as to what kind of haircoat the animal will have, what it will look like, and what its personality is like. By getting an adult cat you miss the teething phases and usually the inappropriate play phases which could potentially cause you injury through biting and scratching.

Kittens' immune systems are not as well developed as those of adult cats, so they are also more susceptible to infections. They require more routine health care during their first year of life than an older cat would. This includes initial vaccines, viral and fecal testing, and spaying or neutering; so the health care costs for a kitten are generally higher than those for an adult cat for the first year.

Time to Get Adjusted

Adult cats are intimidated by changes in their lives. The first day that you bring a new cat into your home, don't be surprised if it heads right under a bed or behind a sofa. It may be harder to lose an adult cat in your home due to its size, but even full-grown cats are capable of wedging themselves into tight spots when they want to hide. Be patient and give the cat a chance to become comfortable with its new surroundings.

As with kittens, you should consider confining a new adult in a room with a litterbox, food, and water for the first day or two when you can't be home supervising it. This way you can monitor habits and be sure that the cat is using the litterbox.

Hey, That's Uncomfortable

Holding and carrying a cat properly is important. Of course you don't want to injure the cat; in turn, if the cat feels insecure it may injure you trying to get away. There are various techniques that work well, and you can master them with practice and experience. Cats seem to have an understanding about the abilities of children and are willing to tolerate more than they normally would with you. If you have children, be sure to work with them and teach them how to handle the cat.

Meow Wow

Whiskers have been called the "sixth sense." The anatomical term for whisker is "tactile vibrissae." These touch sensors are utilized for stalking, measuring, and warning of unseen obstacles. Whiskers are so delicately sensitive that if they move 1/2000th of the width of a human hair, they will send signals to the brain. Whiskers detect wind and reflected air currents, and this information helps the cat to locate its prey. If a cat loses its whiskers, it must depend more on sight for getting around and hunting. Damaged whiskers lead to misjudgment and fumbling. In dim light, cats utilize their whiskers for navigation.

The whiskers and tail of a cat are very sensitive to touch. Do not hold or pull a cat's whiskers. A cat's tail is an extension of its spine, and if you pull too hard, you can cause damage to the end of the spinal column where important nerves controlling urination and defecation are found.

The Best Method

The best way to pick up a cat is to first extend your hand and allow the cat to sniff it. This gives the cat a chance to know who you are. Next scratch the cat between the ears and along the cheekbones or chin. Approaching the cat from the side is less threatening to the animal. Put one hand firmly behind the armpits of the front legs and lift the animal up, then scoop up the hind legs with your other hand from below. Press the cat gently against your body for additional support. A cat that feels secure is less likely to struggle.

This is an example of the proper way to safely hold a cat.

Other OK Methods

It is acceptable to hold a cat, even an adult, by the scruff of its neck. This is the hold that the mother cat used on it as a kitten. Most cats will actually relax as a natural response to being held in this manner. A large cat may be difficult to support well in this way, and you will need to cradle its hind end. If a cat is under something and you want to pull it out, grabbing the scruff and pulling is the safest way.

You can cradle a cat in your arms by scooping it up with one arm at the front of its chest, and the other arm behind its tail. This position should also support the hind legs. For more security, you can hold the hind legs in this position with your hands.

Cats can be cradled upside down like a baby, if they are tolerant. Upside-down cradling is a very submissive posture, and many dominant-personality cats will not allow it.

Another way to hold a cat is over your shoulder like you are burping a baby. In this position, place one hand over the cat's shoulders and the other behind its tail and hold its hind legs.

Methods to Avoid

Cats are pretty tough, but most humans could pull a leg out of joint with force. If you need to pull a cat out from under something, do not pull it out by a limb.

Some cats like to ride on their owner's shoulders, and this is cute when they are kittens, but it doesn't feel good when they grow up and then jump. The animal's weight and claws can be quite uncomfortable. Be careful if you allow a cat to jump or climb up on you.

Skittish Kitty

Each cat has a different tolerance level with regard to being held. Some cats live to be held and carried around. Some will run the other way if they think that you are coming for them. Others will tolerate your attempt at temporary dominance, and then scoot away at the first possible opportunity.

If you have a cat that is scared or injured, and you don't feel comfortable picking it up in a conventional manner, you might try placing a towel or blanket over it first, and then tying to pick it up. When cats cannot see you, they often calm down. For safety reasons, you might then try to transfer the animal to a carrier or box.

When working with a cat, it is important to be gentle but firm. Cats are quite adept at reading their owner's body language. If you are not confident about your ability to pick up or hold a cat, the cat knows it too and will take advantage of the situation.

Let's Meet Your New Friends

Cats are creatures of habit, and they generally would prefer that things stay the way they are rather than face change. The same holds true when introducing a new cat to a household where other pets reside. This is another situation when patience is a must. Sometimes all animal parties involved are amenable to the addition, and other times your former best friend will have nothing to do with you or the new cat.

Cat owners interested in acquiring another cat often ask me whether the sex of the new addition matters. As difficult as it may be for you to find the perfect cat to fit with you, it is even more difficult to try to pick out a friend for an existing cat. I always tell people that they should be getting another cat because they want it, not because they think that their cat needs a friend. If you do get another cat, and it does not get along with your original cat, you still need to be responsible for it. Generalizations can be made that cats of opposite sex in the household get along better, but again each situation is unique.

Meow Wow

Some interesting pet owner demographics to consider: Forty-seven percent of cat owners own two or more cats. Sixty-one percent of cat owners do not have children.

Avoid CATastrophe

Even if a new kitten looks healthy, the stress of moving to a new home can suppress its immune system. It is very common for a kitten to develop an upper respiratory infection within 7 to 10 days of being acquired. If this occurs, have the kitten examined by a veterinarian.

Who Will Fit in Best

Many potential cat owners shy away from acquiring an additional male cat due to fears about urine spraying. This is not a common problem, especially in cats that are neutered before they reach puberty. Female cats can spray too, but they rarely do. Both males and females may eliminate outside of the cat box to mark territory or to show their displeasure in certain instances. It is very uncommon for cats to spray or eliminate inappropriately if they live in single-cat households, but the addition of a new cat can trigger this behavior.

I think it's easier to bring a kitten into a household with an existing adult cat or cats. In this situation, the territory and dominance of the resident cats are established, and they are not as threatened as they would be if they had to compete with another adult cat. Senior cats may not tolerate a kitten jumping on and bugging them, and they usually keep their distance. It is a good idea to put a "young pest" away in another room if needed to give an older cat a break.

For health reasons, it is recommended that a new cat or kitten be examined by a veterinarian before coming into direct contact with other cats. It should be tested for Feline Leukemia, a potentially fatal and contagious feline virus. If the cat is 6 months or older, it should be tested for Feline Immunodeficiency Virus as well. If the new cat came from a shelter, large multi-cat household, or cattery, it would be wise to isolate it from other cats for at least a week in an attempt to control the spread of any contagious diseases.

Steps to Integration Success

Jealousy is a problem to deal with whenever a new cat joins the household. Dogs and other cats will be disappointed if they have to share you with somebody else. Giving the resident animals lots of human attention is essential for a smooth transition.

The first time you bring in a new cat, you should confine it to a room, or keep it in its carrier for at least a few minutes, so that the other animals can sniff and begin an introduction. If there is growling or hissing from either side, talk gently and try to calm the animals.

If you have a dog and are introducing a cat, you will want to have the dog on a leash. Your new cat may have never seen a dog before, or your dog may never have had a cat in the house before, and it is hard to predict how either party will react. Most dogs are just curious and may quickly approach a cat, but doing so can scare the cat—a lot! This type of situation needs to be controlled. Don't leave dogs and cats alone unsupervised until you're sure that neither side will cause problems.

Dogs like to eat cat food and cats like to eat dog food. Everyone always wants what the other guy has. It is not dangerous for this to happen, but each species has different nutritional needs that must be adequately met. Another point to mention is that dogs like to get into litterboxes and eat cat feces, so getting a covered box or placing it in an area less accessible to the dog is recommended. Why does this unappetizing habit occur? Probably because cat diets have higher fat and protein contents, which leads to richer wastes!

There is no perfect acclimation period with animals. If after a short confined introduction all parties seem to be coping, the next step is face-to-face introduction. Let the new cat out of the room or carrier and see what happens. Until you feel completely comfortable with how all parties are handling the situation, the new addition should be confined when not being supervised.

A Little Privacy Counts

Any resident cats should not be immediately forced to share their food, water, or litterbox with the new addition. This is another reason for temporary confinement. In a multi-cat household, competing for food can cause problems such as weight gain and aggression.

Litterbox hygiene is always important, but even more so when there is more than one cat. The best preventive measure to encourage proper litterbox usage is having at least one litterbox per cat. Although two cats may both use two boxes, two boxes soil more slowly than one. A minimum of daily scooping is needed to keep things clean.

The Least You Need to Know

➤ Raising a kitten is a great experience, but requires more work and expense than starting off with an adult cat.

➤ When you acquire an adult cat, you have a better idea of what living with the cat is going to be like.

➤ There are various methods for holding a cat, and making the cat feel secure is important.

➤ Introducing a new cat into a household with other pets should be a controlled process that will minimize stress and disease passage.

Chapter 2

The Lowdown on the Essentials

> **In This Chapter**
>
> ➤ How and what to feed your cat
>
> ➤ Making sure your cat has plenty of water
>
> ➤ How to be sure to give your kitty enough privacy
>
> ➤ Should you let your cat venture outdoors?

Now that you have your cat and have brought it into your home, you need to make sure that you adequately provide for the animal's essential needs. In the wild, cats can adapt to their environment by hunting for food, seeking safety by climbing trees, and finding shelter against the elements. Confined in our homes, cats need help to live harmoniously in our environment.

If you provide the basics of food, water, and shelter, you will be starting your cat off correctly. Monitoring the ways in which the cat utilizes these basic provisions will give you a good idea about the animal's health. Cats are creatures of habit, so any changes in their habits warrants investigation.

Providing Proper Nutrition to Your Cat

Food has a high ranking on a cat's top-10 list. It ranks higher than affection from owners, cravings for catnip, and clawing the furniture! Food is a treat that some owners use to bribe their cats and to get their attention. There is a psychological importance of food to the owner and to the pet, but what about the basic need for food?

Kitty Ditty

The **Association of American Feed Control Officials** (AAFCO) is the organization responsible for creating practical nutritional recommendations for pet food. Any food that you feed your cat should at least meet these minimum standards, and if it does, it will say so on the label.

Is there a magic formula by which to feed your cat? Do you feed canned food, dry food, semi-moist, or a combination? Do you need to be worried about preservatives? Won't your cat get bored if it eats the same thing every day? Can both young and old cats eat the same food? How much should I feed? All of these questions are certainly relevant to making the right feeding decisions.

I am always overwhelmed each time I walk through the pet food aisles of a grocery store or pet supply store. The massive variety of products available seems to grow daily. The pet food market is a multi-billion-dollar business, and lots of companies want a piece of the pie.

There are three categories of cat foods: premium, grocery store, and generic. I would not recommend feeding generic food because often it does not meet the standards of the *Association of American Feed Control Officials* (AAFCO). There are many good brands of food sold in grocery stores, and almost all of these meet the proper standards. The main differences between grocery and premium diets are the ways in which the nutrition is achieved. Premium diets contain higher-quality, more digestible ingredients, which decrease the amount of feces the kitty produces.

Worth a Paws

Once opened, a can of cat food stays fresh for about three days if kept refrigerated. Most cats do not like cold food, so warming refrigerated food in the microwave for a few seconds can help increase its odor and palatability. (Make sure you take it out of the can and heat it in a microwave-safe container!)

What's in That Can?

Cats are carnivores, meaning they eat meat, so they need high levels of protein in their diets. Some people call canned food "meat," but it does not necessarily contain more meat than dry food. Most cats like the taste and smell of canned food, but they do not require canned food to achieve good nutrition. Feeding canned food is an owner's preference.

I think it's important for cats to eat some dry food so that the owner is not a slave, forced to come home and open a can. Canned food is more of a nuisance to feed, and cats that eat canned food tend to build more plaque and tartar on their teeth than those that eat only dry food. The cost of canned food is significantly higher than dry, and canned food is about 85 percent water.

For picky eaters, cats that need to gain weight, or those that need higher water consumption, canned food may actually be a better choice. Cats that are prone to urinary tract problems may benefit from eating canned food due to the high water content, which helps produce more dilute urine. Owners of cats with urinary tract infections should avoid feeding these animals seafood products that contain high levels of minerals such as magnesium because this can contribute to the formation of crystals in the urine.

Not That Dry Cereal Again

Using a feeder that only needs to be filled once a week makes it easy to feed your cat if it does not overeat. We tend to think of cats as grazers that eat a few bites of food at a time, but even grazers can get fat if they consume too many calories. Dry food can be very concentrated, and feeding more than 1 cup a day of some brands to your cat can cause obesity. Most adult, indoor cats tend to gain weight if their bowls are kept constantly full. When deciding how much dry food to feed, check with the food label or consult with your veterinarian. Feeding two smaller meals daily is a good way to control food intake.

Meow Wow

The tongue of the cat is uniquely designed to detect tastes, temperature, and food texture. Different taste buds are specific to different sensations. Sour, bitter, and salty tastes can be detected, but cats apparently cannot detect sweetness.

People today are more aware of their own nutrition and health, and they want to watch what their pets eat. Most dry cat foods are chemically stabilized and preserved. The safety of these chemicals is constantly challenged, and pet food manufacturers defend their safety. A few companies make "all-natural" foods that contain no synthetic ingredients. Whether these diets will improve your cat's health and longevity has not been proven. Fortunately, I have seen many cats that have lived into their 20s and have eaten regular, commercial dry foods their entire lives.

The most common feline feeding regiment is feeding a little canned food once or twice a day, and leaving out some dry food during the intervening periods. Owners might feel like they are spoiling their cats a bit when they do this, but this method is good if portions and between-meal treats are controlled.

If you watch your cat eat, you may see that it does not chew much on the dry food. Some cats ingest too much dry food at once and regurgitate. Cats with this tendency need to be fed smaller portions. They can also benefit from mixing in some canned food, or from adding some water to the dry food. Another strategy to decrease regurgitation is to feed a larger-sized kibble that must be chewed before being swallowed. This slows eating and decreases regurgitation.

Variety Is the Spice of Life

Some veterinary nutritionists feel that a cat should be given some variety of foods during its lifetime, but cats can do well without being fed a smorgasbord of different foods. They do not know that there are unlimited choices available for their feeding pleasure. To try to prevent your cat from becoming too finicky, limit the flavors and types of food that you offer. You can certainly appeal to its preferences, but try to remember who the boss is! If you do choose to change foods, a gradual introduction is recommended. This will decrease the chance of problems.

Avoid CATastrophe

Chocolate, onions, and caffeine are toxic to cats. Although one lick may not be dangerous, cats lack the liver enzymes necessary for metabolizing these products. Larger quantities can build to problematic and poisonous levels in the blood.

Just like humans, there are some cats that have food allergies and cannot eat certain protein sources. If your cat vomits after eating certain foods, look at the ingredients and try offering something different the next time. Many cat foods have similar ingredients, so you may need to consult with your veterinarian for help in finding a suitable diet.

I Want to Help My Kitty Build Good Teeth and Bones

Kittens, adult cats, and senior cats all have varying nutritional requirements. Kittens should eat kitten food for the first 6 to 12 months of their lives. Kitten- or growth-formula foods are generally more calorie-dense, and have higher levels of vitamins and minerals. Senior cats are usually less active and diets formulated for them contain fewer calories, more fiber, and less protein. Adult cats do well on maintenance diets, unless they are pregnant, nursing, or have a medical problem that requires special foods.

Meow Wow

Many "light" feline diets are available for overweight cats. All light diets are not equal, however, and some brands have two or three times the amount of calories per cup than others. To safely put your cat on a diet, create a plan with your veterinarian, stick with it, and take the cat back to the doctor for follow-up checks.

Many owners are faced with the dilemma of having to feed a kitten and an adult simultaneously. The solution to this problem lies in the weight of the adult. If the adult cat is trim, then leaving kitten food out is not a problem. If the adult is over-weight, then the adult maintenance food should be portioned, and the kitten should be supplemented on the side.

Most special and prescription diets are fine for all adult cats but may not be suitable for growing kittens or seniors. Discuss these individual feeding issues with your veterinarian, so that you can tailor a proper feeding program to your cat.

When Your Cat Needs a Stiff Drink

The only beverage that a cat needs to drink is water. As I mentioned in Chapter 1, cats like milk, but it is not good for them since they cannot digest it properly. The amount of water that a cat will drink in a day can vary. Factors that affect water consumption are diet, temperature, and activity level.

Cats that eat primarily canned foods will not drink as much as those that eat dry foods. This is because canned foods have a high water content. Cats normally are not big water drinkers, and they produce very concentrated urine.

An average cat will consume up to 8 ounces of water daily. During high temperatures or after a thorough grooming, a cat may drink more. A cat's body, like that of other small mammals, is 60 percent water.

Unlike humans who know that they need to stay hydrated when they are sick, cats do not drink enough when they are ill and they quickly become dehydrated. Cats often need treatment with injectable fluids to restore their hydration when they are under the weather because it is difficult to make them drink or force enough water orally.

Meow Wow

The sense of taste in cats is probably more sensitive than our own. Some researchers believe that cats like to drink out of running spigots because they prefer fresher-tasting water. If you have a cat that demands you turn on the faucet, you are not alone!

Many cats like to drink fresh running water because it tastes better to them.

Fresh Water Is a Must

Fresh water should be supplied to your cat daily, and water bowls should be cleaned every day. You should subconsciously monitor your cat's water intake, especially as the animal matures. If you notice that your cat is drinking more water than it usually does, this can be a warning sign of diabetes mellitus or kidney problems.

If you do not like the taste of your tap water, consider sharing your bottled water with your cat. Bottled water is a profitable industry, and there are companies today that are producing "designer water" for cats. Distilled water may benefit cats that are prone to urinary tract problems that cause crystals to readily form in their urine. Distilling water removes the minerals that are normally present.

"Alternative" Water Sources

Some cats develop the unpleasant habit of drinking out of toilet bowls. This is only dangerous if you have chemicals automatically dispensed into your toilet water. To discourage this behavior, close the lids on toilets or keep bathroom doors closed.

Drinking out of swimming pools is also a habit with some cats. If your cat goes outside it is difficult to prevent this behavior, but don't worry, the amount of chlorine in this water is not dangerous.

Some Time to Be Alone

Privacy is very important to your cat. Even the most sociable cat needs some time alone. Cats typically like privacy when they groom and when they eliminate. Some cats like privacy when they eat, but others eat more readily when their owners are around.

Proper placement of the litterbox in your home is essential for good usage. Ideally the cat should feel comfortable and undisturbed when it eliminates. Often elimination problems arise when a cat is unhappy about the location of its box. Areas where owners want the box and where the cat wants the box may not be the same. Most cats do not want to eat and eliminate in the same area. Let's face it, you should give in to your cat's preferences.

Bedrooms, secondary bathrooms, and garages are good locations for litterboxes. Many owners want to put litterboxes in laundry rooms. This can work for some cats, but others may be frightened by the noises of the washer and dryer and may choose to eliminate elsewhere.

Timid Kitty

Cats with more timid personalities should be allowed to hide for at least some part of the day. You can work to make your cat more social, but many cats are "scaredy cats" by nature and no amount of training will change this trait. People often tell me that they think their "scaredy cat" was abused before they found it, but it is more likely that the cat was born that way.

Cats that have to acclimate to new cats, dogs, or children in a household should be given time alone. It is not fair to expect that the resident animal should be happy and willing to accept newcomers. This is just not the nature of cats. Cats hate change. They prefer for things to stay the way they are—the way they arranged them! It can take weeks or months for acceptance, or at least decreased fearfulness, to occur.

Give Your Cat a Break

When a new cat or kitten is brought into a household with children, everyone is excited and wants to hold and play with the animal. Being the constant center of attention is not typically what a cat wants. Parents need to control the handling of the cat and be sure that the animal is given an opportunity to rest by itself.

Entering a new home is stressful to a cat, and not getting a chance to regroup and relax merely intensifies the stress. Stress has a negative impact on the animal's immune system, so be sure to give the cat some quiet time and help keep it healthy. If you cannot isolate a cat in a quiet room for a break, you might consider placing it back into its carrier for a while. The carrier can offer safety and solitude.

Using the Potty

Starting off on the right track with a good litterbox setup will make both you and your cat happy. Litterboxes are available in a variety of sizes and shapes. Your cat will probably be more concerned with the type of litter that is present in the box than it will with the type of box you choose.

Litterbox Styles—Functional to Designer

There are two main types of litterboxes: open and hooded. Litterboxes are generally made of plastic. Almost all cats are satisfied with an open litterbox, but each type has its pros and cons.

Litterboxes Compared

Open Box	Hooded Box
Easy to get in and out of	May be harder to get in and out of
Least expensive	More expensive
Easier to scoop out	Harder to scoop out
Less odor control	More odor control
More litter scatter	Less litter scatter
Accessible to dogs and babies	Prevents access to dogs and babies
Takes up less room	Requires more room
Cats may eliminate over the side	Helps to contain urine and feces

The third type of litterbox is electronic. These are open boxes with electronic eyes that detect the cat's presence, automatically rake the litter, and deposit the waste materials into a closed plastic receptacle. These are the most expensive types of litterboxes, and they still require cleaning, although not as often. Most owners of electronic litterboxes are pleased with their function.

A cat should have unrestricted access to its litterbox. Putting the box in rooms where doors may be accidentally closed or in a garage without a pet door will create problems. As mentioned in the previous section on privacy, the location of the box in the house will encourage or discourage its use. Of course you want to put the litterbox in the area that is most convenient for you, but your cat's wishes should be considered first.

The height of the sides of the box can vary and should be evaluated. Kittens and senior cats may have difficulty jumping into boxes with high sides. The same may be true for injured animals. Keep the height of the sides in mind when selecting a box for your cat.

An electronic litterbox does some of the clean-up work for you.

Be sure to get a litterbox that is big enough to accommodate the size of your cat. The cat should be able to turn around and easily scratch and cover up wastes in its box. Try to anticipate the full-grown needs of a kitten when buying the litterbox.

A good rule is to have at least the same number of litterboxes as you do cats in a household. This can pose problems in large multi-cat homes, and even if you have multiple boxes, all cats will use all boxes. One reason for multiple boxes is to spread out odor and wastes so that they do not become too concentrated too quickly and deter a cat from using the box.

What's in the Box

Today, kitty litter is available in numerous varieties. Some are environmentally friendly and some are easier to clean up. You need to determine which factors are important to you when choosing litter and then hope that your cat agrees with your decision.

Some factors to consider are:

➤ Cost

➤ Presence of deodorizers

➤ Size of packaging

➤ Ease of scooping

➤ Ease of disposal

21

➤ Biodegradability

➤ Litter tracking outside of the box

Litters are made from a number of different materials, including clay, pine shavings, and pelleted newspaper. Cats prefer plain types of litters over those with perfumed smells that may be more pleasant to humans.

Clumping litters are some of my personal favorites. Benefits of clumping litter are that urine and feces can be easily removed from the box. It is similar to outdoor sand or dirt, which is what cats are naturally attracted to. If your cat has a urinary tract problem and you are trying to monitor amount and frequency of urination, clumps are easy to evaluate. There is no scientific evidence that clumping litters cause any health problems in cats, although manufacturers of alternative litter types may make such claims.

Litterbox Maintenance

Litterboxes should be scooped at least one time daily, and depending on the type of litter used, completely emptied and cleaned every one to two weeks. Plastic liners are frequently used to help make box emptying and cleaning easier.

Cats like to have a minimum of an inch depth of litter in their boxes, and most like even more. If the litter level drops and you are not ready to empty the box, simply add more litter.

Empty boxes should be washed with soap and water or white vinegar and water. Products containing ammonia should not be used to clean litterboxes because urine contains ammonia, and cleaning with it will simply intensify the odor.

Cats like clean litterboxes, so if your cat eliminates elsewhere in the house, the condition of the litterbox should be one of the first factors evaluated as a cause for inappropriate elimination.

Worth a Paws

The average expected life span of an indoor cat is 13 to 15 years, while outdoor cats may live only 5 to 7 years.

The Dangers of the Great Outdoors

Housing cats exclusively indoors is the best way to keep them safe. Unfortunately, some cats are fascinated by the outdoors and try to sneak out any opportunity that they can. Some cats like to just bathe in the sun outdoors; others like to hunt and visit neighbors. Once a cat has had a taste of exploring the great outdoors, it is hard to keep it inside, but a determined owner can do so.

Dangers that cats face when they venture outdoors are cars, wild animals, territorial cats, unfamiliar dogs, unkind neighbors, bad weather, fleas and ticks, more risk of exposure to toxins and disease, and getting lost. Where I practice in Southern California, the most common cause of death of outdoor cats is coyote attack. If you are prepared to take these risks with your cat, then let it go outside. If you are not, then protect your cat and keep it inside.

If you allow your cat access to the outdoors, it is crucial to place some kind of identification on the animal such as a collar, tag, microchip, ear tag, tattoo, or a combination of these things. It is important to get the cat on a routine where it is brought inside from dusk to dawn to limit the increased dangers of darkness. If you are concerned about the safety of a collar, break-away styles are available and work well.

Avoid CATastrophe

Nationwide, only 2 percent of the cats picked up by animal control agencies are ever reclaimed by their owners. Without identification these cats are considered unclaimed strays. Unfortunately, most unclaimed cats face euthanasia.

Giving cats inside window perches and plenty of interactive playtimes will help keep them stimulated and diminish their desire to go outside. If you want to let a cat out, but at the same time protect it, you might consider training it to walk on a leash or personally supervising the cat outdoors for short periods of time daily.

Some cats are very interested in what is going on outdoors.

The Least You Need to Know

➤ Cats need to eat a diet that is well balanced and meets their basic nutritional needs.

➤ Diet and environment affect the amount of water a cat consumes, and clean water needs to be available at all times.

➤ Let your cat have some privacy; a lack of privacy can cause stress on the animal's immune system.

➤ Selection of a litterbox, kitty litter, and box placement should be with the cat's preferences in mind.

➤ Indoor living can increase your cat's longevity and protect it from many dangers.

Chapter 3

Kitty Boot Camp Begins

> ### In This Chapter
>
> ➤ Training your cat not to bite you
>
> ➤ What you can do to manage scratching
>
> ➤ How to prevent litterbox problems
>
> ➤ Ways to ensure you get a good night's sleep
>
> ➤ How to keep the cat from jumping up on things

Intelligence in the cat is underrated.

—Louis Wain, English painter of cats

Believe it or not, cats can be trained. The reality is that cats are better at training us than we are at training them, but that should not discourage you! Training a cat to live peacefully in your home is not difficult if you and other family members develop a plan and are consistent with enforcing the basic rules.

Positive reinforcement of desirable behaviors is one of the best training techniques for cats, while punishment is one of the worst. Positive reinforcement can be achieved with a food treat, oral praise, or by petting the animal. Startling a cat that is in the process of conducting an unwanted behavior is another effective method because it breaks a behavior pattern. To startle a cat, squirt it with water, blow an air horn, or shake a can filled with pennies.

You Better Not Bite

Teething is part of normal kitten development, so if you acquire a kitten that is less than seven months old, your cat will experience teething. Some cats have more "oral" personalities than others, and teething is a stage to endure. In other cats teething is barely noticeable.

Meow Wow

Cats go through two teething stages during their lifetimes. The first occurs from 4 to 6 weeks of age when kittens develop 26 deciduous (baby) teeth. The second phase occurs from 4 to 7 months of age when kittens lose their deciduous teeth and develop 30 adult teeth. Adult cats have 4 canine teeth, 10 premolars, 4 molars, and 12 incisors.

"Play" Biting

Cats bite as part of their normal play behavior. Anyone who has observed cats (or cats and dogs) at play knows that there is a thin line between play behavior and aggression. Crouching, jumping, and biting is also normal behavior. Kittens learn how to hunt by playing this way. An example of this is when your kitten pounces on you and bites your feet as you are walking down the hall. This is a manifestation of normal behavior and not aggression toward you.

The best way to prevent biting is to never allow a kitten to bite your hands. When kittens are small it seems fun and harmless if they nibble or attack your hands, but this is a behavior pattern that can continue into adulthood. While adult humans can usually physically handle this biting, small children cannot and often become scared of the cat. Moreover, guests may not appreciate having their hands bitten, since your kitty will think of any hand as a toy.

Avoid CATastrophe

Cats have a large number of bacteria in their mouths, so a cat bite should never be taken lightly. If your skin is punctured, immediately immerse the wounded area under running water for three to five minutes in an attempt to flush out bacteria. If the puncture is fairly deep, see your physician for a prescription of antibiotics.

You should have one or two toys that are delegated as "bite toys." Kittens like to bite something soft that they can really put their teeth into. A stuffed sock or stuffed animal is a good substitution for your hands and feet. Put a "bite toy" in the kitten's mouth when it starts to bite. You can teach children to use these toys with the kitten too.

Sometimes, despite giving them something appropriate to bite, kittens will still get wild and out of control. If this occurs, a "kitty time-out" is in order, and can be achieved by closing the kitten in a small room (with or without lights) by itself for 10 to 15 minutes. During this period the kitten can calm down and then be reintroduced to the rest of the home. If the biting behavior starts again, then back into isolation the kitty goes.

The Hunt Continues

Aside from a stuffed toy, kittens should have a toy that they can run and chase after. This type of play will mimic hunting and give your cat some cardio-vascular exercise as well. There is an endless variety of feathers, fur, or materials tied to the end of poles that make good toys. If you have any toys attached to strings, they should never be left out for the cat to play with unsupervised. Cats have a propensity to swallow string, and if it becomes lodged in a cat's intestines, it can create a life-threatening obstruction.

Worth a Paws

If you find that your kitten is attracted to objects that would be dangerous if bitten or swallowed, try to store them away. Using cord protectors or small PVC piping can help prevent electrical cord chewing and burns to the mouth.

Store any potentially dangerous materials and toys in a closed cabinet or closet. Having a kitten around is like having a baby crawling around on the floor. Both like to put anything that they come in contract with into their mouths, and accidental swallowing can occur. Some kittens will bite on electrical and telephone cords. Others have been known to chew buttons off of clothes or even eat coins dropped on the floor.

All Cats Need to Scratch Somewhere

Scratching is another normal cat behavior. If a cat or kitten is not provided with a suitable scratching area, then upholstery and carpeting may fall victim to the desire to scratch. Cats scratch to wear and sharpen their nails, but they also scratch to mark their territory. The oils around the nails leave a scent that is distributed during scratching. You may have visited a zoo or wild animal park and observed lions and tigers performing the same types of scratching behaviors that your own house cat does.

Cats that go outdoors will frequently use trees as their scratching posts, but for indoor kitties alternative objects are needed. The most common materials used as scratching posts are:

➤ Carpet

➤ Sisal or rope

➤ Cardboard

Some cats enjoy using sisal scratching posts.

You may want to experiment with the different materials available and see if your cat has a preference. If the cat has already started scratching certain types of materials in the home, you might even consider building an appropriate scratching post out of the same fabric. Just because you know that an object is a scratching post does not mean that your cat will recognize it as such.

A training program is usually needed to introduce a cat to a scratching post. Different techniques may be required, depending on whether you have a new kitten or an older cat that already has bad habits. If you have a new kitten, try this program:

1. Confine the kitten at night.
2. When you get up with the kitten in the morning, go directly to the scratching post.
3. Entice the kitten to scratch the post by placing its front feet on it or by dangling a toy around it.
4. Reward the kitten with praise and/or a food treat for proper post usage.
5. Never allow the kitten to scratch any other objects in the house.

Within a week or so, you will hopefully have developed a behavior pattern that the kitten will follow. If you no longer want to confine the kitten, allow it out and reinforce good scratching behavior. It also helps to trim the kitten's toenails every two to three weeks to keep them short and less dangerous.

If you have an older cat that has chosen an undesirable location for scratching, try this program:

1. Create a barrier to the area that the cat has
   chosen with plastic wrap or aluminum foil.
   You can also use a thick plastic carpet runner.

2. Place an appropriate scratching post near the
   undesirable location.

3. Entice the cat to use the post by placing its
   front feet on it or by dangling a toy around it.

4. Reward the cat with praise and/or a food treat
   for proper usage.

5. If the cat scratches any undesirable materials
   in the house, squirt it with water.

6. Never allow the cat to scratch any other
   objects in the house.

Worth a Paws

There is a product on the market
called Feliway that is a feline
pheromone spray. Pheromones are
chemical signals that are present in
different animal secretions. The
specific pheromone in this product
was designed to discourage spraying
behavior, but has been effective in
preventing scratching in many
instances and might be worth a try.

Once the cat begins to use the scratching post on a regular basis, you can slowly move
it (about two feet a week) in the direction that you would permanently like to place it.
And as with kittens, trim the cat's toenails every two to three weeks to keep them short
and less dangerous.

Keep It in the Box

I already discussed encouraging proper litterbox use in Chapter 2. I emphasize this
point because litterbox problems are the most common behavior problems in cats.
In turn, failure to consistently use the box is the most common reason that cats are
euthanized or relinquished by their owners. Starting off with good litterbox behavior
is not a guarantee against future problems, but it is a good preventative step.

The factors that contribute to good litterbox behavior are:

➤ Litterbox placement that is convenient for the cat

➤ Allowing the cat adequate privacy when using the box

➤ Filling the box with a kitty litter material that the cat likes to use

➤ Scooping the box at least one time daily

➤ Completely emptying and cleaning the box every one to two weeks

➤ Providing a sufficient number of litterboxes in a multi-cat household

Meow Wow

Dogs come when called; cats take a message and get back to you.

—Mary Bly, English professor and lecturer

When introduced to a litterbox, almost all cats will automatically use it. It is a natural behavior for wild cats to eliminate in dirt or sand, and then cover up their waste products, and in a home a litterbox provides the same option.

Avoid CATastrophe

Cats do not learn from punishment. Never put a cat's nose into wastes that have been left outside the box and then throw the cat into the litterbox. This response could actually make the behavior worse because the animal could directly associate punishment with the litterbox and avoid the box even more.

Showing a cat to its litterbox should be the first thing you do when the cat enters your home for the first time. Place the cat in the box and observe the animal's reaction. You can then watch whether the cat can easily exit the box. If you have a kitten, you should take it to the box every few hours and praise or reward good use. It is recommended to confine a new cat or kitten in the room with the litterbox at night until you feel comfortable that it is using the box on a routine basis.

Most cats will urinate twice daily and have a bowel movement once daily. If a cat regularly consumes the same diet, the pattern will be very consistent. If it does not appear that your cat has eliminated in its box following its typical routine, you may want to search your home for alternative elimination sites.

Cats that are allowed outdoors may prefer to eliminate outdoors and only use a litterbox when forced to. If the outdoors is your cat's preference, make sure that the animal has adequate access. Owners of outdoor cats often install "kitty doors" to allow their pet to come and go as it pleases. If you have a kitty door, don't be surprised if other neighborhood cats try it out! At some point you could find yourself face to face with a curious kitty stranger.

Meow Wow

Cats that eliminate outside of their litterboxes are not always displaying bad behavior. Cats that have urinary tract problems often urinate outside of their boxes to attract your attention. If your cat urinates inappropriately, you should have its urine analyzed and the animal examined by a veterinarian to rule out a medical cause.

Restful Sleep for All

Although kittens seem to bounce off the walls and spend endless time exploring, in reality they spend the majority of their day sleeping. This is also true of adult cats that seem to carry on a never-ending search for the perfect nap location.

Cat Naps

Humans like to sleep at night, but this is not always the case with our cats. Cats tend to be *nocturnal*. Their nature is to hunt, and the best hunting time is in darkness. If your cat sleeps in your bedroom, this can pose a problem. As soon as you reach your precious deep sleep, kitty may decide that it is playtime and bat you on the nose.

Kitty Ditty

Nocturnal is a word used to describe something that functions or is active at night.

Owners frequently complain to me about how their cats wake them up at night and are perplexed with what to do. The answer is simple: Close your bedroom door and don't allow your cat access while you sleep. This is an unacceptable solution to some owners, so my next recommendation is to set up a playtime before you want to go to bed, and then try to exhaust the cat with interactive play. If this becomes a pattern, then the cat is more likely to sleep through the night.

Meow Wow

Cats possess night vision superior to that of both dogs and humans. Being able to detect prey in dim light is very important. Rods and cones are specialized cells in the eye. The rod to cone ratio in cats is 25:1, and in humans it is 20:1. The increased percentage of rods allows the cat to see in $1/6$th the light needed by humans.

Managing the Kitty Night Owl

If you give your cat attention and get up when it wakes you, you are actually reinforcing its behavior by doing exactly what the cat wants you to do. Who is in charge here? The best thing you can do is to ignore the cat. However, since cats can be persistent, you may have no choice but to get up and shut the cat out of the room. Keeping a squirt bottle by the bed and simply squirting the cat with water if it bothers you is another alternative.

Worth a Paws

Just as you want your cat to allow you enough sleep, you need to be sure that it is getting enough sleep. This is not a common problem unless you have young children or another pet in the home that do not leave the cat alone.

Some cats will scratch or paw at a door that is closed in an attempt to get in. If your cat does this then you may need to confine it somewhere else in your house so that you do not hear it. If the cat has claws and they are damaging a door, you may want to consider Soft Paws, vinyl nail caps glued over a cat's natural nails, during the training period.

As I've mentioned, cats are creatures of habit, so breaking an undesirable behavior pattern at an early stage is important. If you allow your cat to bother you at night for months and then decide that you cannot take it anymore, the animal *can* be re-trained but it may take a long time to change the behavior.

In situations where the behavior-modifying techniques that I've mentioned do not work, a veterinarian may prescribe a mild anti-anxiety or tranquilizing drug to aid in the training process. Drug intervention should be the last step because almost all cats can be trained or prevented from bothering you at night.

A Preference for Your Pillow

Many owners are disappointed when the adorable cat bed they buy for their pet goes unused. Some cats like to sleep in cat beds where they can roll up into a ball and be left undisturbed, but others would prefer your bed or sofa.

Many cats like to rest on your furniture. Others select less conventional beds.

You can train a cat to use a cat bed by trying to initially place it in a location where the cat would normally sleep. Gently pet the cat and try to get it to relax in the bed, then leave the animal alone and see if it will go back to the bed on its own. You may need to repeatedly place the cat in the bed to encourage use.

If you do not want your cat leaving its hair all over your furniture, you might want to place a towel or cat throw on areas frequently used to lay or nap. Grooming your cat on a regular basis, which will be discussed in Chapter 4, helps decrease shedding. If you want to completely prevent a cat from lying on furniture, you might need to cover the object with aluminum foil or sticky tape to discourage use. (Of course, this might discourage your use as well!) Close the doors of rooms that you want to keep the cat out of if possible. The water squirt bottle can be used to help train the cat to keep off the furniture.

Cats are clever animals though, and the more you try to keep them from going somewhere, the harder they will try to get in. Giving the cat good alternative bedding is the best way to keep it off the other furniture.

The Counters Are Off-Limits

Cats love to jump up on things. They surprise us at times with how high they will go. We often wonder, "What is their motivation?" It may be curiosity, or it may be a desire to get a better perspective on the activities going on around them. Regardless of the reason, it is common for cats to get up on things that we may wish they would not.

I have heard people complain when they observe cats jumping up on kitchen counters in someone else's home. I then wonder whether their cats do the same thing in their homes, but at a more opportune time!

As with any behavior you wish to change, it is important to be consistent with what you allow the animal to do. If you hate when the cat jumps up on your kitchen counter, chase it down immediately and be sure that your spouse or roommate does the same thing. If some members of the house allow the behavior, then the cat can be confused or even think that you are playing with it when you chase it down.

Avoid CATastrophe

Another good reason to keep your cat off the counters is to prevent burns. Cats have been known to jump up on ranges and burners and burn their feet. If you are cooking and your cat likes to jump up, do not leave the animal unsupervised in the kitchen.

What's Cooking, Baby?

Your cat will be less tempted to get up on your counters if there is nothing there of interest. Keep your food stored away. Always feed your cat on the floor and not on any table or counter that you do not want the cat on regularly. Put dishes in the dishwasher and empty food packaging in closed garbage cans so that these things do not tempt the cat.

If your cat continues to jump up, it is crucial to catch it in the act and squirt it with water, yell, or clap your hands to startle it. Push the cat off if it does not jump down on its own. Try to find what attracted the cat in the first place and remove it.

What Else Can You Do?

For cats that insist on continuing to jump up, the next step is to cover the counter with double-sided sticky tape. Cats do not like the way the tape feels, and this adverse stimulus should discourage the behavior. I used to frequently come home in the evening and have to peel tape off of my cat's hair until he got the idea.

Commercially available pet-repellant sprays may or may not work to prevent jumping up on things. Covering objects with aluminum foil can work, since cats do not like the sound the foil makes when they jump on it. I do not recommend the electrified "scat mats" for use with cats because of the potential stress and trauma from the shock to the animal.

If you are not sure whether your cat is exploring in your absence, check tabletops and counters for hair and paw prints. These are clues that point to a guilty kitty. If you are not making progress with preventing jumping behavior, consider confining the cat when you are not home and watching it when you are. Also be sure that you are giving the cat enough attention and playing with it. Some cats will jump up and have you chase them down as a game just to get your attention.

The Least You Need to Know

➤ All kittens bite when they teethe, so give them appropriate items to bite and do not let them bite your hands.

➤ Scratching is a normal behavior that needs an outlet, so to prevent destructive scratching, provide your cat with a scratching post right from the start.

➤ If you want your cat to regularly use its litterbox, you must scoop it at least once daily.

➤ Place the litterbox in a location that is convenient for the cat and fill it with a litter type that the cat likes to use.

➤ You can get a full night's sleep if you keep your cat out of your bedroom or train it to leave you alone at night.

➤ Cats like to jump up on things, but this behavior can be discouraged and prevented.

Part 2
Basic Health Care

Now that you know how to take care of your cat and stop any unwanted behaviors, the next step is preventive health care. Preventive care involves keeping the animal clean and healthy, and protecting it against preventable problems.

Since our feline friends cannot tell how they feel or why they are acting a certain way, it is good to know what to expect. Identifying problems with your pet can be difficult due to the stoic nature of cats, so knowing what to specifically look for is extremely helpful. It is also very important to have a good working relationship with a veterinary clinic, which is a valuable resource for care and education on cats.

Chapter 4

Is Your Cat Having a Bad Hair Day?

In This Chapter

➤ Learn how to groom your cat yourself

➤ Decide the best way to handle a matted coat

➤ Giving your cat a bath

➤ Can a professional groomer help you and your cat?

The beauty of a cat comes not only from its graceful movement but also from its haircoat. The haircoat of a cat is usually divided into short, medium, or long categories. People like to think that shorthaired cats do not shed as much as longhaired cats, but this is not the case. Unless you have a hairless Sphynx cat, all cats shed. The Devon and Cornish Rex breeds of cats have kinky coats that shed less than others, but any animal with hair sheds.

Cats are clean animals, and most cats groom themselves regularly. But depending on the cat and the coat, your furry friend may need help taking care of itself. Complete grooming of a cat may involve combing, brushing, de-tangling, shaving, bathing, and drying. This sounds like a lot of work, but many owners are able to do what is needed to keep their cat looking good. For those who have trouble, professional grooming services are available.

Kitty Ditty

Polydactyl is a term used to describe an animal with more than the normal number of toes. Cats that have extra toes need more nail trimming than average cats. The extra toenails usually don't get worn down and can grow into their footpads.

Start with the Claws

The first step in any grooming procedure is trimming the animal's toenails. This can be a benefit to both you and your cat. If cut too short, a cat's toenail will bleed. If this occurs, you have cut the quick (see the following figure). Proper technique for toenail trimming is to push on the top of the toe to extend the nail, and then cut off the white hook with a pet nail trimmer. If you are inexperienced, you might want to start off cutting small amounts of nail and increase over time as you gain comfort with the procedure. You can have a veterinarian or groomer demonstrate the technique for you.

An average cat has five toes on each front foot and four on each rear. A *polydactyl* cat will have more. Toenail trimming should be started when your cat is a kitten so that it becomes used to it. Cats know if you are not confident, so if you are having problems with nail trimming, you may want to stop, regroup, and start over. Your cat will take advantage of the situation if it senses your anxiety and make it even harder for you to trim its nails by squirming. You might consider cutting just a few nails at a time or trying to cut the cat's nails while it is sleeping.

When you trim a cat's toenails, be careful not to cut the quick. The quick will look like a pink triangle.

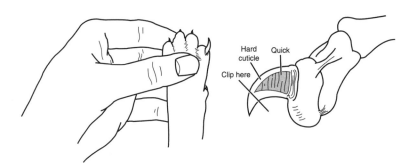

Hard cuticle   Quick

Clip here

Should You Comb or Should You Brush?

Tools that can be used to comb or brush a cat come in numerous sizes, shapes, and colors. Most people are familiar with conventional combs and brushes, but mitts, rakes, and grooming cloths are also available. What tool you use depends on the length of coat and the tolerance level of the cat. Many cats love to be combed, while others turn into little tigers when the comb comes out.

Worth a Paws

Most cats benefit from being combed or brushed at least once a week. The hair you remove helps decrease shedding and hairballs.

Start Off Young and Bribe

It is a good idea to introduce a comb or brush to your kitten within a few days of bringing it home. Start by allowing the animal to sniff (and bite) the tool and see what it is. Gently comb the animal around the neck and back. If you are met with hissing and claws, stop and talk calmly to the cat. You may need to hold the cat by the scruff of its neck when you comb it in order to keep it still. Short, frequent combing sessions will help to train the kitten.

Kittens that do not like being combed may allow a soft-bristled brush to be used instead. Kittens that are trained to allow grooming are more tolerant of grooming as adults. It is much easier to handle a two-pound kitten than an unhappy 10-pound adult, so it is worth the energy to work on training the young.

If you are having a tough time trying to comb your cat, you might want to enlist the support of a friend or relative to help hold it. Giving a food treat to the cat after a successful brushing session will positively reinforce sitting still for grooming. Some cats like to be combed while they are eating. Eating can provide a good distraction to the animal, and give you an opportunity to get a few strokes in.

Useful Flea Combs

The only grooming tool that I think is essential for every cat is a flea comb—your cat does not have to have fleas in order to benefit. A flea comb has dense fine teeth. The most user-friendly flea combs have easy-to-hold handles and metal (versus plastic) teeth. A shorthaired cat can be combed from its head to the tip of its tail with a flea comb, but this tool is too fine to use on longer-haired animals.

I routinely use a flea comb on every cat I examine. Its purpose is twofold: to determine if fleas are present, and to check for scabs, scales, and dead hair. Owners often look at me in amazement when I comb off a significant amount of hair from their cat, but the fine teeth of the flea comb are excellent at catching stray hairs and getting below the surface hair. If fleas are present, flea dirt and live fleas are caught in the dense teeth of the comb.

41

Flea combs can be useful for removing small knots in short hair, but the pull is too strong for mats on cats with more hair. If your cat gets food or other substances on its coat, a flea comb can be used to comb the materials off of the hair.

Flea combs are valuable grooming tools, especially for shorthaired cats.

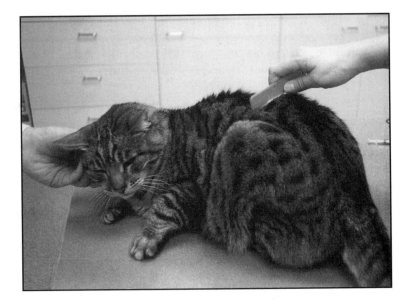

The disadvantages of a flea comb are:

➤ It can break hairs easily if used too vigorously.

➤ It can be painful to use on longhaired cats or those with matted fur.

➤ If the fine teeth become bent, they can scratch the cat.

What About Your Longhaired Cat?

For cats with medium to long hair, a medium to coarse metal comb is needed. Many owners like to use slicker brushes (short metal bristles), but the problem with this tool is that it can ride on top of the coat and leave hairs matted underneath. Metal rakes are useful in longer coats, especially if there is a lot of hair to comb out.

One way to ease the stress of combing a hairy cat is to pick smaller areas to work on, and comb one area a day or every few days. Even cats that are tolerant of combing have limits as to the amount of time they are willing to put up with the procedure.

Hairballs

Any cat can have hairballs, but the more hair a cat ingests when self-grooming, the more likely it is to spit up a hairball. *Trichobezoars* are normal, and using hairball remedies may decrease their frequency but not eliminate them. The main reason to use hairball remedies is to prevent a hairball from causing an intestinal blockage.

Kitty Ditty

Trichobezoar *is the technical term for a hairball. This word is formed from the prefix* tricho-, *derived from the Greek, meaning "hair," and the suffix* bezoar, *which is a concretion of materials formed in the intestines.*

Traditionally, hairball remedies were malt petroleum pastes that came in tubes. Today these pastes are found in different flavors, including tuna, and even come in pump dispensers. Psyllium, a type of fiber, is also a useful hairball remedy. It is available in pre-measured capsules, in bulk form, and as chewable tablets. These products are available through veterinarians and pet stores. A food called Science Diet Hairball Control Formula has been developed for the purpose of reducing hairballs, and it contains cellulose, another type of fiber. No scientific studies are available at this time to support the claim.

Ouch, That Hurts!

Even fastidious cats have a hard time licking and keeping all hairs in place. Regular combing and brushing is the best way to prevent matting, but many of us don't have enough time to comb our pets every day. If you're able to comb your pet even a few minutes a day, it can prevent a more time-consuming and painful problem later on.

Matting in Longhaired Cats

It is easy for matting and knotting to occur in cats with medium to long coats. To prevent matting, concentrate combing on the areas more likely to mat. These areas are the armpits, abdomen, behind the ears, the tail and under the tail, and behind the back legs. Mats will grow to a more unmanageable size if not removed.

Unfortunately, cats tend to get mats that are very close to their skin. It is tempting to grab a pair of scissors and cut them out, but this is not the right first step. The best way to remove mats is:

1. Try to comb the mat out with a coarse metal comb by starting at the edge of the mat and then working in closer to the skin.

2. If you cannot get a comb through the mat, try to work your fingers through it to separate the hairs.

3. If the cat is in pain from the pulling or if you are not making any progress, work a comb between the skin and the mat.

4. Cut the hair along the comb on the side away from the skin. This will prevent you from cutting the cat's skin.

5. Gently comb out the shorter remaining hairs.

It takes weeks to months for hair to grow back. Often the skin under a mat appears red and inflamed. This is due to dirt and moisture getting trapped and irritating the skin. It also occurs if some pulling is needed during the mat removal process.

Your cat is not going to be happy when you start working on matted hairs. Be careful and stop combing if you are in risk of being bitten or scratched. Get help from a friend or relative, or turn the job over to an experienced groomer.

Matting in Shorthaired Cats

Most shorthaired cats need little grooming, but some can get matted too. This most frequently occurs in older animals that do not groom themselves enough and in obese animals that cannot reach many areas themselves. These animals need more routine combing. A persistent owner armed with a flea comb can remove most of the matting that occurs on a shorthaired cat.

The matting that occurs on shorthaired cats tends to be located along the end of the spine and tail base. The hair may be greasy, dry, and scaly all at the same time. This is because a cat distributes the oils along the hairs when it grooms itself, and it can't reach these areas. Don't be surprised if your overweight cat starts biting or licking the air when you start combing these areas. Combing these areas is like tickling the cat in a spot it can't reach, and boy, does that feel good!

Bath Time!?

Surprisingly, some cats like water and will tolerate baths, but for most cats a bath is a hair-raising experience. Owners often ask me how frequently their cat should be bathed. There is no set schedule for bathing a cat.

Factors to consider when deciding about a bath are:

➤ Greasiness of the coat

➤ Presence of fleas

➤ Dirtiness of the coat

➤ Smell

➤ Discoloration

Many cats live to a ripe old age without ever receiving a bath, but I think all cats look and smell better after being bathed. Baths can play a role in treating some dermatologic conditions and removing external parasites such as fleas.

It is important to use a proper shampoo on your cat. Most shampoos for human hair do not have the proper pH balance for a cat's skin, and should not be used. Baby shampoo is acceptable to use, as are specially formulated pet shampoos. Many of the insecticides found in flea shampoos can be toxic to cats or young kittens, so be very careful if you want to use a flea shampoo. Make sure that it is labeled for use with cats and kittens. With the advent of safe, effective, once-a-month flea preventives, flea shampoos should not be a necessity.

Avoid CATastrophe

Before starting a bath you should trim your cat's toenails. This will decrease the potential for injury if the cat gets upset. You should also comb out any mats in the hair because they will tighten and be harder to remove after they are wet.

Steps to bathing a cat are:

1. Place a towel or mat at the bottom of the tub or sink so that the animal does not slide.

2. If possible, use a faucet that has a sprayer attachment.

3. Gently wet the cat's coat with warm water. Hold the cat by its scruff if necessary.

4. Massage the shampoo into the coat.

5. Use a toothbrush with some lather to clean the cat's face, being careful not to get any soap in the animal's eyes. If shampoo does gets in the animal's eyes, rinse with saline solution in a bottle.

6. Let the animal soak for a couple of minutes.

7. Rinse thoroughly with warm water.

8. Squeeze the excess water out of the coat and down the legs and tail.

9. Thoroughly towel-dry the cat.

10. Use a blow-dryer on low or medium to dry the coat. Higher settings can cause burning if you are not careful.

11. Comb or brush the hair during the drying process.

If you are fortunate enough to have a cooperative kitty, the process will go well. For cats that are scared or anxious, though, the process can be a disaster if you are not careful. Expect the cat to try to get out of the sink. Consider wearing an apron or old clothes in case you get splashed or have to grab a wet cat. Close the door to the room you are bathing in to help prevent kitty escape.

Give Up?

You may be reading this chapter and thinking, "You've got to be kidding! There is no way that I would be able to groom my cat." If this is true or if you have been unsuccessful in your grooming endeavors, you should consider taking your cat to an experienced groomer.

Not all groomers like working with cats, so it is important to find one who does. There are some groomers who have mobile vans and will come to your house, park in your driveway, and work on your kitty there. Other groomers work in grooming shops, pet stores, and veterinary hospitals. There are groomers who have completed courses on pet grooming and have certificates. There are others who have learned by experience.

Worth a Paws

Persians are the most popular type of purebred cat. To maintain their beautiful long coats, they need frequent grooming. Most owners are not capable of keeping Persian hair under control themselves. Ask other Persian owners about what is involved and consider selecting a different breed if you don't have the time or money to have the animal regularly groomed.

How to Pick a Groomer

The best groomer is one who has worked with cats and has access to a veterinarian in case of need. Medical assistance may be required if the cat is nicked accidentally with sharp grooming tools or if it needs to be sedated so that a proper job can be performed. Many cats freak out with strangers or are so badly matted that the grooming process is painful. In these cases sedation is recommended so that neither the animal nor the groomer gets injured.

If you have a cat that you don't feel comfortable grooming, it should be groomed at least every three months. The shorter the interval between grooming sessions, the less matting can occur. Some cats become so matted that they need to be shaved. Depending on the location of the matting, the shaving may involve one area or the entire body.

Giving Your Cat a Perfect Hairdo

Different breeds of dogs typically have different haircuts, but the same is not true for cats. Most cats do not get haircuts unless they are matted or have difficult-to-manage coats. There is really only one haircut for a cat—the body shave. If a cat is body shaved, the entire trunk is typically shaved closely. Options exist on how far down the legs and tail the animal is shaved and how much of the neck or mane hair is removed. If you have never had your cat shaved and you request it, ask to see a sample of what a shaved animal looks like so that you are not shocked with the results.

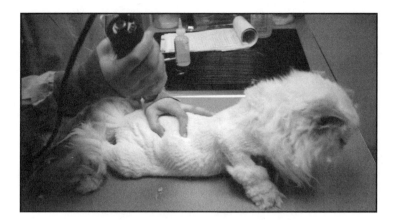

A groomer giving a cat a body shave.

The finished product of a body shave. If possible the mane, legs, and tail are left with long hair.

Don't be surprised if you take a matted cat to a groomer and body shaving is suggested. A shaved cat may not look as good to you as a cat with all its hair, but the pain and discomfort associated with combing out a lot of mats may be extreme. The skin is also very traumatized when there is significant matting, and you could end up with a ragged, patchy coat after combing. Even after shaving, the pattern may look irregular where mats were removed, but you've saved your cat from a lot of agony.

Many owners take their cat to a groomer simply for a bath and brush. Aside from the procedures listed for bathing a cat yourself, a groomer may place cats in cages with dryers on the door before finishing with hand drying. Groomers usually have assistants to help them with combing and drying because many cats need four hands to finish. Even though cats do not require bathing, clean, fluffed hair does look better. Why get your cat mad at you when you can blame someone else?

The Least You Need to Know

➤ Always trim your cat's toenails before beginning any grooming procedure.

➤ Combing is generally better than brushing for removing excess hair and preventing mats.

➤ Longhaired cats need more intensive and frequent grooming than shorthaired cats.

➤ Matting can be painful to a cat, and care is needed when removing mats.

➤ If you cannot or do not want to groom your cat yourself, seek the help of an experienced groomer.

Chapter 5

How Do You Know if Your Cat Is Sick?

In This Chapter

➤ Your cat is not eating

➤ Your cat has a fever

➤ Your cat is acting funny

➤ The common clinical signs of illness

➤ Are there any safe household remedies?

➤ Learn tricks for medicating your cat

Our feline friends cannot tell us how they feel, so it is important to have some understanding of the signs of a sick cat. Cats are generally stoic animals, and often they do not let us know that they are sick until the disease has progressed. Observant owners can learn to identify subtle changes in their cat's routine and behavior that may be indicative of illness.

The difficult part of identifying changes is first trying to determine what is normal for the cat. Cats do not think or act like a human would in many situations, so many cat activities seem strange to us. An example is vomiting hairballs. If a human spit up hair, it would be very abnormal, but for a cat this is a normal event.

This chapter will introduce you to some of the ways you can detect problems in your cat. It will also help you figure out when you should consult with a veterinarian.

Kitty Ditty

Anorexia is a term used to describe a lack of appetite for food. Veterinarians will use this term when owners tell them that the cat is not eating or eating very little.

Avoid CATastrophe

Cats, especially overweight animals, can develop a condition called hepatic lipidosis if they do not eat. Cats with hepatic lipidosis break down their body fat for energy, but the fat overwhelms the liver, injures the normal liver cells, and makes the cat sicker. Early intervention with anorexic cats is needed to stop hepatic lipidosis from occurring.

Is Your Feline Anorexic?

Being finicky and not eating are two different things. Some cats hold out for their favorite foods and this makes them finicky, but *anorexic* cats do not care what you put in front of them. If a cat does not eat for 24 hours, you should be concerned. If the lack of appetite lasts more than 48 hours, you should have the animal examined by a veterinarian.

When Your Cat Won't Eat

If your cat is not eating, you need to determine if there is a problem with its diet or if the cat is sick. Some reasons why a healthy cat may not eat include:

➤ Spoiled food

➤ Ants or other insects in the food

➤ You bought the wrong flavor

➤ Competition at the food bowl

➤ Food for humans or treats have affected appetite

➤ Food bowl is in a bad location

➤ Hunting and eating prey or snacking at a neighbor's house

If none of these reasons are valid, it is likely that the animal is sick. Reasons why a sick cat may not eat are:

➤ The cat is congested and cannot smell the food

➤ The cat has a fever, causing a loss of appetite

➤ Bad teeth or other dental disease is affecting the cat's ability to eat

➤ Liver or other gastrointestinal disease is causing nausea

➤ The cat is dehydrated and too weak to eat

How to Make Your Cat Eat

Sick cats do not eat well, so it is important to encourage them. Offer yummy foods, such as canned food, tuna fish, deli meat, or baby food. Warming food slightly for a few seconds in a microwave oven can help by increasing the aroma of the food. Hand-feeding, talking gently, and petting the cat can stimulate eating too. If a cat seems uninterested in eating, do not leave food sitting out for more than an hour. Pick it up and re-introduce it a few hours later. You can hand-feed your cat by offering it some soft food on a spoon or on your finger, and encourage the animal to lick it off.

When none of these suggestions proves successful, a trip to the veterinarian is war-ranted. Veterinarians may use prescription appetite stimulants and/or force-feed an anorexic cat. Force-feeding is typically accomplished by using a syringe without a needle and squirting some type of strained diet into a cat's mouth. For cats that are difficult or too sick to orally force-feed, feeding tubes can be placed into the esophagus or stomach.

What About Water?

Water intake is extremely important. If an animal cannot keep water down, it should be taken to a veterinarian immediately. This can be a sign of an intestinal obstruction. A cat that does not eat or drink can become seriously dehydrated within a day. Vomit-ing and diarrhea can contribute to water loss by the body, and these clinical signs also cause dehydration. If your cat is not drinking, you can give it some water with a syringe or eye dropper, but it is almost impossible to get enough water into a cat this way.

Veterinarians can re-hydrate cats by injecting sterile balanced electrolyte solutions under the animal's skin. This practice is called subcutaneous administration. Fluids can also be directly injected into the body through a vein using an intravenous catheter, commonly known as an IV. Intravenous treatment requires hospitalization but is necessary for more seriously dehydrated patients.

Kitty's Nose Is Warm

A warm, dry nose or warm ears are not accurate indications of a fever in a cat. The only way to be certain about the presence of a fever is by actually measuring a cat's temperature.

Meow Wow

The normal body temperature of a cat is higher than that of a human. The normal range of temperature is from 100.5 degrees F to 102.5 degrees F.

To take a cat's body temperature, you should do the following:

1. Using a rectal thermometer, shake the mercury down below 99 degrees F.
2. Lubricate the tip of the thermometer with petroleum jelly.
3. Insert the thermometer into the animal's rectum.
4. Hold the cat as still as possible and leave the thermometer in place for two minutes.
5. Remove the thermometer and read.

You may need two people to take a cat's temperature with a rectal thermometer.

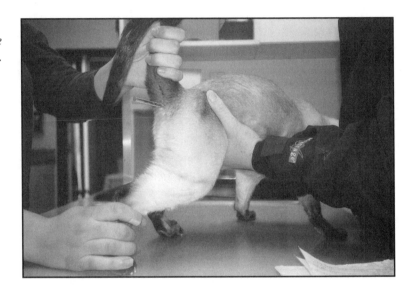

Inexpensive digital thermometers are available at drug stores and can be used rectally in cats. Human ear (tympanic) thermometers are not accurate in cats. Special ear thermometers are available for animals, but they are expensive and sold through veterinary distributors.

What Causes a Fever?

In a cat, a fever is generally considered to be a temperature reading above 103.0 degrees F. Increased body temperature does not always mean that the animal is sick, but if the cat has a fever, you should try to find out why.

Increased body temperature can be due to:

➤ High environmental temperature

➤ Stress or excitement, such as putting the cat into a carrier and taking it to the veterinarian

➤ Intense playing or running

➤ Bacterial infections

➤ Viral infections

➤ Seizures due to increased muscle activity

What You Should Do if Your Cat Has a Fever

If you suspect that your cat has a fever, be sure that the animal is in a cool place. Do not give any over-the-counter medications made for humans to reduce a fever in a cat. If the cat is alert and acting normally, check its temperature again in an hour. You can hose a cat down with cold water to bring its temperature down, but this rather radical treatment should be reserved for cases when the temperature is above 105 degrees F. You can also apply rubbing alcohol to the animal's footpads to cool it, but if the cat then licks its feet, it will drool a bit.

Whenever a cat has a fever, it is best to have the cat examined by a veterinarian as soon as possible. The doctor will try to determine what triggered the fever and then offer options for treatment. Cold fluids can be injected into a cat to cool it down. If a fever persists for more than 24 hours, more extensive nursing care and diagnostic testing is probably warranted.

Avoid CATastrophe

Never give a cat aspirin, acetaminophen (Tylenol), ibuprofen, or any other anti-inflammatory medication made for humans. Cats lack the enzymes needed to metabolize these drugs, and ingestion is potentially life-threatening. If you accidentally treat your cat with one of these drugs, seek veterinary care immediately.

When Your Cat Is Acting Funny

We've come back to the issue of deciding what is normal behavior for a cat. Each cat is an individual with unique habits and preferences. Owners of adult cats have a good idea of what is normal for their cat with regard to eating, drinking, playing, and sleeping; but for the new kitten owner, these behaviors may not yet be established.

Cats are creatures of habit, so if your normally "bouncing off the walls" kitten couldn't care less when you come home from work, it is likely not feeling well. In general, cats that are sick become quieter than usual and seclude themselves. They seem like they do not want to be bothered with even regular daily activities.

Irritability

Sometimes when cats are not feeling well they become more irritable. Signs of irritability are:

➤ Hissing or growling

➤ Striking out with a paw and claws

➤ Biting

➤ Moving away from you when normally they would not

➤ Less tolerance of other people or animals in the house

If your cat becomes more irritable, try to determine if the animal is not feeling well and wants to be left alone or if the behavior change does not have an apparent trigger. In either case, you will likely need to have the animal examined by a veterinarian to see if a more specific cause for irritability can be determined. A veterinarian can treat any underlying medical problems and work with you to solve behavioral problems.

Failure to Respond

Cats are usually very alert and tuned in to the activities around them. If your cat suddenly becomes disinterested or unresponsive, this is not normal. As cats age, their activity level is reduced, but if vision and/or hearing are not impaired, they still react to things around them.

Diseases that affect the nervous system are not that common in cats, but they do occur. Any sick cat with behavior changes should have its nervous system assessed by a veterinarian. Diseases that affect other organ systems or electrolyte imbalances can also cause behavior changes.

Typical Signs of Illness

There are many clinical signs that a sick cat can exhibit. Some common clinical signs of illness in cats are:

Anorexia	Constipation
Bad breath	Coughing
Bleeding	Diarrhea
Bloating	Drinking more than normal
Bloody urine	Fever
Colds	Gas
Conjunctivitis	Head shaking

Itching	Sneezing
Jaundice	Straining
Excessive licking	Swelling
Limping	Vomiting
Nasal Congestion	Weight loss
Redness (of skin, eyes, face)	Worms
Seizures	

How Bad Is It?

One isolated episode of any of the common clinical signs does not indicate a sick cat. Every owner has a comfort level with evaluating the signs that their cat shows, but whenever there is uncertainty, consult with your veterinarian.

Signs that last more than a day or that are progressive indicate problems that are unlikely to be resolved without treatment. Cats are very protective and defensive by nature, so they hide their illnesses well. Often cats do not let us know that they are sick until a condition is quite advanced.

When to Go to the Emergency Room

There are a few clinical signs that warrant immediate attention. These include difficulty breathing, inability to urinate, uncontrolled bleeding, an inability to stand, seizures, and vomiting blood. Signs like these can be indicative of life-threatening problems. If you think that your cat may have sustained a severe trauma such as being attacked by a larger animal, hit by a car, or falling from a roof, get the cat to a veterinarian as soon as possible.

The cost of emergency services is more than services provided during regular business hours. Emergency veterinary clinics provide aggressive diagnostics and treatments. Be sure to discuss any recommendations with the doctor and try to understand what is being done and how necessary it is so that you will not be surprised when you see your bill. You need to feel comfortable with your animal's treatment.

Worth a Paws

Even if your regular veterinarian closes his hospital at night and on holidays, he should be able to provide you with a source of after-hours emergency care. Veterinary clinics have an answering service or message machine that can provide you with a phone number for emergencies and/or refer you to an emergency clinic. Emergency clinics can also be found in the Yellow Pages.

Checking Out Your Medicine Cabinet

Cats are very sensitive to medications, but they can be safely treated with a few products for humans. It is important to read labels and check ingredients before treating a cat. Call your veterinarian's office before giving your cat any medications. If the animal is not responding to your care within 24 hours, don't wait to get help.

Cleaning Cuts

Any small wound or abrasion can be safely cleaned with hydrogen peroxide. This solution can fizz and bubble when it comes in contact with blood, but it does not sting like rubbing alcohol does. Another disinfectant that you may keep around the home is a Betadine solution. This type of solution has an iodine color and can cause staining, so be careful where you apply it.

Ointments and Creams

After a wound, puncture, or abrasion is cleaned, it is safe to use a triple antibiotic ointment on it. One common product is Neosporin, which can be safely used topically twice daily.

Hydrocortisone cream or ointment can be applied to a minor rash that is itchy to a cat. This drug is useful for itching and inflammation if there is no infection, but if bacteria or fungus are present, it can make the infection worse.

Cleaning Around the Eyes

Many cats, especially Persians, get some discharge, which forms in the corners of the eyes and can be hard to remove. It is best just to use warm water on a cotton ball or tissue around the eyes and nose. A saline solution that people with contact lenses use can also be used to clean the eyes and nose. Some breeders use mild boric acid solutions to keep the area around their cat's eyes clean.

Kitty Has an Upset Stomach

If you have a cat that is vomiting, but still able to hold water and small bits of food down, you can try treating with Pepcid a/c. A cat can take $1/4$ to $1/2$ of a 10-mg tablet once daily. If you think the vomiting is due to a hairball and you do not have any type of hairball remedy, try $1/2$ teaspoon of white petroleum jelly on the cat's nose. Cats hate to have a dirty nose and will lick it clean, thereby ingesting some lubricant.

Some types of diarrhea will respond to treatment with Kaopectate. A 5-pound cat can take one teaspoon (5 ml) of the medication up to three times daily. The main ingredient is attapulgite, which absorbs bacteria and irritants.

One other drug for humans that can be safely used for a short period is Imodium. This drug should only be given in small amounts; the dose is $^1/_8$ teaspoon for a 10-pound cat three times daily, for no more than two days.

Again, it is always best to call your veterinarian before giving your cat any type of medication.

Kitty Is Constipated

It is normal for a cat to have a bowel movement at least once daily. Cats that pass less frequent, dry stools need help. You can also use a hairball remedy because it can act as a laxative.

Cats can become constipated due to diet, dehydration, or just by grooming and ingesting too much hair. If you think that your cat is constipated, you can buy a veterinary psyllium product or you can get plain Metamucil and give one to three teaspoons daily. One tablespoon of canned pumpkin pie filling can also work as a laxative.

Avoid CATastrophe

There is a subtle posture difference when a cat urinates versus defecates. If you observe your male cat straining to eliminate, and you are not sure that it is constipated, you should consult with a veterinarian immediately. Male cats can get life-threatening urinary blockages, and straining may be the only sign that they show.

Kitty Gets Carsick

Whether it is stress or motion sickness, some cats vomit when you travel with them in a car. You can give a cat Dramamine, $^1/_2$ of a 25-mg tablet 30 minutes before travel to calm the stomach. This drug is an antihistamine, so your pet may be sleepy after administration. Removing food and water for a few hours before travel also decreases the likelihood of vomiting during a car ride.

Kitty Was Just Stung by a Bee

It would be unusual for a cat to have an *anaphylactic* reaction to an insect bite or sting, but it would be normal for redness and swelling to occur at the site. Benadryl can be given to cats to help prevent the localized allergic reaction that occurs. You can give $^1/_2$ of a 25-mg tablet to a cat or 12.5 mg of the liquid. Be sure that the medication you are using is diphenhydramine only because many antihistamine preparations also contain acetaminophen, which can be potentially life-threatening to a cat.

Kitty Ditty

An **anaphylactic** reaction is a severe and potentially fatal allergic reaction. It can occur within seconds of contact to an allergen.

Worth a Paws

Cats like to keep themselves clean. If you apply any topical cream or ointment to a cat's skin, expect the animal to lick it. Using topical products sometimes draws a cat's attention to an irritated area and the skin can become more irritated if the cat licks it too much. Sometimes cats don't know when to stop.

Chlortrimeton, which is chlorpheniramine, can be used in cats. It comes as a 4-mg tablet and a cat can take $1/2$ tablet twice daily. This antihistamine could be used for an allergic reaction or for itchy skin.

Encounters with Oil

Cats that go outside often crawl into spots that they shouldn't. One of the problems that can occur is that they become covered in oil or grease from the underside of a car. These products will make the cat sick if it licks much of them off.

A safe way to remove grease or oils from a cat's coat is to bathe the animal in Dawn dishwashing liquid. It is not normally recommended to use any type of detergent on a cat, but this one is safe because it does not contain phosphates, which are dangerous to cats.

A Spoonful of Sugar Helps the Medicine Go Down

One of the challenges of feline medicine is getting medications into our patients. As most cat owners know, their loving kitty can turn into a wild animal when it comes to taking medicine. There are some hints that can make medicating easier.

Worth a Paws

Varying the medicating routine can help. If you give medicine at an exact time each day and go through the same preliminary steps to prepare, your cat may get smart and be out of sight when the time comes. Giving a treat as a reward after medicating can serve as positive reinforcement to the cat.

The most important aspect of getting medicine into a cat is the confidence of the owner. This may sound strange, but believe it or not, your cat knows when you are intimidated and will take full advantage of the situation. A positive attitude about getting the medicine into the cat's mouth is necessary for success. If you start the process with doubts, you will likely fail.

There Must Be an Easier Way

When I dispense medication to a client, if there are alternatives, I will ask if there is a preference for liquid or tablets. If the client is unable to give the medication that I prescribe, the cat may not get well, so I need to try to make it as easy for the owner as possible. If an owner has not medicated the cat before, a doctor or staff member will give the cat the first dose and demonstrate the procedure.

Medicating cats is more easily achieved if you put the animal up on a table or counter. By doing so you are taking the cat off of its "turf" and giving yourself an advantage. The harder that you try to hold a cat down to medicate, the more it will resist. Minimal restraint is best. Wrapping a cat in a towel like a baby is necessary in some cases.

Liquid Medication

Liquid medications can be dosed with either an eyedropper or a syringe without a needle. How quickly you will be able to squirt the medicine into the cat's mouth depends on the volume that is administered. Small volumes, up to 0.5 ml, can usually be given in one squirt. Larger volumes may need to be split into three or more squirts. You do not need to pry a cat's mouth open to give liquids. Simply insert the tip of the dropper into the corner of the mouth, lift the cat's chin, and squirt slowly.

Liquid medication can be given to a cat by placing a dropper at the corner of the mouth.

Owners frequently ask if they can mix the liquid medication into the cat's food. I generally do not recommend this because cats have a great sense of smell. When they detect a foreign substance in their food, they will not eat. Many of the liquid antibiotic drops are "fruity" and have sweet tastes and smells. They are not the perfect complement to a tuna dinner.

"Pilling" a Cat

Tablets or capsules can sometimes be crushed and successfully mixed into food, but learning to directly pill a cat is better. When I teach owners to give pills I ask whether they are right- or left-handed and then demonstrate with the same dominant hand.

Worth a Paws

Many cats will gag and foam after being medicated. This can be due to the bad taste of the medication, not swallowing initially, or stress. Foaming is only rarely due to an allergic reaction to the medication, so do not panic if your cat begins to drool.

Avoid CATastrophe

Never administer any kind of medication to your cat without first consulting your veterinarian. Do not assume that a remedy that has been recommended in the past for a particular symptom will again be appropriate should the same or similar symptom recur. Many medical conditions resemble one another, but their treatments may be very different. Don't guess at what treatment is right for your cat.

For example, I tell right-handed people to put the cat on a table parallel to their body with the head facing toward their right side. The cat's head needs to be grasped with the left hand around the cheekbones, and then tilted so that the cat's nose is pointing toward the ceiling. When done correctly, the cat's mouth will automatically open, and the more coordinated right index finger can pop the pill over the back of the cat's tongue while the middle finger holds the lower jaw down. In this situation, you are not opening the cat's mouth with your hands; you are using leverage to position the mouth open.

Plastic pill guns are available if putting your finger into the cat's mouth is dangerous or unsuccessful. Ask your veterinarian for one of these tools if you think you need it. Coating a pill with butter is another option. It will make the pill taste better and slide more easily down the throat. Some cats will lick up pills that are coated in hairball lubricant, because they like the taste of the lubricant
so much.

Doesn't It Come Another Way?

More and more veterinarians are utilizing compounding pharmacies. These pharmacies will take medications and re-formulate them into liquids that cats prefer or into sizes that are easier to administer. If you are having difficulty with medication, find out if it can be re-formulated. This can add cost to the product, but it is worth it if you are then able to get it into your pet.

A final option is to board an animal during treatment. This ensures that the medication is given properly.

The Least You Need to Know

➤ Cats that do not eat for more than 24 hours are probably sick; if the condition last longer than 48 hours, seek veterinary care.

➤ Dehydration can occur when cats do not eat or drink, and vomiting and diarrhea exacerbate the condition.

➤ Never give any type of aspirin, acetaminophen, or ibuprofen to cats for pain or fever.

➤ Cats like routine, so if their behavior changes, look for signs of illness.

➤ A veterinarian should examine your cat if clinical signs are not isolated events.

➤ It is always safer to have your veterinarian recommend or prescribe treatment for your cat, but in a few instances, it is acceptable to try some specific household remedies.

➤ Let your veterinarian know if you are having trouble medicating your cat so that other options can be explored.

Chapter 6

Annual Health Care for Your Cat

In This Chapter

➤ What is a complete physical exam?

➤ Which vaccines should be given and when

➤ How to keep teeth and gums healthy

➤ Does your cat have worms?

As much as cats seem like they don't need us, they do if they want to live long, healthy lives. In the wild they can do a good job of taking care of themselves, but the longevity of a housecat is much greater than that of its wild cousins.

The quality and length of a cat's life can be extended by some routine health care. Although it is said that cats have nine lives, they only have one that you can help along. By ensuring that your cat receives veterinary examinations, needed vaccines, dental care, and parasite control, you can offer your cat optimal preventative health care.

Kitty Ditty

You may hear a veterinarian use the term **palpation** during a physical examination of your cat. This term is used to describe the way the doctor uses her fingers to feel and touch different body parts and assess them.

Did Your Cat Pass Its Physical?

Cat owners often ask me what they can do to provide the best possible care for their pet. I tell them two things—keep it indoors and be sure that a veterinarian examines it at least once a year. For years, owners have mistakenly believed that vaccinating their cat was the best they could do, but this is not the case. Studies show that vaccinating cats annually may not be necessary. Some cats have adverse reactions to vaccines and are better off without getting annual boosters. The issue of vaccination will be more thoroughly discussed in Chapter 8.

Good owners can be very observant about their cats and notice changes that occur, but a veterinarian can objectively evaluate the animal on a regular basis. It is difficult for owners to assess subtle changes, such as weight loss that occurs slowly over a period of time, but a veterinarian can consult records and monitor trends.

What's Involved in an Annual Exam?

A veterinarian should examine a cat annually, from the tip of its nose to the end of its tail. Each doctor may have her own routine when conducting a full physical exam, but the best exams are thorough exams.

A full physical exam should include:

1. Measurement of body weight
2. Measurement of body temperature
3. Evaluation of the eyes, ears, and nose
4. Opening the mouth and assessing the teeth and gums
5. *Palpation* of external lymph nodes
6. Evaluation of the coat and skin
7. Evaluation of muscle tone and body condition
8. Listening to the heart and lungs with a stethoscope
9. Examination of the legs, paws, and claws
10. *Palpation* of the abdomen
11. Examination of the rectum and genitalia
12. Examination of the tail

Depending on the individual cat and how cooperative it is and the skill of the veterinarian, this examination can take anywhere from 2 to 10 minutes. In most situations, a veterinarian can conduct the exam without help, but when the patient is wiggly, scared, or aggressive, more hands are needed.

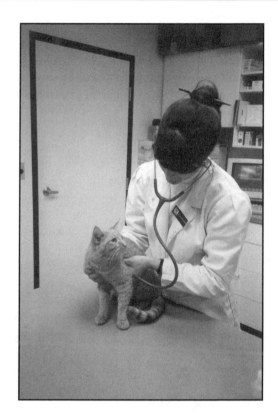

A veterinarian should carefully listen to the heart and lungs of a cat during a physical exam.

Meow Wow

When cats are hot or frightened, they are only able to sweat from their feet. The footpads are the only place containing moisture-secreting sweat glands. If you notice damp footprints on your veterinarian's exam table, you will know why.

Does It Hurt?

A routine physical exam is not painful to your cat. If the animal squawks and squirms, it is probably just resisting restraint rather than showing discomfort. Animals that have not been fully examined by a veterinarian before are generally less cooperative than those that previously have, but some cats are so frightened that they act worse at each successive veterinary visit.

Worth a Paws

If you have a cat that "acts up" when taken to a veterinary clinic, you should consider medicating it beforehand with a mild tranquilizer. It is not good for the cat to be stressed, and it is more difficult—if not impossible—for the veterinarian to do a good job with an uncooperative patient.

Let the professional veterinary staff handle your cat during any veterinary visit. Many animals become scared and defensive when they are outside their own homes and become fractious. Owners are often bitten or scratched by their own cats when they try to help hold the animal during an exam. Experienced animal assistants and veterinarians are trained to manage these situations. The best way that you can assist is by talking to your pet in a calm, reassuring voice.

At the end of a physical exam the veterinarian should discuss any abnormal findings and assess the general health of the cat. If you do not understand what the doctor has told you, be sure to ask questions. I personally like it when clients ask me questions because then I know that they are paying attention to what I have told them.

I also like it when clients come to the physical exam appointment armed with questions. This prevents a client from going home and wishing that he had asked the doctor something about the cat that he forgot during the appointment.

Meow Wow

Your veterinarian and her staff should be a resource for information on all aspects of caring for your cat, including nutrition and behavior. Bring any questions that you have on these issues along to discuss during your cat's annual physical exam.

All Those Needles!

Vaccines are an important aspect of preventive health care. However, many people wrongly believe that vaccines are more important than the hands-on exam by the doctor. Low-cost vaccine clinics have flourished on this premise, and as a consequence many cats do not receive adequate health care.

How Do Vaccines Work?

Antibodies obtained from their mothers protect newborn kittens from many diseases. This maternal immunity decreases between 8 and 12 weeks of age, and the kitten then needs other protection. The purpose of vaccinating is to "teach" the kitten's immune system to fight specific infectious agents. In almost all cases, vaccinating at 8 and then again at 12 weeks of age is adequate. Vaccination at these times provides protective immunity to the disease agents in the vaccine. This immunity protects against most symptoms connected with the disease agents but may not fully prevent infection. It can take up to 14 days after the vaccination for full immune function to occur. It is questionable how long the protective immunity lasts after that.

The vaccine manufacturers have recommended annual re-vaccination based on studying the duration of immunity for a few weeks to months. They have not been required by the USDA to determine longer durations of immunity except in the case of the rabies vaccine. Although rules have changed for establishing minimums, maximum duration of immunity studies are not required, thus we do not know exactly how long a vaccine will protect a cat.

Worth a Paws

The American Association of Feline Practitioners and the Academy of Feline Medicine (AAFP/AFM) published feline vaccination guidelines in 1998. These recommendations base vaccine administration on a cat's individual risk factors, history, and age. They question the necessity of vaccinating every cat every year. Discuss your cat's vaccination needs with your veterinarian.

Have Vaccines Been Linked to Cancer?

An increasing incidence of a type of tumor called fibrosarcoma has been noted in locations where vaccines are routinely administered to cats. Research is being conducted and a national veterinary task force exists to determine the relationship between vaccines and fibrosarcomas. The incidence of vaccine site fibrosarcomas is estimated at one to three out of every 10,000 vaccines administered, which is an extremely low number.

The veterinary community feels that the risk of disease from *not* vaccinating is much higher than the risks associated with vaccinating, but a re-thinking of how, when, where, and why we vaccinate cats has resulted. This is an extremely controversial issue for veterinarians, and not all veterinarians are in agreement over which vaccine protocols should be followed.

Kitty Needs Shots

One year after the initial vaccine series has been completed, the cat should receive booster vaccines. Vaccination in subsequent years should be based on the cat's risk of exposure and individual lifestyle. Detailed explanations of the vaccines are found in Chapter 8.

My vaccine recommendations for kittens are:

1. Feline Rhinotracheitis, Calici, Panleukopenia (FRCP) at 8 and 12 weeks.
2. Feline Leukemia (FeLV) at 10 and 14 weeks.
3. Rabies vaccine if required by law or if the cat goes outside at 16 weeks.

My vaccine recommendations for adult cats are:

1. FRCP annually to every three years.
2. FeLV annually if the cat has a risk of exposure to outside cats.
3. Rabies every three years if required by law or if the cat goes outside.

Vaccines exist that protect against FIP, Bordetella, and ringworm. I do not routinely recommend these vaccines, but would consider their use on an individual basis if risk factors exist.

Meow Wow

The AAFP/AFM has standardized vaccine sites to help identify causes of local adverse reactions and to aid in the treatment of vaccine-associated sarcomas. Abbreviated, these site recommendations are: FRCP vaccines should be administered over the right shoulder, FeLV in the left rear leg, and rabies in the right rear leg.

Adverse Responses to Vaccines

Adverse responses to vaccination do occur. Common, self-limiting reactions are pain or swelling at the injection site. If this type of reaction does not resolve within six weeks, it should be evaluated by cytology and/or biopsy. You should consult with your veterinarian if any type of reaction occurs post-vaccination.

Allergic reactions can occur in some cats after they have been vaccinated. These reactions can range from mild to severe anaphylaxis. If your cat has previously had any type of allergic reaction, you should alert your veterinarian and discuss possible preventive measures. These could include splitting up administration of multiple vaccines to different visits, pre-medicating with an antihistamine and/or a corticosteroid, or discontinuing certain vaccines.

A Cheshire Cat Smile

In a perfect world cats would brush their teeth every day just like we do. The reality is that cats cannot brush their own teeth, and many owners are not willing, too busy, or don't know how to brush their cat's teeth. Like humans, cats develop dental disease as plaque and tartar builds on their teeth. It can progress to gingivitis, which is inflammation of the gums.

As dental disease progresses it can lead to bacteria entering the cat's bloodstream and affecting other parts of the body. Some experts attribute the frequent occurrence of kidney disease in senior cats to occur as a result of long-term exposure to bacteria in the blood. Dental abscesses and infected jawbones may also be a result of dental disease.

A veterinarian examines a cat's teeth and checks for signs of dental disease.

Brushing Your Cat's Teeth

Owners can brush their cat's teeth, and many different products exist for use on cats. If you are able to brush your cat's teeth at least once a week, it will deter plaque and tartar buildup and therefore decrease dental disease.

Avoid CATastrophe

Do not use toothpaste made for humans on cats. Toothpaste for humans is not meant to be swallowed. Pet toothpaste can be swallowed and will not cause problems when ingested.

Here are some tips to follow if you want to brush your cat's teeth:

➤ Start brushing your cat's teeth at a young age—it makes training easier.

➤ Use a small bristled pet toothbrush or fingerbrush without toothpaste during first attempts.

➤ Try to rub the cat's teeth at the tooth's gum line two or three times a side, both upper and lower teeth.

➤ Add a pet toothpaste to the brush if you are meeting with success.

Other Ways to Keep Teeth Clean

Dry foods tend to cause less plaque buildup than canned foods, so feeding a primarily dry diet (see Chapter 2) can help the teeth. Feline diets that are formulated to prevent plaque buildup are available and can be fed for maintenance or as a treat. Specific dental treats are also available, but none of these items will knock the existing plaque off of the teeth.

Do You Need to Take Your Cat to a Dentist?

Your veterinarian should be able to provide routine dental examinations and care. Some veterinarians are able to perform restorations and root canals. Some can even perform orthodontics! If veterinarians choose to pursue it, board certification in dentistry can be obtained.

During your cat's annual physical exam, its teeth and gums should be examined and evaluated. Your veterinarian should let you know the condition of your cat's teeth and if dentistry is needed. Each cat builds plaque at a different rate, but almost all cats need to have their teeth professionally cleaned by the time they are 4 years old. How frequently the animal will need the procedure repeated varies, but many cats need their teeth cleaned every year. Cats with bad gums may even need cleaning every six months.

If your veterinarian tells you that your cat needs a dental, he is usually talking about cleaning, polishing, fluoride treating, and removing any infected, eroded, or broken teeth. These procedures are performed with the cat under general anesthesia, but on an outpatient basis with the animal coming in the morning and going home at the end of the day. Your cat's teeth are cleaned the same way that yours would be by a dentist, but unfortunately cats are not willing to open up and say, "ahhh."

Is Dentistry Safe?

When dentistry is properly performed, many precautions are taken. You should discuss any fears that you have regarding the procedure with your veterinarian. Age is not a valid reason to decline a dental procedure for your cat. The risks associated with the bad teeth and infection is harder on the cat's body than dentistry and anesthesia.

Meow Wow

Owners frequently tell me how fabulously their cat is doing post-dentistry. They tell me that they did not realize how uncomfortable their cat was until after the procedure was performed. Even if your cat is eating well, it doesn't mean that its teeth don't hurt.

Pulling Teeth

Unlike in humans, it is very difficult to save a cat's damaged teeth with any type of filling material. When significant damage to a tooth has occurred, your veterinarian will likely recommend that it be extracted. Extractions can be performed during the same anesthesia as dental cleaning. A combination of hand tools and a power drill may be used to properly extract a tooth.

Cats do not have the same cosmetic need for teeth that we do, but their teeth do play a role in picking up food and holding it in their mouths. Owners naturally are very concerned about their cat's ability to eat if multiple teeth need to be removed, but believe it or not, even cats without teeth can eat dry food once their gums have healed. They can make a mess because food drops out of their mouths, but they are happy.

Parasite Control

There are two types of parasites: internal parasites such as gastrointestinal worms, and external parasites such as fleas. It is common for kittens and outdoor cats to have parasites, but adult indoor-only cats have little exposure to these bothersome creatures.

When Your Cat Has Worms

It is recommended that all kittens have their feces checked for worms. During a fecal examination, the sample is examined for worm eggs and protozoal parasites. The common intestinal parasites are:

Avoid CATastrophe

Over-the-counter de-worming medications are available that can be effective against some types of worms, but they are not effective against tapeworms. If you choose to use a non-prescription de-worming medication, read the label carefully to make sure you are treating for the right worm, and giving the appropriate dose.

➤ Roundworms

➤ Coccidia

➤ Giardia

➤ Tapeworms

➤ Hookworms

➤ Whipworms

Eggs for roundworms, hookworms, and whipworms can be found in feces when examined under a microscope. It is not common to see tapeworm eggs; you are more likely to see the worm segments. The segments look like rice when they are fresh and then like sesame seeds when they dry out.

Coccidia and giardia are protozoal parasites—one-celled organisms that can be seen microscopically. Both are common parasites, but giardia is more difficult to find in a fecal examination.

All gastrointestinal parasites can cause diarrhea, but this symptom will not always occur. It is possible for your cat to have worms without you knowing it. During a routine physical exam, a veterinarian should look under the cat's tail to check for tapeworm segments. A fecal exam should be performed on all kittens, and during an adult cat's annual visit, it is a good idea to have a fecal sample checked.

Veterinarians can diagnose and specifically treat intestinal parasites. Some parasites can be eliminated with one treatment, but others need successive days of treatment or repeated treatment two weeks later. Parasites are not present in every fecal sample, so if your veterinarian recommends repeating a fecal check, there is good reason.

Worms are not deadly to a cat, but they make absorption of nutrients less efficient and they can cause diarrhea. Small kittens with large numbers of worms are affected the most, and their growth and condition can be impaired. Protozoal parasites are more dangerous than worms if uncontrolled because they can cause dehydration and more severe diarrhea.

Flee, Fleas!

In the 1990s, there have been great advances in products that are effective against fleas. Some of the safest and most effective products are only available through veterinarians.

Aside from causing discomfort to your cat, fleas can cause:

➤ Allergic dermatitis

➤ Anemia

➤ Tapeworms

➤ Discomfort to you and other pets

Cats are very sensitive to many chemicals, so any time you use an over-the-counter flea product, be sure to read the label and be careful. It is best to get professional advice regarding flea control, and your veterinarian and staff are a great resource.

Types of flea control products are:

➤ Flea combs

➤ Oral, injectable or collars with growth regulators

➤ Spot-on adulticides

➤ Shampoos

➤ Dips

➤ Sprays

➤ Foams

➤ Powders

➤ Collars

➤ Home treatments

➤ Yard sprays

Worth a Paws

Program, Advantage, and Frontline are products that have revolutionized flea control. Although expensive and available only through veterinarians, they are very effective and safe. Flea experts recommend using a growth regulator, such as Program, and an adulticide, such as Advantage or Frontline, in combination to prevent the emergence of resistant fleas.

Cats that stay indoors generally have fewer problems with fleas than cats that go outside. It is more difficult to control fleas in a multi-pet environment. These factors are all important in deciding which flea control products to use. The flea has historically developed resistance to all products developed to eradicate it, so it will be interesting to see what happens with the newer products available. Will fleas continue to beat the system?

Fleas like to live in warm, moist environments. They can live inside all year-round, and in warmer climates they can survive outside all year. The best way to monitor a cat for fleas is to comb it regularly with a flea comb. The comb will catch fleas in its teeth and also trap flea dirt. If you find signs of fleas, continue to comb and try to pick them all off or you can use the comb as a gauge of your success with other products.

Meow Wow

Fleas and tapeworms are two parasites that have a connection. Cats get tapeworms by ingesting fleas that are carrying tapeworm larvae. Humans cannot get tapeworms from their cats; a human would have to eat a flea to get the same tapeworms.

Other Parasites That Can Make Your Cat Itch

Cats can be infested with other external parasites, including mange and lice. Luckily, these feline-specific parasites are not usually contagious to humans. Your veterinarian can make recommendations on ridding your cat of these parasites.

Cats do not carry pinworms. If you have a child with pinworms, do not blame your cat; they came from another source.

The Least You Need to Know

➤ Your cat should receive a full physical exam by a veterinarian at least once a year.

➤ Vaccines are important to providing immunity to your cat, but you should work with your veterinarian to develop an individual vaccine program.

➤ Good dental health can improve your cat's longevity and its quality of life.

➤ Internal and external parasite control is needed to keep your cat healthy.

Chapter 7

Does Your Cat Need to Go Under the Knife?

In This Chapter

➤ What you should know about declawing

➤ What you should know about neutering

➤ What you should know about spaying

➤ Do you need to fix your cat's hernia?

There are a few elective surgeries that you will consider during the first year of your cat's life. These are routine procedures that are performed at a veterinary clinic. Any surgical procedure involves some risks and anesthesia, but experienced veterinarians and modern drugs decrease the potential for problems.

Many cat owners look for deals on the prices for these procedures, and prices can vary greatly. Keep in mind that to use good drugs, monitor the patient adequately, and to perform the procedure in a sterile and painstaking manner does involve expense. When prices are low, corners need to be cut somewhere.

The Draperies Are in Shreds!

In veterinary medicine, declawing cats is a controversial issue. Declawing is a surgical procedure that permanently removes the toenails. Scratching is a normal cat behavior, and some people feel that it is cruel and inhumane to remove a cat's body parts just because it makes the owner's life easier.

Many owners routinely have kittens declawed in order to prevent problems later when the cat uses prized household possessions as scratching posts. Not every cat engages in destructive scratching though, and most can be trained to scratch in an appropriate location.

Meow Wow

In England it is illegal to declaw a cat. The British have stricter laws than we do in the United States regulating cosmetic and surgical procedures performed on animals.

Worth a Paws

Veterinarians can use pain-relieving drugs to help with discomfort after surgery. Oral pain relievers can be prescribed, but the application of a patch that releases small amounts of drug continuously is becoming more and more popular. Ask your veterinarian about pain relief and your cat.

What's Involved in Declawing?

When a cat is declawed, the last joint on each toe is amputated. Many people think that declawing involves cutting the nail very short, but it actually requires removal of bones. There are a few different surgical techniques to do this, and each veterinarian has his or her preference.

Most of the time, only the front claws are removed in a declaw, but in some situations owners ask that all four feet be done. No matter which surgical technique is employed, there is some pain involved with declawing. If an owner wants to declaw a cat, I urge them to do so at a young age (between 8 and 16 weeks). The pain associated with the procedure is much less in smaller, younger animals.

During the procedure the cat is under some type of anesthesia, surgery is performed, then the feet are bandaged and the animal is hospitalized for at least one night. The recovery period varies and depends on the size and age of the cat. It also depends on the use of pain relievers and the occurrence of any complications.

Some veterinary clinics use a laser, rather than a scalpel blade, to declaw cats. Lasers cut and cauterize tissue at the same time, so healing may occur more rapidly.

Is Declawing Cruel?

There are differing opinions regarding declawing. I personally think that it is a painful procedure, and before declawing your cat, you should try to train it to use a scratching post. If a cat is being destructive or injuring you with its claws, training is not successful, and you are going to keep the cat inside, declawing may be a valid alternative.

Many humane groups and the Cat Fancier's Association condemn declawing, but it is a personal choice for each cat owner. Some breeders and cat rescue groups will require that you sign a contract stating that you will not declaw any cat that you purchase or adopt from them.

During the recovery period it is common for cats to be hesitant to jump and to hold their paws up in the air. These signs all indicate pain. Owners are frequently concerned after the surgery when their cats show these signs, but they need to understand that it takes time for healing and calluses to form around the newly exposed bone and nerve ending.

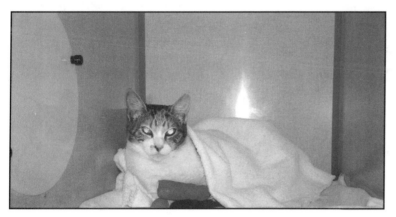

After a cat has had declaw surgery, the paws may be wrapped, and the animal may be hospitalized for one or two nights.

Declawing Alternatives

The most basic alternatives to declaw surgery are trimming a cat's toenails every few weeks, and working on training the animal to use a scratching post. Vinyl nail caps, called Soft Paws, are available and when applied can last about a month. They cover the cat's normal nail with a smooth cap, thus preventing damage. Many veterinarians carry this product and will apply them. Take-home kits are available if you want to apply them yourself.

Digital flexor tenectomy is an alternative surgical procedure, but not one that I favor because I don't think there are enough benefits. Instead of amputating the bone in the toe, a small piece of the tendon that controls the claw is removed. It prevents the cat from protruding or retracting its claws, and it is a less painful procedure since no bone is removed. When this procedure is performed, the cat's toenails still need to be trimmed regularly because the animal cannot control them and the nails will not wear down.

Side Effects to Declawing

It is rare for complications to arise with a declaw, but it is always a possibility. Infections occur infrequently but respond favorably to antibiotic treatment. Swelling of the paws can occur and is controlled with bandaging. If a veterinarian uses careless surgical techniques, regrowth of a toenail or part of a nail can occur.

Studies show that declawed cats do not bite any more than clawed cats. Declawing does not directly change a cat's behavior either. Declawed cats can still climb (but not as well), and their defensive mechanisms are reduced, so they should not be allowed outside unsupervised.

Avoid CATastrophe

Two deadly viruses, Feline Leukemia Virus and Feline Immunodeficiency Virus, are much more common in intact male cats. This is because the viruses are passed by direct contact, especially through biting, and biting and fighting occur most often between two male cats. Neutering can help prevent the spread of these diseases.

Prevent a Paternity Suit

Part of being a responsible owner is sterilizing your cat, whether it is male or female. Men who own cats are sometimes empathetic to their male cat and do not want to castrate it, but this is ridiculous. Cats have sex to reproduce, not because they derive any pleasure from it.

Neutered cats live happier, healthier lives and make much better house pets than intact animals. If you have ever smelled the urine of a tomcat, you will understand why you would not want one in your home. Once tomcat urine soils something, the odor cannot be removed. It is even hard to deal with the smell of tomcat urine after a litterbox has been emptied!

What Is Neutering?

When a male cat is neutered, he is castrated and both testicles are surgically removed. By doing so, the main testosterone-producing organs are taken out of the body.

Why Neuter?

Testosterone is responsible for:

➤ The terrible odor of tomcat urine

➤ Wide facial "jowls"

➤ Thicker skin

➤ Increased territoriality

➤ Marking of territory by spraying

➤ Aggressive tendencies, including fighting between male cats

➤ The tendency to roam farther from home

➤ Stud tail—the greasy spot at the tail base

All of these problems are eliminated or at least decreased by neutering. A male can no longer produce sperm without testosterone, so he is infertile.

Will Neutering Change Your Cat's Personality?

Neutering does not change any of the good aspects of a cat's personality. It can take the aggressive "edge" off of an animal, but an affectionate male will still love you after being neutered. The evening after surgery your cat could still be feeling the effects of anesthesia and may act differently, but that resolves by the next day.

The beneficial effects of neutering are not seen immediately, and if you neuter a kitten that has not reached puberty, you will not see any changes. Neutering a young animal prevents behavioral and odor problems from occurring. If you neuter a cat that has reached puberty, it will take a few weeks for behaviors and odors to change as the current testosterone level declines.

Owners sometimes ask me whether their cat could receive a vasectomy instead of castration. Although one of the purposes of neutering is to prevent reproduction, the main reasons are to decrease the undesirable behaviors associated with testosterone. If an animal were to have a vasectomy, testosterone would still be present and so would the associated undesirable behaviors.

When Should You Neuter?

The general recommendation for neutering a cat is at 6 months of age. This is before an average cat would reach puberty. Many humane groups and breeders will neuter kittens, if they have two testicles in their scrotums, at 8 weeks of age. This procedure prevents the cats from mating. This early-age neutering is considered safe, and it does not cause problems later on in life.

Most veterinarians neuter cats on an outpatient basis: The animal will come in the morning, have surgery, and then go home the same evening. Neutering is a surgical procedure usually performed under injectable anesthesia without sutures. There is little aftercare, and a post-surgical visit is not needed.

Cats with Only One Testicle

All male cats have two testicles, so if they are not in the scrotum, they are somewhere else. During normal development, the testicles move from inside the abdominal cavity to outside into the scrotum. When this does not occur, the testicles are considered "retained." Most male kittens are born with testicles in their scrotums. If testicles are still retained at 8 months of age, it is unlikely that they are going to descend.

Retained testicles still produce testosterone, but *cryptorchid* cats are less fertile than normal cats. Because testosterone is present, these animals should definitely be neutered. Cryptorchidism is heritable, and animals possessing this trait should not be bred.

Kitty Ditty

Cryptorchid is the term used to describe a cat with only one testicle present in the scrotum. The term monorchid could also be used. If a male cat has neither testicle in the scrotum, he is called a bilateral cryptorchid.

The surgical procedure for a cryptorchid cat is similar to a spay. The retained testicle is either going to be in the abdominal cavity or somewhere along the path through which it would normally descend, such as the inguinal canal. The cost involved in this procedure is higher than for an uncomplicated neuter because lengthier surgery will be needed to find the testicle.

Prevent Unwanted Pregnancy

Cats are very efficient at reproducing, and once an animal has reached puberty, it is sexually mature and can reproduce. Female cats do not usually reach puberty before 6 months of age, but during the spring mating season and in multi-cat households, occasionally puberty comes earlier.

Is Your Cat a Hussy?

Female cats go through some bizarre behaviors when they go into heat. Most cats get very friendly, rub up to you and other animals in the family, and even stick their rear ends up in the air. They can howl and writhe on the floor, even look like they are in pain, during a heat cycle. Cats do not bleed when they are in heat. At my veterinary clinic we frequently get calls from new cat owners who are in a panic after observing these behaviors in their cat.

Meow Wow

Cats are seasonally polyestrus. Their heat season generally runs from February to September, and females can cycle every two weeks during this time unless they are bred or stimulated to ovulate. This explains how cats can produce a new litter of kittens every few months.

What Is Spaying?

Most veterinarians perform *ovariohysterectomy* surgeries on an outpatient basis. Although these are routine procedures, people do not realize that an abdominal surgery is being performed. A cat is placed under general anesthesia, usually with some type of gas anesthetic, and an abdominal incision is made. The ovaries and the uterus are removed, and the surgery site is closed with sutures. The sutures can be absorbable or they can be removed in 10 days, depending on the preference of the doctor.

Kitty Ditty

When a cat is spayed, it has an **ovariohysterectomy,** in which the animal's uterus and ovaries are removed.

When to Spay

If possible, you want to spay a cat before it goes through heat even one time. This can be achieved by spaying at 6 months of age. As with male kittens, early-age sterilization is possible as young as 8 weeks of age. There are no benefits to having a cat experience a heat cycle, and certainly there is no benefit for a cat to have a litter of kittens. These are myths.

The Benefits of Spaying

Aside from stopping annoying heat cycles, spaying will prevent your cat from contributing to pet overpopulation. Female cats that have experienced one or more heat cycles are more likely to develop malignant breast cancer than spayed cats. Intact female cats are at risk for pyometra—a life-threatening uterine infection. An infection like this cannot occur if there is no uterus.

Avoid CATastrophe

There are many sad statistics regarding pet overpopulation. Each year tens of thousands of cats are euthanized in the United States because no one wants them. Be a responsible cat owner and have your pet sterilized before it can contribute to the pet overpopulation problem.

Spayed female cats are less likely to roam in search of a mate, and they are less likely to be aggressive. As with male cats, sterilizing will not change any of the positive aspects of the animal's personality.

There are always some slight risks involved with surgery and general anesthesia, but for a young, healthy cat they are negligible. If complications were to occur, they would most likely be due to an underlying health or congenital problem or poor surgical techniques. This is another reason why you should think about factors other than cost when choosing a doctor to perform the surgery.

An ovariohysterectomy is an irreversible procedure, so once a cat is spayed, she will never be able to reproduce. Some cat owners want to "experience" the birth of kittens, especially if they have children themselves. Instead, I think they should visit their local animal shelter and see what happens after the miracle of birth when homes are not found for the kittens.

On occasion, the owner of a purebred kitten tells me that he wants the cat to have kittens, so that he can recoup his money. I think that this is another terrible reason to breed a cat. Responsible breeders sell purebred kittens as pets because they are not optimum show quality. They want you to sign a contract that you will not breed the animal. You should buy a pet purebred cat because you want it, not because you want to make money. If any complications arise in the pregnancy and measures such as a caesarian section are needed, the litter will end up costing you money instead.

Hernias in Cats

Some kittens are born with hernias, which are holes in a muscle that should normally be solid. These defects are usually not very serious and can be corrected as an elective procedure.

Types of Hernias

The most common type of hernia is called an umbilical hernia and occurs when the kitten's belly button does not close properly. The hole that is left is usually quite small, and it appears as an out-pocketing at the middle of the belly covered by skin. If you touch it, it feels soft. You can even reduce the hernia temporarily by pushing the abdominal fat back into the small hole in the body wall with your finger.

Inguinal hernias can be a congenital defect or they can occur secondary to trauma. An inguinal hernia appears as an out-pocketing in the groin region.

Two other hernias are occasionally found in cats. These are diaphragmatic and pericardial-diaphragmatic hernias. These types of hernias occur in the chest cavity and must be found through an x-ray. You might suspect one of these in an animal that is having some difficulty breathing. Breathing is affected because abdominal organs that would normally be held back by an intact diaphragm are able to move into the chest cavity and compress the lungs.

Diaphragmatic hernias are most often due to trauma, when the diaphragm, which is the muscular band separating the chest and abdominal cavities, is damaged. This is an injury that needs to be surgically repaired.

Pericardial-diaphragmatic hernias are congenital defects. In this condition, the diaphragm is connected to the pericardium, which is the sack surrounding the heart. This malady sounds serious and looks terrible on an x-ray, but the surgical repair can be more dangerous than living with the defect.

How Serious Is a Hernia?

Umbilical hernias are not an emergency, and they can be repaired when the animal is sterilized. Repairing an umbilical hernia involves a few sutures in the abdominal wall and the skin. A spay incision can usually be extended to include and then close an umbilical hernia. In a male cat, a hernia repair will be at a separate site than castration surgery. If your cat has an umbilical hernia, ask your veterinarian what would be involved with repair at the time of sterilization.

Inguinal hernias are usually not emergencies either, but because they can enlarge, they should be repaired. Diaphragmatic hernias should be repaired as soon as it is safely possible. A pericadial-diaphragmatic hernia should be left alone unless it affects the animal's ability to breathe.

What if It's Not Fixed?

The risk with any hernia is that if it gets larger, organs can get trapped in abnormal locations and be damaged. It is rare for an umbilical hernia to get larger, and if surgery is not performed, it could scar down with a bubble of fat protruding, or it could stay open and continue to feel like a soft out-pocketing throughout a cat's life.

The Least You Need to Know

➤ Declawing involves amputating a piece of bone from each toe, and it is a safe but painful procedure.

➤ There are alternatives to declawing, but if you choose the procedure, you should keep your cat indoors.

➤ Neutered male and spayed female cats make healthier, better pets.

➤ Don't panic if your kitten has an umbilical hernia, it can be easily fixed when the animal is sterilized.

Chapter 8

Vaccinating Your Cat

In This Chapter

➤ Learn about the different types of vaccines available

➤ Learn about the diseases that vaccines prevent

➤ Understand which vaccines your cat may benefit from

➤ Learn about vaccine schedules

When you get a vaccine reminder card in the mail from your veterinarian, you probably think that it looks like a bowl of vegetable soup. What are FRCP, FeLV, and FIP? Many owners don't inquire about what these letters stand for and tell the veterinarian to go ahead and give the cat all the shots it needs. I don't think that this is a good idea.

As a cat owner it is useful to have some basic knowledge of the diseases that you protect your cat against with vaccines. You may be surprised to find out that vaccines are not as protective as you have been led to believe, and that giving vaccines annually may not be in your cat's best interest. The purpose of vaccinating is to "teach" the cat's immune system to fight specific infectious agents. Does the system need to be reminded each and every year?

Annual vaccination of your cat has always been veterinary standard practice, and owners have been taught to vaccinate their pets each year. However, during the 1990s the veterinary profession has begun to question the need for annual vaccination. This is in light of new information regarding the duration of immunity derived from vaccines, and adverse vaccine reactions, including tumors, that may be associated with sites of vaccination.

What You Should Know About Vaccinating Your Cat

The American Association of Feline Practitioners and the Academy of Feline Medicine took a bold step and created an advisory panel on feline vaccines. They published feline vaccination guidelines in January 1998. The following information highlights some of the guideline recommendations. Your veterinarian may or may not be familiar with these specific guidelines, but discussing your individual cat's vaccination needs is important.

The AAFP/AFM Feline Vaccination Guidelines state that, "The objective of feline vaccination protocols should be to vaccinate more cats in the population, vaccinate individuals less frequently, and only for the diseases for which there is a risk of exposure and disease." Assessing an individual cat's risk of infection is a cornerstone in developing a vaccine protocol. The three items that need to be evaluated are the patient, the patient's environment, and the infectious agents.

Evaluating Risk

When making a decision about vaccination, risk factors to consider are:

➤ Age

➤ Number of cats in the household

➤ Exposure to outdoor or free-roaming cats

➤ Boarding

➤ Catteries (cat breeding facilities)

➤ Shelters

Because they have immature immune systems, young kittens are more susceptible to disease than adult cats. Initially, kittens are protected by antibodies they receive through their mother's milk. The first milk that a queen produces is called colostrum, and it is rich in protective antibodies. These antibodies provide maternal immunity and are absorbed into a kitten's system during its first 24 hours of life. Maternal immunity wears off by 12 weeks of age, and kittens must then develop antibodies on their own. Antibodies are developed after vaccination and after exposure to infectious diseases.

The number of cats in the home environment and the chance of exposure to other cats also play major roles in assessing risk. The chance of exposure to infectious agents in a household with one or two cats is significantly less than in a larger multi-cat household. Cats that go outdoors and come in contact with free-roaming or other indoor/outdoor cats face a higher risk of disease exposure.

Cats that are housed in boarding facilities, catteries, or shelters have a greater opportunity of being exposed to infectious agents. This is due to stress, crowding, and simply the number of cats in the facility. Cats that come from different environments can bring different infectious agents with them.

It can take up to 14 days post-vaccination for full immune function to develop. So, if you vaccinate your cat for the first time today, it will not have protective immunity until at least 14 days after the initial vaccine series has been completed.

How Diseases Are Spread

Infectious agents are viruses, bacteria, and fungi—microorganisms capable of causing diseases. Infectious agent exposure can occur by many routes. Each agent has its own method of passage between cats. Airborne infections are more likely to affect cats housed in boarding facilities, catteries, or shelters. Diseases that are spread by direct cat-to-cat exposure are more likely in cats that go outdoors, where uncontrolled contact between cats can occur.

Avoid CATastrophe

Introducing a new cat into a home has the potential for introduction of new infectious agents. This is especially true if the cat has come from a cattery or shelter. To try to prevent problems, isolate a new addition to the household for at least one week and have it examined by a veterinarian before introducing it to your other cats.

The decision to vaccinate for a particular infectious disease agent should be based on reviewing the patient's risk assessment. Currently, vaccines exist to protect against nine different infectious diseases in cats, and several manufacturers produce vaccines. The infectious agents are:

➤ Rhinotracheitis virus (feline herpes)

➤ Calici virus

➤ Panleukopenia virus

➤ Chlamydia (pneumonitis)

➤ Feline Leukemia Virus

➤ Rabies virus

➤ Feline Infectious Peritonitis virus

➤ Bordetella

➤ Ringworm

The Core Vaccines

The AAFP/AFM guidelines have created two categories of vaccines: core and non-core. A core vaccine is recommended for all cats based on several factors, including severity of disease, potential risk to humans, prevalence of disease, and safety and efficacy of the vaccine. A non-core vaccine may be appropriate in certain situations, but is not recommended for all cats.

The four infectious diseases that have been deemed "core" are Feline Panleukopenia virus, Feline Rhinotracheitis virus (feline herpes), Feline Calicivirus, and Rabies virus.

Feline Rhinotracheitis, Calici, and Panleukopenia

Most owners know this as the FRCP or three-way vaccine. The general recommendations for this core vaccine are:

1. Vaccinate kittens at their initial veterinary visit (6 to 8 weeks).

2. Vaccinate again every three to four weeks until the kitten is over 12 weeks of age.

3. Give a booster one year later.

4. Booster every three years unless the cat has a higher risk of exposure such as boarding or traveling to cat shows.

Injectable vaccines are drawn into syringes before they are administered.

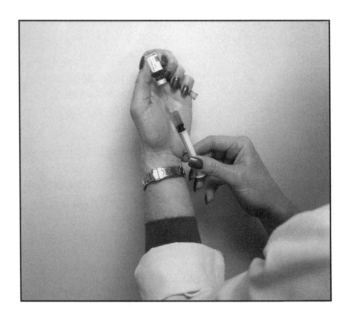

Feline Panleukopenia is "feline parvo," and the virus is usually fatal to affected cats. It is shed in feces and transmitted through fecal-oral contact. Panleukopenia virus can contaminate cages, bowls, and litterboxes and be spread through poor hygiene. Most vaccines available for this agent stimulate complete protective immunity. Clinical signs associated with panleukopenia can include fever, anorexia, vomiting, and diarrhea. Death can be rapid due to severe dehydration and electrolyte imbalances. The most characteristic finding is an extremely low white blood cell count when a complete blood count (CBC) is run.

Feline herpesvirus and feline calicivirus are estimated to cause up to 90 percent of upper respiratory disease in cats. These diseases are rarely fatal but are extremely prevalent. Transmission occurs through sneezing and aerosol spread, by direct contact, and by contaminated objects. The most common signs are sneezing, anorexia, and conjunctivitis (inflammation of the tissues around the eyeball).

Meow Wow

Feline herpesvirus does not cause disease in humans. Humans can be affected with Herpes simplex, which causes fever blisters, and Herpes zoster, which is responsible for chicken pox and shingles.

Cats can develop chronic herpesvirus infections that cause long-term, intermittent bouts of sneezing and conjunctivitis. Feline calicivirus infection can also cause limping or severe gum disease in some cases.

Topical vaccines may be administered in an intranasal (in the nose) or intraocular (in the eye) manner. The benefits of topical vaccination are stimulation of more rapid protection and no chance of injection site tumor. The disadvantages of topical vaccination are the possible triggering of mild sneezing, coughing, and conjunctivitis. This type of vaccine can be useful in boarding, cattery, and shelter situations when quicker and more frequent upper respiratory disease protection is needed.

Worth a Paws

Vaccination against herpes and calici viruses does not prevent infection but does reduce the severity of the associated clinical signs. In addition to the traditional injectable form of vaccination, a topical vaccination is available for these viruses. Topical vaccines may be administered in an intranasal (in the nose) or intraocular (in the eye) manner.

Rabies

Rabies is placed into the core vaccine category because of the potential for a rabid cat bite to cause human infection. Rabies is transmitted primarily through bite wounds. The virus is present in the saliva of infected animals. Clinical signs associated with rabies infection are behavioral changes, pupil dilation changing to constriction, drooling, and stumbling. Infected animals can die within four days of developing clinical signs. Once clinical signs develop there is no effective treatment for rabies.

Avoid CATastrophe

A few species of animals are more likely to carry rabies than others. Always use caution if you come in contact with bats, skunks, or raccoons (especially during the day) because they are common carriers. These animals can carry rabies but not develop clinical signs.

Normally friendly and affectionate animals can suddenly and unexpectedly turn aggressive and agitated when infected with rabies, and normally aloof cats can become very friendly. The incubation period of the virus—the time from bite wound to clinical signs—is variable. Rabies is introduced into a cat's body by a bite, spreads up nerves to enter the central nervous system, then spreads to other body tissues. For some reason the virus likes to go to the salivary glands.

Rabies vaccine can be administered to kittens over 12 weeks of age, one year later, and then every three years. Certain states have laws that require cats be vaccinated against rabies, while others do not. Each locale may also have different rules regarding quarantine of animals that bite humans. Healthy, nonvaccinated animals that bite humans may be under observational quarantine for 10 or more days.

Non-Core Vaccines

The decision to vaccinate with one or more of the non-core vaccines should be based on the previously discussed risk factors. Non-core vaccines are not necessary for all animals. They should be considered for those cats that have a risk of exposure to the particular disease. You should discuss the pros and cons of vaccination with your veterinarian.

Discuss the vaccine needs of your cat with a veterinarian.

Chlamydia

Chlamydia psittaci is a bacterial infection that causes upper respiratory disease in cats. Transmission is through direct cat-to-cat contact. The most common clinical sign is severe conjunctivitis. Vaccination does not prevent infection with chlamydia, but it can lessen the associated clinical signs.

Kitty Ditty

Don't be alarmed when you hear about feline chlamydiosis caused by Chlamydia psittaci. This is not the same agent that causes venereal disease in humans, which is Chlamydia trachomatis.

The prevalence of Chlamydia psittaci in the United States is considered to be low. Some veterinarians feel that vaccines for Chlamydia produce a relatively high adverse reaction rate. Chlamydia is commonly the fourth component of a four-way booster vaccine (FRCPC—Feline rhinotracheitis, calici, panleukopenia, and Chlamydia). At this time, the duration of immunity conferred with vaccination is unknown, and annual vaccination is recommended only for those animals at risk.

Feline Leukemia Virus

Feline Leukemia Virus (FeLV) is a potentially fatal virus of cats. It is passed by direct cat-to-cat contact or by a queen to her kittens. Testing and identifying FeLV-positive cats is essential to controlling infection. Clinical signs associated with FeLV are non-specific and can range from anemia to immuno-suppression to tumor formation. FeLV can cause latent infections, which hide quietly in the cat but may cause clinical signs months to years later.

Kitty Ditty

FeLV and FIV (Feline Immunodeficiency Virus) are both members of the retrovirus family. Tests exist for both, but a vaccine is only currently available for FeLV.

Vaccination is recommended for cats that test negatively for FeLV but live in environments where possibilities for exposure to the virus exist. Some veterinarians recommend that all kittens receive initial vaccinations to FeLV because their exposure risk may not yet be defined. For example, even though you do not want your kitten to go outside, things might change and the animal could end up going out at some point in the future. You would want it to be protected in this situation.

The vaccination schedule for FeLV is as follows:

1. Vaccinate at 9 weeks of age or older.

2. Repeat vaccine four weeks later.

3. If the cat remains in a high-risk environment, continue vaccinating annually.

Cats at risk for exposure to FeLV include cats that go outdoors, stray cats, feral cats, open multi-cat households, FeLV-positive households, and households with unknown FeLV status. Vaccination confers fair to good immunity to the cat, and this varies between manufacturers.

Feline Leukemia vaccines are administered in the left rear leg muscle.

Kitty Ditty

On its own, FECV is not a life-threatening virus, but it can cause diarrhea and is contagious among cats. In some catteries and multi-cat households, every cat will have an antibody titer, which indicates exposure, to a feline corona virus.

Feline Infectious Peritonitis (FIP)

FIP is a fatal virus of cats. This virus' mode of transmission is not definitively known, but the current theory is that it is passed through oral or nasal contact with feces infected with Feline Enteric Corona Virus (FECV), a common virus, which then mutates in certain individual cats to become FIP. A mutation is a change in the virus's genetic code. Transmission may also occur from a queen to her kittens.

Circumstances that may influence whether or not FECV mutates to FIP are:

➤ Age of the cat (most susceptible cats are less than one year old)

➤ Breed of cat

➤ Genetics

➤ General health

➤ Immune status

➤ Environmental stresses

Unlike FeLV, reliable screening tests for FIP do not exist; therefore, assessing protection from vaccination is difficult. Efficacy of the FIP vaccine has been controversial because some studies support protection and others fail to demonstrate significant protection. Fortunately, the incidence of FIP in pet households is low.

The AAFP panel was unable to come to a consensus regarding what constitutes an "at-risk" cat. One at-risk category would be cats in households where FIP had been previously diagnosed, and vaccination could protect cats that have not already been exposed. This vaccine is administered initially in two doses, three to four weeks apart in cats over 16 weeks and then boostered annually. FIP vaccine is only available in an intranasal form.

Bordetella

Bordetella bronchiseptica is a bacterium that is better known for causing kennel cough in dogs. It has been cultured from cats with upper respiratory infections and also in cases of pneumonia. Within the veterinary community there is debate as to the necessity for this vaccine because Bordetella does not seem to cause disease in many pet cats.

The highest incidences of Bordetella are in purebred catteries and in animal shelters. Pet cats do not appear to be at a high risk for infection. Discuss the need of this vaccine with your veterinarian.

Ringworm Vaccine

The final vaccine currently available for cats is for *Microsporum canis*, a fungus that causes ringworm. *M. canis* can affect both cats and humans, but generally infections are limited to skin rashes. Although ringworm is a somewhat common infection, most veterinarians feel that the vaccine is an optional part of a treatment program. Complete treatment aimed at preventing and eliminating the fungus can involve oral, topical, and premise treatment.

While the vaccine may decrease the visible lesions on the cat's skin caused by the fungus, it does not necessarily make a cat less contagious to others. The duration of immunity conferred by the vaccine is questionable as well.

How to Determine if a Vaccine Is Causing a Problem

I discussed the existence of vaccine site fibrosarcomas and other adverse reactions to vaccines in Chapter 6. The AAFP/AFM has standardized vaccine sites to help identify causes of local adverse reactions, and to aid in the treatment of vaccine-associated sarcomas. Abbreviated, FRCP vaccines should be administered over the right shoulder, FeLV in the left rear, and rabies in the right rear; all should be administered as far down the leg as practical.

If any type of lump, bump, or swelling occurs in an area where you think a cat may have been vaccinated, you should have it examined by your veterinarian. It is not uncommon for a temporary reaction to occur, but if it lasts for more than a month, a biopsy of the lesion should be performed. If a veterinarian has given different vaccines in different sites, then a negative response can be localized to a specific vaccine.

If your cat has an allergic reaction or vomiting and lethargy after vaccination, discuss splitting up the administration of multiple vaccines or discontinuing vaccination altogether. The purpose of vaccines is to help protect your cat, not make it sick.

The Least You Need to Know

➤ It is not necessary for every cat to have every vaccine every year.

➤ There are risk factors that should be evaluated when determining how to vaccinate your cat.

➤ There are core vaccines that should be given to all cats.

➤ Vaccines do not always provide complete protection from a disease, they may simply decrease the severity of the clinical signs in an infection.

Chapter 9

How to Choose a Veterinarian

In This Chapter

➤ The importance of facilities and location

➤ Getting the recommendations of friends and neighbors

➤ Bedside manners

➤ How much can you afford to spend?

➤ What does it mean if a practice is specialized?

Most veterinarians have earned a four-year undergraduate degree and then attended veterinary school for four years to receive their doctorates. All veterinarians receive similar basic training in veterinary school, and after graduation pick the type of practice and job that they want. Veterinarians are well-educated professionals, and each has his own personality and level of experience.

If you have other pets or have had other pets in the recent past, you may have already developed a good relationship with a veterinarian. It is a good idea to familiarize yourself with a veterinary clinic so that you can get your new cat checked out right away. If you have a positive experience, this clinic will be a resource for questions or problems that may occur later on.

Selection Basics

If you live in a metropolitan area and look in the Yellow Pages, you will see listings for numerous veterinarians. How can you choose the perfect one? There are many factors to consider, and each of them will have a different value to you.

Location

We all have busy lives, so we often choose to work with businesses that are conveniently located for us. Each individual is willing to drive a certain distance to buy something or to receive a service, and this can vary depending on the situation. The same holds true for obtaining veterinary care.

I think that location is a valid reason to choose a veterinary clinic because you are more likely to utilize services that are easier to obtain. You might want to consider investigating veterinary clinics that are close to your home or work or even along the way.

Worth a Paws

You should consider visiting a veterinary clinic and touring the facility before bringing your cat there. If a doctor is proud of the clinic and how it is run, this should not be a problem, but it is best to call ahead so that you don't show up in the middle of an emergency.

Face Value

The way a veterinary facility looks is a reflection on the philosophy of the clinic owner. A neat, clean facility requires more maintenance and care, so extra effort is needed. You may infer that the doctor will want to provide extra care and effort to treat your cat.

The size of the facility is not as important as what it contains. A basic veterinary clinic has a reception area, exam rooms, treatment area, ward for cages, surgery room, isolation area, pharmacy, and doctor's office. Depending on where you live, real estate costs and the availability of good locations will determine where veterinary practices are found. A bigger facility is not always a better facility.

First impressions are always important, but they need to be put in perspective. If you enter a veterinary hospital and there is a strong urine smell, it could be due to a tomcat left as a patient (which is not a problem), or it could be due to urine-soiled floors and dirty litterboxes (which definitely *are* problems). Dirty counters and floors don't look good, and they may make you question the cleanliness of the areas where your cat will be treated. Do remember, though, that it is hard to control hair and debris in the middle of a hectic day at a veterinary clinic.

A client bringing her cat to a veterinary clinic.

Is This a Full-Service Clinic?

Most veterinary clinics offer a variety of services, including:

- ➤ Medical care
- ➤ Surgery
- ➤ Dentistry
- ➤ Boarding
- ➤ Grooming
- ➤ Nutritional counseling
- ➤ Flea control
- ➤ Behavior consults
- ➤ In-house laboratory
- ➤ X-rays
- ➤ Pharmacy

Worth a Paws

Cats do sleep about 23 hours a day. If the cages are small in a boarding facility, find out if there is any opportunity for a cat to get out and stretch. The cleanliness and ventilation of the boarding area is more important than the size of the cage.

During the course of your cat's lifetime, there is a good chance that it will need most of these types of services at one time or another. Having a competent full-service facility makes your life a little easier. If you utilize multiple services, the staff and doctors will become familiar with you and your cat and will be able to serve you better.

Depending on the size of the facility and the staff, services such as boarding and grooming may be available. Before boarding your cat, I would recommend previewing the boarding area. Cages vary in composition and size, and you will want to have a good idea of the accommodations offered.

What About Referrals?

When choosing a veterinary clinic, it is a good idea to ask friends and neighbors with cats for recommendations. You can consult with the local veterinary association, and you can even search for veterinarians who have a special interest in cats by browsing the Internet Web site for the American Association of Feline Practitioners (http://avma.org/aafp).

A veterinary clinic's reputation is very important, and conscientious doctors want to be respected in the community. If someone tells you to avoid a clinic, find out specifically why and evaluate the validity of the reason. It is always best to make the final judgment yourself.

Feeling Comfortable

All of the factors that I have previously discussed are important when choosing a veterinary facility, but I think that the most important factors are the customer service and communication offered to clients by the doctor and clinic staff. These less tangible qualities require extra effort and care.

Effective Communications

A client must be able to have effective communication with the clinic staff and veterinarian. Clear lines of communication will ensure that your cat receives the care that you want, and that you can be given recommendations on the best service and treatment options available.

Many people call around before deciding to use a veterinary clinic, and a decision to utilize a facility may be based solely on communicating with a receptionist. If the receptionist is knowledgeable and friendly, you may feel comfortable with going there without knowing anything about the doctor. This is another example of how a first impression can influence you. If you want to know about the doctor and staff and get more information, just ask.

A good veterinary receptionist spends time listening and talking to clients.

This Was a Good Experience

During your first visit with the veterinarian you can evaluate your experience by answering the following questions:

1. Did the doctor handle your cat kindly and compassionately?
2. Did you find the doctor easy to communicate with?
3. Did the doctor have a professional appearance?
4. Did the doctor listen to you?
5. Did you understand the diagnosis and recommendations for your pet?
6. If medication was prescribed, did the doctor show you how to administer it properly?
7. Did the doctor spend enough time with you and answer your questions?

A good veterinary clinic will have a competent support staff comprised of receptionists, technicians, and assistants. These staff members will be able to answer most of your questions or find out the answer if they are not sure. The veterinarian may not always be available to answer your questions outside of a scheduled visit, so it is worth asking a staff member. You might be able to get help right away.

Meow Wow

The most highly trained staff member at a clinic, aside from the doctor, is the licensed animal health technician. These technicians have been educated, passed a certification exam, and are legally able to perform many procedures. Their knowledge and training in animal care are comparable to those of registered nurses.

Should You Look for a Deal?

Each different veterinary clinic will have different prices for the services that they render. This can be frustrating if you are shopping around by phone and trying to assess which clinic has the best prices. A veterinarian will set his prices based on many factors, including facility, staff, level of expertise and continuing education, location, anesthetic and products used, and competition.

Some clinics try to bring you in the door by quoting a low price over the phone, but then tacking on extra costs for ancillary services that they require. It is important to try to compare costs for the exact same services, using the same drugs and techniques if you are shopping around.

Do You Get What You Pay For?

I am biased in the fact that I feel that a good veterinarian is a professional who has to charge a fair price to offer you high-quality services. If you want to have a procedure performed on your cat, you need to decide if price or quality is the most important issue. When low prices are charged, something has to be sacrificed. When fair prices are charged, you should be getting the best care. Note that veterinarians will often try to work out a payment plan for expensive, nonroutine procedures.

In a vaccine clinic, you might wait in line while a veterinarian goes down the row and injects animals without looking at them. Of course getting a vaccine in this manner is relatively inexpensive because no expertise or care is provided. A veterinary hospital is not being maintained. Your questions are not being answered. You could even be hurting an animal that is not in good health. By going to a vaccine clinic you may also be stressing your cat more than it would be in a regular veterinary visit because it is not protected in a room by itself without other animals around. In this type of situation, you are getting what you pay for—not much.

Your Cat Is Unique

As I mentioned in Chapter 6, the annual physical exam and consultation that you have with a veterinarian will greatly benefit your cat's health and improve its longevity. These visits are certainly more important than a rigid vaccination schedule. There is value to the information your veterinarian can provide when assessing your cat individually. Aside from the physical exam, there is value in discussing behavior and nutrition. There is also value in the doctor's observations of trends in your cat's weight, body condition, and general health.

Many clinics offer wellness plans for cats. These plans are tailored for certain life stages. Wellness plans can provide a package of services at a discounted price rather than getting each service separately. The plans are good deals if your cat can benefit from the included services, but not if there are unnecessary add-ons. If you choose a wellness plan from a good veterinarian, you might be able to detect problems with your kitty as they arise and begin treatment at an earlier and more beneficial stage.

Worth a Paws

If you are dropping a cat off for a procedure or if a veterinarian recommends multiple treatments or procedures, ask for a written quote if you're not offered one. This will protect both you and the veterinarian by ensuring that you both have the same expectations.

Veterinary Specialists

As we enter the 21st century, specialization in business and knowledge continues. Although all veterinarians graduate from veterinary school with the same degree, some decide that they want to become more highly trained in a particular discipline and attain board certification.

Meow Wow

Currently there are 21 different specialties in which a veterinarian can become board certified. Less than 10 percent of the approximately 60,000 veterinarians in the United States are board certified.

What Is a Cat Practice?

Veterinarians have the option of working on one or on many species. Regular small-animal and mixed-animal practices are able to capably handle feline patients, but with the increasing popularity of cats as pets, many veterinarians are dedicating their practices strictly to felines. Any veterinarian can become a feline practitioner, so if you want to differentiate between doctors, you may want to check other credentials.

If you are interested in a feline-only practice, it's a good idea to contact the veterinarian and investigate what makes the practice special. A veterinarian can affiliate with three different organizations relating to feline medicine. They are:

➤ The American Association of Feline Practitioners (AAFP)

➤ The Academy of Feline Medicine (AFM)

➤ The American Board of Veterinary Practitioners (ABVP)

Any veterinarian can affiliate with the AAFP and receive current information on feline care through newsletters and conferences. The AFM is a subgroup within the AAFP comprised of veterinarians who have completed certain amounts of continuing education and have belonged to the AAFP for three or more years. The AFM provides even higher levels of feline continuing education to its members and is involved with research grants and feline practice guidelines.

If a veterinarian truly wants to call herself a "feline practice specialist," the only way to achieve this status is by becoming board certified through ABVP. Becoming board certified requires a lot of work and dedication, and I think it shows the optimal commitment to feline medicine.

Meow Wow

To become board certified in feline (or in canine and feline practice) through ABVP, a veterinarian must have been in practice at least six years, completed a certain amount of continuing education, obtained letters of recommendation, written publishable case reports, and passed a certification exam.

What if Your Cat Has a Special Problem?

Your regular veterinarian may not have the facilities or the experience to handle certain diseases that your cat may face. In these situations, he may refer you to a board-certified specialist. You may decide yourself that your cat needs a second opinion, and it is always best to get one from a specialist. Some board-certified specialists have their own private practices, some work in groups, and others work at veterinary teaching hospitals.

Some of the board-certified specialties that are frequently consulted are internists, surgeons, neurologists, ophthalmologists, dermatologists, cardiologists, and oncologists. If you live in a metropolitan area, it is very likely that one or more of each of these veterinary specialists is available in the surrounding area.

Emergency Providers

There are veterinarians who offer emergency services themselves and others who refer clients to emergency clinics that are only open after hours, weekends, and holidays. Some emergency facilities employ veterinarians who are board certified in emergency medicine and critical care.

In a true emergency, if possible, you want to utilize a facility that has a doctor and staff already on the premises and ready to go. The cost of emergency services is usually significantly higher than those received during regular business hours, but the same is true in human medicine.

Even though you may not be thinking clearly in an emergency, try to understand the diagnosis and treatment options available. Question the veterinarian if you are unsure and be clear on your choices before making decisions.

Holistic Veterinarians

Aside from offering typical Western medicine, there are some veterinarians who practice holistic care. I will be the first to admit that traditional medicine and the tools that are currently available cannot cure all health problems. Because of this, some veterinarians are turning to alternative medicine.

Types of alternative veterinary care include:

➤ Herbal remedies

➤ Acupuncture

➤ Dietary supplements

➤ Nontraditional diets

If you seek alternative care, find out how the veterinarian has gained her knowledge. There are veterinary organizations comprised of doctors interested in alternative health care, but this is not a regulated practice. Many of the treatments may be effective, but there are not many conclusive scientific studies supporting their efficacy.

The Least You Need to Know

➤ Choose a veterinarian whose location, facilities, and services fit your needs.

➤ Your friends and neighbors may be able to refer you to a good veterinarian.

➤ You will be most happy using a veterinary clinic that has a helpful staff and that communicates with you clearly.

➤ Be aware that the costs of veterinary services may be related to the quality of care received.

➤ There are veterinarians who are board certified in certain specialties, including feline practice, and this status shows a strong commitment.

Part 3
From Kittenhood to Old Age

People grow and mature as they age, and the same is true for cats. Kittens are toddlers, adolescents, and then all grown up within their first year of life. Since cats mature at such a rapid rate, they can be promiscuous at a very young age! You want to be able to keep them from getting into trouble.

Today, cats are living significantly longer lives than they were only 20 years ago, and making their golden years comfortable is important. Being familiar with the changes that a cat will go through and what to expect toward the end of their lives will help prepare you for the inevitable. These next chapters will take you through the life stages of the cat.

Chapter 10

Kitty Adolescence

In This Chapter

➤ Observe your cat's normal behaviors

➤ Differentiate between normal and abnormal behaviors

➤ What to expect during your kitten's first 6 months

➤ Options for sterilizing your cat

Kittens develop very quickly and are grown-up cats before you know it. I felt silly when I got a new kitten last year and wanted to stay home with him all of the time. My husband thought I was crazy, but I told him that the kitten would be all grown up within a few months and I didn't want to miss him being a kitten. I guess that is what people say about their own children, so it is a natural feeling for parents!

Knowing what to expect with regard to kitten development is helpful so that you can work on training your kitten properly and be able to intervene if behaviors get out of hand. You have the best chance of molding your kitten into the perfect pet when it is young.

You Call This Normal?

Starting off with a new kitten is a lot of fun, but if you are a first-time cat owner, you may have questions about what normal behavior is. Kittens seem to work at two speeds—full power and stop. They seem to have unending energy, and then they crash and sleep very soundly.

Avoid CATastrophe

Kittens love to chew on things, especially when they are teething. Be sure to put coins, paper clips, rubber bands, ribbon, needles and thread, and the like securely away when your kitten is not supervised. I have had the unfortunate experiences of removing numerous objects from the intestinal tracts of young cats.

Oral Personality

The mouth is a very important organ for a kitten. A newborn kitten will start using its mouth within an hour of birth when it starts nursing. Kittens nurse every few hours around the clock for the first couple of weeks of life. Most kittens begin to wean to solid food at 4 weeks of age and can be fully weaned by 6 weeks. It is normal for kittens to eat dirt or kitty litter during the weaning process, but they learn quickly that these substances don't taste very good. Kittens have all of their baby teeth by 6 weeks of age.

Kittens teethe and lose all of their baby teeth from 4 to 7 months of age. During this period it is common for kittens to chew on everything in sight, including your hands and feet. It is best not to let a kitten chew on you. The more it does, the more likely it will think that skin can be chewed on. Even if you don't mind, your friends and relatives will not appreciate it when your kitten chooses to chew on them.

Define a Scratching Post

If you are persistent, you can train a kitten or cat to use a scratching post. Many owners tell me that their kitten scratches everything in the house except for the scratching post, but when I ask them how they are training their kitten to use the post, they say that they didn't know that they had to. But how would a cat know the difference between furniture and a cat scratching post?

It is normal for cats to scratch. It helps them sharpen and shed nails and leaves a territorial scent. Even declawed cats will go through the motions of scratching. Owners should do their best to teach their kitten appropriate scratching behavior before relying on declawing to solve the problem. (See Chapter 3 for some tips on training a cat to use a scratching post.)

Kittens Just Want to Have Fun

Kittens have a strong need to play, and their play activities include:

➤ Running

➤ Pouncing

➤ Jumping

➤ Stalking

Some kittens will play on their own, but all kittens need interactive play. If you work and there are no other pets in the household, your kitten will get bored during the day. You may get annoyed when the animal will not leave you alone when you get home, but there is a lot of pent-up energy that needs to be released.

Kittens will burn off energy playing with each other, but you may want to tire them out before bedtime. That way you'll get some sleep too! (Photograph by Andy Jones)

If you have two or more pets in the house, you will likely observe some pretty rough play behavior between them. Many owners are concerned about the animals hurting one another, but usually the involved parties know the rules. There is a fine line between playing and fighting, but animal play behavior can involve chasing, biting, and rolling around.

It is a good idea to spend at least five minutes of intense playtime with your kitten or cat twice a day. The best times are before you go to work or leave to run errands in the morning, and then near bedtime. Cats are nocturnally active, so you want your cat to be tired at bedtime.

It is normal for a kitten to hunt and stalk your feet. This is not a sign of aggression, but a sign of frustrated hunting behavior. If a kitten stays indoors and does not have another animal to jump on and bite, your feet will do. Keep a stuffed sock or stuffed toy handy for use in these situations, and when the kitten attempts to pounce on you, substitute the toy as the attack victim.

Naughty Kitty!

Kittens can be like bad children. They like attention, and they may engage in behaviors that they know will irritate you. Believe it or not, cats will seek negative attention on purpose, especially if they are not getting enough attention otherwise. There are differences between irritating and abnormal behaviors. The best way to prevent abnormal behaviors is early identification and taking action to prevent patterns from developing.

Who's the Boss?

If you didn't already know it, your cat owns *you*. In most households the cats do better jobs of training people than vice versa. Problems arise when the cat wants to be dominant over people or other pets in the household.

During kitten health examinations, I think that it is important to assess the animal's personality and tolerance levels. This helps me to discuss the animal's behavior with the owner and stop unwanted traits early. When a kitten is intolerant of being held in a submissive posture, bites or screams when being handled reasonably, or always has to have its paws on top of your hands, I become concerned about over-dominance.

Meow Wow

It is common for hand-raised orphan kittens to be intolerant or dominant toward people. As unlikely as this seems, humans do not discipline kittens in the ways a mother cat or siblings would. This lack of training and establishment of authority can lead to bad behavior. Hand-raised orphan kittens should be exposed to other cats and people at very young ages when possible.

Worth a Paws

You are reinforcing bad behavior if you let go of a cat every time it screams or snaps at you. Of course you should not intentionally put yourself in a position where you would be hurt. But, if you give in, you let the cat know that it is the boss, and not you. Learn how to firmly and safely hold a cat that acts badly.

Ways of taming a dominant kitten are:

➤ Hold it in a submissive posture for a few minutes each day.

➤ If the kitten screams and cries, safely hold onto it until it calms down.

➤ If the kitten gets wild and out of control, confine it for a "kitty time-out."

➤ Reward good behavior with praise or food treats.

➤ Practice touching toes, opening mouths, combing fur, and touching ears to desensitize the kitten to contact in these locations.

➤ Ask your veterinarian for advice.

Attack Cat!

Aggressive cats hiss, growl, lay back their ears, arch up, and then attack. This differs completely from the aggressive "hunting" behavior of the playing cat. The types of aggressive behaviors in cats are:

➤ Aggression between males

➤ Pain-induced aggression

➤ Fear-induced aggression

➤ Maternal aggression

➤ Territorial aggression

➤ Competitive aggression

➤ Learned aggression

➤ Sexual aggression

➤ Predatory aggression

Avoid CATastrophe

Cats have a lot of bacteria in their mouths. If a cat bites you, clean the area vigorously with running water for several minutes and then consult your physician. Doctors usually recommend immediate treatment with antibiotics, so don't wait to see your physician.

Genetics, hormones, and food can all be causes of aggressive behaviors and aggression may be stimulated by particular sights and smells. Neurotransmitter levels and electrical activity in the brain can trigger or reduce aggression. If you have a cat that you feel may be acting aggressively, you should have it evaluated by a veterinarian as soon as possible. Consultation with an animal behaviorist may also be needed. Certain types of aggression can be cured by removing specific stimuli or by neutering, some can be controlled with medication, but others may not be treatable.

Missing the Litterbox

Using a litterbox is a natural behavior for a kitten, and it comes from the inborn desire to bury waste and learned patterns as to where this should be done. If a kitten is not using the litterbox, train it to do so as discussed in Chapter 3.

Cats that have eliminated outdoors at some time in their lives may inappropriately choose houseplant containers for their waste disposal location. They would also need to be trained to a litterbox and plants and soil removed from the house or covered up during the training process.

Some popular breeds of cats, such as Persians, may have genetic problems that make litterbox training difficult. If you are buying a cat from a breeder, ask about the animal's litterbox behavior and try to catch problems early.

A True "Scaredy Cat"

Many cats are very timid by nature and can be difficult pets to own. Often owners tell me that they have adopted a cat that they think has been abused because it is so fearful, but, in fact, it is more likely that the cat's timidity is an inherited trait.

Characteristics of a timid cat are:

➤ Very tense and rigid when picked up

➤ Resents restraint

➤ Remains immobile rather than explores a new area

➤ Hides from people

➤ Runs when it hears noises

➤ Plays less than typical cats

Some cats may have actually undergone traumatic experiences that cause them to be fearful. And for some of these cats, the timidity subsides with time, but others may never change. Oral anti-anxiety drugs and behavior modification with desensitization can help in some situations, but some cats have timid personalities that will last their lifetimes.

Kitten Growth Stages

The maturation that occurs during a kitten's first 6 months of life correlates to the first 15 years in a human. From birth to 6 months, a kitten changes from a newborn to a sexually mature animal.

Birth to One Month

During this period a kitten develops from total dependence on its mother for food, warmth, and elimination, to being able to handle these things on its own. Newborn kittens can neither see nor hear and rely on smell and stimulation from the queen. They crawl and then learn to walk by 3 to 4 weeks of age, with some very clumsy days along the way.

Four to Six Weeks

Kittens can begin to ingest solid food and eat on their own during this time. They also begin independent litterbox usage. This period is a very important time in the socialization process. Kittens that are not exposed to humans and other animals (including cats) at this stage can have a hard time adjusting later on in life. Kittens that are outdoors and trained by their mothers can learn early hunting behavior during this time. Baby teeth develop and the kitten's eyes change from blue to their permanent color.

Six to Eight Weeks

This is the earliest time for a kitten to be taken from its mother and littermates and introduced into a new home. A kitten of this age should be able to care for its own basic needs. In a new home, a kitten may be initially scared and lonely, but it should be able to adapt.

Eight to Sixteen Weeks

During this period kittens adjust to their independence and become stronger and more curious. They go through rapid growth and usually gain about one pound per month. They begin to jump, climb, and scratch. Owners can make a big impact with training their kitten during this time.

Worth a Paws

Six months of age is generally recommended as the best time to sterilize a cat, but sterilization at an earlier age is being performed more frequently without problems. By 6 months cats have been vaccinated, become physically developed, and should be healthy and strong. Most cats have not completed puberty by this time.

Sixteen to Twenty-Four Weeks

This is teething time, when a kitten loses its baby teeth and gets its permanent adult teeth. Biting and chewing behaviors can increase. The animal's coat fills out and there is more interest in grooming. Most kittens do not reach behavioral sexual maturity until after 6 months of age, but they can be physically mature before then.

Looking for Love

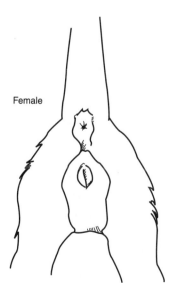

Female

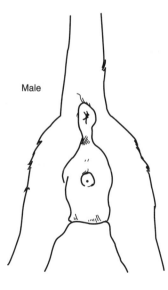

Male

Males and females have different genitalia, although in newborn kittens it can be hard to distinguish between the two sexes. Note that the genital opening in the male is circular, whereas that of the female looks like a slit.

Cats go through physical maturation before they are behaviorally ready to reproduce. The time of year has an effect on reproduction, as cats are *seasonally polyestrus*. Veterinarians recommend that cats be sterilized before they begin sexual behaviors for many reasons. Some of the important reasons are:

➤ Neutered animals tend to be calmer and more easy-going.

➤ Neutered animals stay closer to home.

➤ Neutered animals fight less and are less protective of their territory.

➤ Cycling of sex hormones can trigger some health problems.

➤ The odor of sexually mature male cats is unbearable.

Male "Coming of Age"

Male kittens start producing low levels of testosterone at about $3^1/_2$ months of age. They can produce sperm by 5 months of age, but they are not usually able to copulate before they are 9 to 12 months old. The behaviors that begin as the kitten starts sexual maturation are:

➤ Neck gripping

➤ Pelvic thrusting

➤ Mounting

Most male cats have two testicles descended into their scrotums at birth. If the testicles have not reached the scrotum by 8 months of age, it is unlikely that they ever will. Even if a testicle is retained, it should be removed when the animal is neutered. The surgical procedure used with a cryptorchid cat, if the testicle is in the abdominal cavity, is similar to that used when spaying a cat.

Castrated male cats should not show any changes in their personalities, but may exhibit changes in their behaviors, especially if they have been previously sexually active. Experienced cats may stop sexual behaviors within a few days, but others may show minimal behavioral changes. It is best to neuter a cat before it starts sexual behaviors in order to prevent patterns of behavior from developing.

Kitty Ditty

Seasonally polyestrus means that during certain seasons of the year, cats can go through their heat cycles multiple times.

Female "Coming of Age"

Once a female cat begins to cycle, she is able to conceive. The *estrous cycle* is the hormonal cycle that defines female "heat." Cats do not bleed when they are in heat, and the signs of heat in a female cat are all behavioral. Most indoor cats will begin to cycle at 5 to 9 months of age.

The kitten's environment plays a role in the onset of puberty, and factors such as exposure to tom-cats, cycling females, or increasing amounts of light will trigger earlier estrus. Although some cycle all year-round, most cats in North America cycle between mid-January and late September.

Proestrus is the short one to three days before estrus. A female cat in proestrus may:

➤ Show a general increase in her activity

➤ Roll and rub on objects and people

➤ Spray urine

➤ Lay on the ground, vocalize, and knead with her paws

➤ Howl

➤ Not yet allow a male to mount her

The proestrus period allows a female cat to let males know that she is available!

There are no health benefits in allowing a female cat to go through estrous cycles or produce kittens, but there are benefits to sterilization. Aside from the obvious benefit of not having to cope with a cat that is exhibiting different (and often annoying) behaviors, spayed female cats are not at risk for uterine infections. Female sex hormones also increase the risk of breast cancer in older female cats, but breast cancer is rare in cats that never experience a heat cycle.

Cats that are in heat can still be spayed, but the surgery is slightly more involved because the blood vessels around the uterus are engorged. A cat that is spayed during her heat cycle will still show behavioral signs for a few days after surgery.

Kitty Ditty

The **estrous cycle** in a female cat is comprised of four stages—anestrus, proestrus, estrus, and metestrus. Estrus is the only time period in which a female will allow copulation and can conceive.

Worth a Paws

Although some neutered males can still exhibit some sexual behaviors months after surgery, neutered females will not show sexual behaviors if their ovaries and uterus have been properly removed. If you have a spayed female cat that is acting like she is in heat, consult with your veterinarian. An ovarian remnant may be the cause.

The Least You Need to Know

➤ Biting, scratching, and pouncing are all normal kitten behaviors that need to be directed appropriately.

➤ Dominance, aggression, timidity, and eliminating outside of the litterbox are all treatable behaviors, although some cats are not responsive to treatment.

➤ Many developmental and behavioral changes occur during the first 6 months of a kitten's life.

➤ You don't need to wait for a kitten to exhibit signs of sexual maturity before having the animal sterilized.

Chapter 11

Kitty Sex Life

In This Chapter

➤ Conception in the cat

➤ The stages of pregnancy

➤ The options with unwanted pregnancy

➤ What occurs at birth

Cats are very efficient at reproduction and are able to have multiple litters with multiple births each year. Most cats go through puberty at an early age—somewhere between five and nine months. Females can be fertile for about 7 years, while males may be able to reproduce for 11 years or more.

The large numbers of feral (wild) cats demonstrate that in an uncontrolled environment, cats will keep reproducing. Today's methods of sterilization are surgical and thus not easily applied to the vast numbers of feral cats. Researchers are working on new methods of feline contraception including oral medications and even vaccines. These methods may help kitty overpopulation in the future.

The Act

Male cats can be continually sexually active once they have reached puberty. Females, however, are only sexually active when they go through their heat cycles.

Kitty's in the Mood

Female cats will only accept a male mounting them and copulating when they are in heat. When a female cat is in heat, she does not bleed like a dog, rather she has changes in behavior. The changes can include:

➤ Increased vocalization

➤ Rolling on the ground and crying

➤ Lying with her rear end pushed up in the air

➤ Acting more affectionate

➤ Attempting to escape the house and get outside

Most females reach puberty after 6 months of age, and cycle every two weeks until they are bred or induced to ovulate. If a female is not in heat, she will not stand still for a male. If she is in heat, she will allow a male to mount her, then after intromission occurs, she will bite and strike at him to leave her alone.

A female cat can ovulate multiple eggs each breeding, and she can be quite unparticular about her partners, allowing multiple males to mount her during her cycle. This makes it possible for different males to sire kittens in the same litter. A female may allow two to four different breedings to occur during a few days of a heat cycle.

A Tomcat's Always in the Mood

Intact tomcats are ready to do their duty at all times, but they are not the decision-makers. They may attempt to mount females that are not in heat, but they will be rebuffed. As a dominant behavior, some male cats even try to mount other male cats.

An average healthy male is usually fertile. Problems with male reproduction may be caused by:

➤ Lack of libido

➤ Low sperm counts

➤ Hair caught around the penis

➤ Cryptorchidism

➤ Lack of coordination

If someone is trying to breed their male cat, they will most likely put it with an experienced female for the first attempt. Often when two kitty virgins are put together, neither knows what to do and the male can get frustrated and lose interest if he is not successful.

Meow Wow

Most professional cat breeders keep one or two intact males in their catteries with four or more females. Keeping a tomcat can be a smelly experience, and because the male can be used to breed multiple queens, fewer males are needed to have a good breeding program.

The entire mating process of cats can last a few short minutes and can be repeated multiple times within a day. Cats do not care who their partners are, and the female could not care less about the male after he has done his duty.

If you have ever observed cats mating, it is actually a rough activity. The tom will mount the female and bite her in the neck. After intromission, the queen will scream, turn around, and bite the male until he releases her.

When Your Cat Is Pregnant

If in heat and given the opportunity to be with an intact male, chances are that a female cat will get pregnant. There are many physical changes that a female cat will experience during a pregnancy. The average cat's gestation period is 63 to 65 days.

The tom takes no role in raising his kittens, and some toms are even aggressive toward kittens. On the other hand, a queen will be very protective of her babies. You may remember Scarlet, the mother cat that made headlines in 1996. Scarlet entered a burning building five times to save her five kittens, although she was severely burned in the process. A mother cat will also protect her kittens from you. If you are caring for a feral queen, be careful of how much you handle her kittens because she may reject them.

Signs of Pregnancy

An inexperienced cat owner may be unaware of the signs of heat. Some cats put on more of a show than others do. If you have a cat that has come in and out of heat and suddenly seems to stop cycling, be suspicious of pregnancy.

Cats do not need a lot of owner care to maintain a pregnancy. They seem to do fine on their own. Other than allowing a queen to eat what she wants and trying to keep her protected from illness, you can leave the rest to her.

What to Look For

Inasmuch as cats are only pregnant for about nine weeks, things happen fairly quickly. The progression of signs is:

1. Increased appetite and weight gain

2. "Pinking up" of the nipples within two weeks of being bred

3. More rounded appearance of the abdomen

4. Engorgement of the mammary glands

A veterinarian can palpate a female cat's abdomen and confirm a pregnancy three to four weeks into gestation. The fetuses develop bones at about 54 days of gestation, so an x-ray at this time can tell how many kittens will be born. X-rays do not damage the fetuses, and they can be useful if you want to know what to expect.

A pregnant queen that is almost ready to deliver has a very distended abdomen.

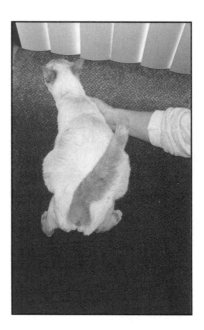

Can You Terminate Your Cat's Pregnancy?

Breeders of purebred cats know when their females are cycling and try to plan their pregnancies. They try to mate cats that are not too closely related and to produce offspring that have certain characteristic traits. Owners of pet cats may want their female to have a litter, and they have the right to do so, although again I would suggest that they visit their local animal shelter first and see the result of too many kittens and not enough good homes.

Sometimes time just gets away from an owner, and his cat is in heat and pregnant before he's had a chance to have the animal sterilized. What are the options?

Ovariohysterectomy

Pregnant cats can be safely spayed (see Chapter 7), but most veterinarians do not like performing the surgery when a cat is close to full term. If you know that your cat is in heat and that it got outside, it can be spayed within a few days and before significant fetal development has occurred.

If you are already noticing that the cat's belly is distended and pregnant, chances are that the cat is at least six weeks pregnant. The risks of spaying a pregnant cat are slightly higher than performing the surgery on a non-pregnant animal, due largely to blood loss and increased surgery time. However, if you do not want kittens, spaying at this time should be considered.

Medical Intervention

Currently there are no safe and reliable medications that will terminate a feline pregnancy. Drugs are available that will cause the pregnancy to abort, but they can also potentially harm the queen. For the safety of the queen, let her have the kittens if you are set on breeding her again, or have her spayed after the litter is born.

Kitty Birth Control

Veterinarians do not prescribe birth control medications to cats because of the risks that they carry in contrast to the safety of surgical sterilization. There is one drug that is occasionally used by breeders, called megesterol acetate, to suppress a female's heat cycle.

Because most hormones have multiple functions, there are possible side effects to any hormone treatment. Cats that receive even small doses of megesterol acetate run the risks of:

➤ Developing diabetes mellitus

➤ Developing pyometra, a uterine infection

➤ Mammary gland enlargement

➤ Mammary cyst development

➤ Mammary cancer

➤ Decreased fertility in the future

Worth a Paws

You can monitor a queen's rectal temperature twice daily if you are not sure when she will deliver. Twenty-four hours before delivery, most queens have a drop in body temperature to about 99 degrees F.

The Birth of Kittens

You expect that a queen will soon be delivering when she shows interest in creating a nest where the kittens will be born. You can express milk from her mammary glands a day or two before she delivers. When kittens are born, they weigh only a few ounces and are extremely fragile. They are very dependent upon their mother for survival because their eyes are closed, their ears are not completely developed, and they can only crawl. An average litter contains three to five kittens.

A litter of newborn kittens.

How Long Does Labor Last?

The length of a queen's labor depends on whether she has had kittens before and how many kittens she is having. The period from the start of contractions to the end of labor can be minutes, hours, or even a day if multiple breedings were responsible for the litter.

If a queen is having contractions for an hour without producing any kittens, veterinary help should be sought. Just like humans, cats can experience problems with delivery called *dystocia*.

Dystocia can be caused by:

➤ A weak or sick queen

➤ A kitten turned backwards in the birth canal

➤ A kitten that is too large to pass through the birth canal

➤ A dead kitten in the uterus holding the others back

Responding to a Difficult Labor

Take your cat to your veterinarian if she has been in labor for an hour without passing any kittens. A veterinarian will take an x-ray to see where the kittens are and to see if any abnormalities can be detected. He will also want to check the queen's blood to see if she is having any problems, such as low calcium, that prevent her from having normal contractions.

Kitty Ditty

Dystocia is a term used to describe difficulty during the birthing process. A cat that has a prolonged, non-productive labor, has gone 67 days without going into labor, or has a kitten stuck and protruding from the vulva would experience a dystocia.

A doctor may induce the queen with drugs or even consider performing a caesarian section depending on the situation. If there are no apparent problems, the first step is to induce labor. If induction is not successful, a caesarian section is necessary. When surgery is performed, there is increased risk that the kittens will not survive.

What Occurs During Labor?

You may observe passage of a mucus plug when a cat starts into labor. Contractions will follow and kittens will be born. The queen will lick and remove the placenta from the kitten; if she does not, the kitten can suffocate and you need to intervene. The queen will then bite off the umbilical cord that connects the kitten to the placenta.

The queen may then continue labor and produce more kittens. She will also continue to lick and clean the kittens that have been born and gently nudge them toward her nipples so that they can begin nursing. Kittens are able to nurse within an hour of being born.

Avoid CATastrophe

If you have a queen that likes to roam, try to confine her in a room with her kittens so that they don't become neglected. Also be careful about flea control. If a queen has fleas, they can jump to the kittens and cause life-threatening anemia.

The queen may eat her placenta, and as unappetizing as this looks, it is very normal. She may have a vaginal discharge for up to two weeks postpartum. The discharge might look like blood or might even be green and mucoid, but it should not look like pus. If it looks like pus, consult with your veterinarian.

123

Meow Wow

Kittens receive their initial immunity to disease by absorbing antibodies present in their mother's colostrum. Kittens are only able to absorb the antibodies in colostrum during their first 24 hours of life. It is very important for kittens to nurse their mothers as soon after birth as possible.

Examining Newborns

Unfortunately, kittens can be stillborn. If a kitten is not crying and wiggling after the placenta has been removed, pick it up and try to see if it is alive. You can gently shake it upside down to try to clear its mouth and throat. Touch the chest to check for a heartbeat. Check for jaw and muscle tone by opening the mouth and moving the limbs, and if all feels limp, the kitten is probably not alive.

Within a few hours of kittens being born, you should look them over for any apparent birth defects, or you can take them into your veterinarian for an assessment. Things to check:

1. Open the mouth and look for a hole in the roof of the mouth. This would be a cleft palate.
2. Check to see that there are four legs and a tail.
3. Check the umbilical cord and make sure that a hole is not present at the abdominal wall.
4. Check under the tail and see if there is a rectum and a set of genitalia.

Kittens that are unhealthy at birth generally do not survive. Queens may abandon or cannibalize kittens that are not healthy.

Raising an Orphan

Mother nature knows best, and kittens that are cared for by their mothers have better chances of survival than orphan kittens that are raised by humans. If you find kittens that have been abandoned by their mother or have kittens that are not being cared for by their mother, be prepared for a lot of work and possible disappointment. But if all goes well, there are few more rewarding experiences than raising an orphan kitten into a healthy cat.

Feed Me

Newborn kittens need to eat every two to three hours. They have very small stomachs and require small amounts of food on a regular basis. You do not want to give cow's milk to a kitten because it will cause diarrhea and dehydration. There are a few different brands of kitten milk replacer formulas that are available through veterinarians and pet stores. There are also pet nursing bottles with small nipples. Kitten milk needs to be fed warmed, but not hot—just like the milk you would give to a human baby.

Kittens can be fed kitten milk replacer solutions through a special bottle.

Potty Me

Kittens do not have control over their urination and defecation until they are about 4 weeks old. From birth to that time, their mother normally stimulates them to eliminate by licking their genitalia. Of course, you don't have to go this far, but you can simulate the sensation by using a warm, damp washcloth, turning the kitten over, and gently rubbing the genitalia until urine and feces pass.

Keep Me Safe and Warm

Kittens do not have any body fat to keep themselves insulated. They usually pile on top of each other next to their mom and share her heat. If you have an orphan, you need to keep it warm by using a hot water bottle or a heating pad set on low covered with a towel. You also need to keep it in a box and in an area free from drafts.

Except when you are handling it, a newborn kitten should be confined in a small box with a towel. Because newborns cannot see, it is essential to know where they are at all times and keep them out of trouble.

The Least You Need to Know

➤ A female cat's heat cycle controls when mating will occur.

➤ The gestation period of the cat is 63 to 65 days, and a pregnant cat goes through rapid physical changes.

➤ There is no guaranteed safe medical abortion or birth control for cats available at this time.

➤ Labor is usually uncomplicated in the cat, but if problems occur, seek veterinary help.

➤ Raising an orphan kitten is a lot of work, but it can be a rewarding experience.

Chapter 12

How to Care for a Feline Senior Citizen

In This Chapter

➤ The average life span of a cat

➤ The possible causes of death in an older cat

➤ Ways you can keep your senior cat comfortable

➤ Know how to assess your cat's quality of life

➤ It is normal to grieve the loss of a pet

Even with nine lives, cats do not live forever, although we'd like for them to. When you have shared your home with a cat for years, it becomes an integral family member to which you develop strong emotional attachments. Cats provide undemanding and unending love. They are always there for you.

You can prevent many problems that could shorten your cat's life by following the suggestions on care that are offered in this book. Cats are very good at disguising their problems, so as they age, you need to be even more attuned to changes in their every-day activities and behaviors. Early detection of problems is the key to improving longevity and quality of life.

How Long Will Your Cat Live?

There are many formulas for calculating a cat's age in relation to human age. An old standby is that seven cat years are equal to one human year, but in actuality, the first few years of a cat's life are equivalent to more than seven years each, and the later years are equal to fewer.

Owners want to know what the life expectancy is for their cat, and in general I tell them that it is between 13 and 15 years, especially if the cat stays indoors. However, we have many 19- and 20-year-old patients, and our oldest is 24! If a cat goes outside, the expectancy is shortened because of the increased risks the cat can face. It is exposed to more diseases and dangers such as poisons and cars.

The following table compares the age of a cat with that of a human.

Cat Years	Human Years
1	16
2	21
3	26
4	30
5	34
6	38
7	42
8	46
9	50
10	54
11	58
12	62
13	66
14	70
15	74
16	78
17	82
18	86
19	90
20	94

When Is Your Cat Old?

There are many different opinions on what determines "old." There is no consensus on the age that a cat becomes a senior, but a "Panel Report on Feline Senior Care" published in 1999 by the AAFP/AFM recommends initiation of a senior preventative health care program by 7 to 11 years of age. By 12 years almost all cats start experiencing the effects of aging.

There are certain diseases and conditions that occur in cats due to degenerative processes. Each cell in an animal's body is programmed to last a certain amount of time, and this occurs in each animal at a different rate. Some animals look and act old at

10 years, while others are fit and spry at 15 years. Certain organs seem to age at a faster rate than others do, and this is perhaps why certain health problems are more common in older cats.

Keeping Up on the Aging Process

Cats need the most veterinary and owner care when they are kittens and when they are seniors. Middle-aged cats are usually healthy and take pretty good care of themselves, and can get by with once-a-year visits to the vet for their physical exams.

Regular veterinary examinations will objectively note gradual changes, which can add up to significant changes over a period of time. Even if you've lived with your cat for years, you may not notice subtle changes that occur in its conformation and health as it ages.

Worth a Paws

The "Panel Report on Feline Senior Care" published by the AAFP/AFM recommended health care protocols based on a cat's age and clinical signs. For cats 7 to 11 years and up, semi-annual physical examinations and annual diagnostics were recommended. Other issues that are addressed in the report are behavioral changes, pain relief, anesthesia concerns, nutrition, dentistry, and coping with pet loss. An awareness of all of these issues is essential to providing optimal care to senior cats.

An owner waits for his cat to be examined.

129

Senior Health Care Program

A preventative health care program for "healthy" animals could include a complete history and physical exam and some diagnostic testing, including a CBC, blood chemistries, viral testing, urinalysis, and possibly blood pressure measurement. I think it's beneficial to start a program like this around 9 years of age.

By establishing baseline values on body condition and different organ function, changes can be detected as the animal ages. If an animal has an illness, monitoring should be performed at least every six months.

What Will Cause Your Kitty's Demise?

Although you may not like to think about it, it's a good idea to be familiar with the possible problems that a senior cat can develop. As with any disease, early identification is useful to help slow the disease and to prevent related maladies. There are six diseases that are particularly common in senior cats:

- ➤ Hyperthyroidism
- ➤ Chronic renal failure
- ➤ Hypertension
- ➤ Cancer
- ➤ Diabetes mellitus
- ➤ Inflammatory bowel disease (IBD)

Liver disease, heart disease, neurological diseases, and lung disease are also found in senior cats, but their frequency is greater in geriatric humans than cats.

Hyperthyroidism

Hyperthyroidism is very common in senior cats and is usually the result of a benign growth on one or both of a cat's thyroid glands. The thyroid produces hormones that affect general metabolism and organ function, so an overactive gland makes excessive levels of hormones.

Hyperthyroid cats can have ravenous appetites but lose weight. They can have rapid heart rates, arrhythmia, vomiting, and diarrhea. This disorder is diagnosed by a blood test, and treatment is aimed at suppressing the gland medically, or removing the overactive tissue by surgery or radiation.

Chronic Renal Failure

Chronic renal failure is a degenerative process that slowly impairs the important functions of the kidneys. The kidneys are responsible for filtering the blood and producing urine. They are also responsible for water and electrolyte balance in the body. Kidney function is measured through urinalysis and blood testing, but these tests don't even start to indicate problems until more than 50 percent of all kidney function has been lost.

Cats with chronic renal failure typically drink a lot, urinate a lot, and lose weight. Treatment of chronic renal failure is aimed at maintaining an animal's hydration and electrolyte balance as well as controlling some secondary problems (anemia, dental disease, and weight loss) that can occur.

Owners can help to prevent kidney disease by feeding a good diet that does not over-acidify the urine in senior cats and providing plenty of water. The most common clinical signs of kidney disease are increased thirst and increased urination. As kidney disease progresses, the cat becomes thin, dehydrated, and develops a terrible odor from the mouth.

The kidneys are organs that do not regenerate, so once they are damaged, disease will progress. By intervening with diet, fluids, and other treatment, the process can be slowed but not cured. It is hard to know how quickly problems will progress, so monitoring changes in *blood urea nitrogen* (BUN) and *creatinine* will give a veterinarian an idea of the stage of degeneration. If detected in early stages, kidney disease can be managed, possibly for years. Management requires active owner participation in fluid supplementation and animal care.

Kitty Ditty

Blood urea nitrogen (BUN) and **creatinine** are products that attain higher levels in the blood when cats have kidney disease. Abnormally high values of these products are not even detectable until more than 50 percent of kidney function has been lost.

Hypertension

High blood pressure (hypertension) does occur in cats. Most often it is secondary to hyperthyroidism or chronic renal failure. Testing a cat's blood pressure can be tricky because cats are generally stressed when they go to a veterinary clinic, and stress increases blood pressure. Hypertension can be addressed by controlling the primary disease and by use of oral medications.

Cancer

Cats are living longer now than they ever have, and this increases the risk of cancer. Cancer is an unregulated growth of new cells. The cause of most cancers in cats is not known, just as in humans. Some types of *neoplasia* are rapidly progressive, while others are slow. Some types are external and observed by owners, and others are detected through palpation of an animal by a veterinarian during a physical examination.

Each year leaps and bounds are made with cancer treatment. The same types of drugs and therapies that are used on humans are available for cats. There are veterinary oncologists who specialize in animal cancer treatment.

The prognosis differs for each type of cancer. The treatment modalities available for cancer include:

➤ Chemotherapy

➤ Surgery

➤ Radiation

➤ Cryotherapy

The goal of treating cancer in animals is to prolong life while maintaining a good quality of life. It is not simply to keep an animal alive. If an animal is having problems handling the treatment, it is changed or discontinued. Veterinarians do not want the treatment to be worse than the disease.

Cancer will cause various clinical signs depending on its location. Most cats with cancer will have weight loss, elevated white blood cell counts, and anemia. The blood tests available today are not geared to specifically detect cancer. Testing for cancer markers in the blood of cats is not as advanced as it is in humans, but expect the technology to be available in the future.

Kitty Ditty

Neoplasia is another term used to describe cancer. "Neo" means new, and "plasia" means abnormal growth. There are two types of neoplasia: benign, which means non-aggressive and unlikely to spread and cause problems; and malignant, which means aggressive and likely to metastasize to other organs.

Diabetes Mellitus

In diabetes mellitus, the body is unable to properly use glucose. A cat will eat and produce glucose in the blood, but that glucose will not be transported into cells for nourishment, so even though a cat is eating, its body is starving. Diabetic cats will have voracious appetites, and they typically drink a lot of water, urinate a lot, and lose weight. The clinical signs associated with diabetes are similar to those of chronic renal disease. Most diabetic cats need to be treated with twice-daily insulin injections because insulin allows glucose to enter the starving cells in the body.

Inflammatory Bowel Disease (IBD)

Inflammatory bowel disease (IBD) is a problem that affects the lining of the stomach and/or intestines. Cats with IBD typically have vomiting and/or diarrhea that does not respond to conventional remedies. To definitively diagnose IBD, biopsies of the stomach and intestine are needed. Biopsies can be obtained through the use of an endoscope or through exploratory surgery. Treatment for IBD involves reducing inflammation and controlling infection and usually long-term medication. The prognosis for cats with IBD is good, but IBD can progress in some animals to a type of cancer called intestinal lymphosarcoma.

Liver Disease

The liver is a vital organ responsible for digestion, vitamin and mineral storage, metabolic processes, and detoxification of substances. If it is not too severely damaged, the liver can regenerate.

In a geriatric cat, the liver can become inflamed, infected, or cancerous and stop functioning normally. Signs of liver disease in the cat include jaundice, vomiting, weight loss, and anemia. Blood tests and palpation of the liver provide clues, but most liver disease can only be diagnosed by a liver biopsy. Biopsies can be obtained through a exploratory surgery or by a needle guided by ultrasound.

Heart Disease

Cats don't have heart attacks, and they do not develop arteriosclerosis like we do, in which the arteries become clogged and blood flow to the heart is impaired. Most feline heart disease occurs in young and middle-aged cats. When a geriatric cat experiences heart failure, it is usually in connection with another illness.

As mentioned earlier, a common disease in older cats is hyperthyroidism, and when this condition is not controlled, heart failure can occur. The heart muscle simply wears out after being overstimulated for a period of time. When the heart fails, the rhythm is affected, fluid can pool in the chest, and circulation can become impaired.

Signs of heart disease include weakness, panting, open-mouth breathing, and coughing. Diagnostic tools available to evaluate heart disease include:

➤ X-rays

➤ Electrocardiogram (ECG)

➤ Cardiac ultrasound

133

Neurological Disease

Strokes are not very common in cats, so when neurological signs are present, other diagnoses need to be considered. A stroke occurs when oxygen flow to the brain is impaired and brain cells are damaged. A stroke could affect an animal's ability to walk, eat, and eliminate, so if improvement in clinical signs is not seen within a few days, the prognosis is poor.

Seizures are more common in older cats than strokes. Seizures are periods of abnormal electrical activity in the brain. If an older cat has a seizure, possible causes would be hypertension, metabolic imbalances, or cancer. When routine diagnostic testing does not pinpoint a cause, other tests are available.

To evaluate the neurological system of a cat, other tests that are available are:

➤ Cerebral spinal fluid tap (CSF)

➤ Magnetic resonance imaging (MRI)

➤ Computer-assisted tomography (CAT scan)

Lung Disease

Cats that have had life-long asthma or long-standing infections can develop scarring in their lungs. As they age, the scarring can progress and cause respiratory collapse. Cats can die suddenly from respiratory collapse. If an animal's lungs are unable to inflate properly, oxygen cannot enter the blood and suffocation can occur.

Fluid also prevents the lungs from expanding. Other disease processes can cause fluid to build in the lungs or within the chest cavity. These are also life-threatening. Cats that are having problems breathing will often sit upright, cough, breath with their mouths open, and act in distress. They need immediate veterinary help. X-rays of the chest cavity and needle aspiration of fluid or lung tissue can help diagnose the cause of lung disease.

Keeping Your Old Friend Comfortable

As different parts of the body wear out, it may be difficult for a cat to maintain its regular activities. If you are an owner of an older cat, you want to be sure to make things as easy as possible for the animal.

It is common for vision and hearing to be impaired as a normal part of the aging process, although it is unusual for a cat to go completely blind due to aging. If vision is compromised, the animal can usually see better in daylight than at night. It will do better if items such as food bowls and the litterbox are kept consistently in the same areas, since the animal is already familiar with their locations.

Although it is best to keep all cats indoors, it is extremely important to do so if your cat is deaf. While this deaf cat is obviously alert, it can't hear approaching traffic. (Photograph by Chris Van Camp)

Complete deafness occurs occasionally in older cats. You should not let a deaf cat go outdoors because it will not hear noises that would normally alert it to danger.

Hydration

Because kidney disease is so common in older cats, maintaining good hydration can make a big difference with how your cat feels. At my clinic, we work with many owners who learn to give their cats fluid injections at home to help maintain or improve their pet's hydration.

It is difficult to make a cat drink under the best of circumstances, but it is even harder when the animal is dehydrated and weak. Depending on the cat and the owner, giving *subcutaneous* fluid injections can be easy. If this is something you would be willing to try, you should discuss the procedure with your veterinarian.

Kitty Ditty

The term **subcutaneous** is derived from "sub," meaning below, and "cutaneous," meaning related to the skin. Instead of going directly into a vein, materials injected in this manner are absorbed by the blood vessels under the skin.

It is not difficult to administer subcutaneous fluids to a cat, and a good number of owners do it themselves.

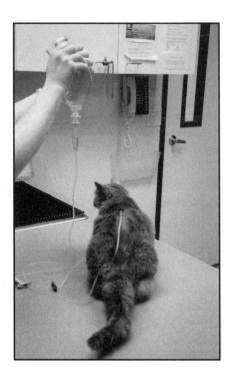

Avoid CATastrophe

If a cat is eating a lot and still losing weight, take the cat to the veterinarian. This clinical sign could indicate hyperthyroidism, diabetes mellitus, kidney disease, or another significant disease.

Nutrition

Because they are not building muscle and are less active than younger cats, senior cats need less protein. As a cat ages, the digestive and absorptive processes of the gastrointestinal system can become less efficient. Many companies produce "senior" or "geriatric" diets geared for these situations.

Dental disease is common in older cats and can affect how much and what a cat will eat. Dental health should be assessed at each veterinary visit, and diet changed to accommodate the cat's dental function.

Softer foods that require little or no chewing may help an older cat. For a cat with a poor appetite, dense foods that provide a lot of nutrition in a small quantity can be appropriate. It is always important for a senior cat to eat and at least maintain its body weight.

Aching Bones

It is inevitable that joints will develop at least some mild arthritic changes over time. Arthritis, or degenerative joint disease (DJD), can cause pain and restrict a cat's movement. If a cat cannot get around well, it may not be able to perform its normal functions.

Arthritic cats that spend time outdoors are in danger because they cannot run and jump as well as they might need to in a dangerous situation. When joints hurt, it is more difficult to jump down from places the cat has jumped up on. It is a good idea to start keeping an older, achy cat indoors for its own protection.

The location and type of litterbox might need to be changed for an arthritic cat. You want to make it as easy as possible for the cat to get in and out. Consider uncovering a hooded box or getting a box with lower sides if the cat is having a hard time using it.

The placement of food and water bowls should also be considered. If a cat cannot move its head and neck well, elevating the bowl could make a big difference in the animal's ability to eat and drink.

A Comfy Place to Lay

Older cats can lose body fat and muscle. They can become less insulated against cold temperatures, and they can develop "bed sores" when bony parts rub on hard surfaces that they lay on. Be sure that your cat has something soft and warm to lie on.

Keep Your Cat from Being Eaten Alive

As horrible as it sounds, insects like to take advantage of weaker animals. Older cats may not be able to move away or scratch when insects bother them. Insects want to get a meal as easily as possible, so if an animal is not shooing them off, they are going to stay and eat.

Worth a Paws

Observe and take note of where your older cat likes to lie. If it is a hard surface, try placing a towel, throw rug, or kitty blanket on it to make your cat more comfortable.

Check your older animal for fleas, and use flea control when needed. If the cat goes outside, monitor the areas it uses for sleeping and make sure that ants are not bothering the cat. Also check to make sure that flies are not bothering an outdoor cat. Flies can lay their eggs on animals that are not moving away, and the eggs will hatch into maggots about 12 hours later.

Knowing When to Let Go

Each owner will have different feelings about how far he is willing to go financially and emotionally with the treatment of his cat. There is no right or wrong when it comes to treating a geriatric cat with a life-threatening illness. For some owners a year or two more of life is worth it; others are ready to say goodbye when the news is bad.

I always tell owners that there is never a "perfect" time to make a decision about a cat's life. It is uncommon for a cat to die comfortably and quietly in its sleep, and in most situations, an owner is faced with making a decision about euthanasia.

Quality of Life

The phrase "quality of life" is used a lot, but people don't always know what it means. My interpretation is that if an animal is able to eat, drink, eliminate, and get around reasonably well, then its quality of life is probably pretty good. When these basic functions cannot be performed, then quality of life is in question.

Unfortunately, in many older cats, one part of their body is not working at all, but otherwise they're in good health. Under these circumstances, making a decision is difficult for an owner. We cannot truly assess how much pain an animal is in with most diseases, so we use their clinical signs as a guide.

Euthanasia

When an animal is "put to sleep," it is given an overdose of an injectable barbiturate anesthetic agent. If the injection is given intravenously, the animal dies within 20 seconds. Everything in the cat's body slows to a stop, including the heart, so the process is painless.

Each of us has different feelings about death and what it means. A few things to consider with euthanasia:

➤ Do you want to be present when your cat is given the injection?

➤ Do you want any special arrangements made for the body?

➤ If there are young children in the family, how will you explain it?

➤ Will you need help coping with the loss of your pet?

As much as you do not want to plan for your cat's death, when the time comes, it is often hard to think clearly. It is best to be prepared so that you do not have to make a hasty decision.

Are You Crazy to Be This Upset?

I am upset any time I have to put a cat to sleep. Certainly it is the worst part of the job of being a veterinarian. I am able to derive comfort from the fact that I know that I am able to end animal pain and suffering through euthanasia. Anyone who has ever been close to a pet knows how much it hurts emotionally when a pet dies, but people who have not had pets often do not understand.

It's Okay to Cry

I think it is normal to want to cry when a pet you have loved and shared your home with dies. I personally feel sadder about putting a cat to sleep when the owners are not upset. I think that it is great to let your emotions out whether you are a man or a woman. Why should you have to keep them bottled up? Those of us in the veterinary profession do understand how painful it is to make a decision about a pet's life.

Do Others Share the Grief?

All family members, even those who may have previously claimed not to care about the cat, will feel some sort of loss with the animal's death. It is good to talk about it when possible. If there are children in the family, let them know that you are sad too, but that all living creatures will die at some time.

If you live alone, you should tell others about the loss of your pet so that friends and relatives can help you and be supportive of your feelings. Although no one else you know may have felt the same way about the pet as you did, other support options are available. These include:

➤ Local pet loss support groups

➤ Pet loss support hot lines available by phone

➤ Internet Web sites dedicated to pet loss

Should You Get a New Pet?

Each person should go through a grieving period, but the length of time will vary. A new cat will never replace an old one, but each animal should find its own place in your heart. I personally think that owners that feel a void from the loss of a pet should consider a new pet because they obviously have a lot of love that another pet would benefit from.

You may or may not want to get the same color, sex, or breed of cat. The decision is up to you, but remember the new cat is not a replacement, it is a new family member. You must also remember that if you get a kitten, the behaviors and your responsibility to the animal will be different from those that you have been accustomed to.

The Least You Need to Know

➤ Indoor cats have an average life span of 13 to 15 years.

➤ Your cat is considered "senior" when it is 9 years or older.

➤ Cats die from a variety of illnesses, but many of them are chronic, degenerative diseases that can be slowed if detected at an early stage.

➤ With a little effort, there are ways in which you can help keep an older cat more comfortable.

➤ Euthanasia is a painless way that a pet's life can be ended.

➤ Crying and mourning over the loss of a cat are normal feelings that should not be suppressed.

Part 4
The Body Systems and Their Diseases

A cat's body is a finely honed machine that is capable of many great feats. You probably don't think too much about the individual parts of the body that all have to synchronize together every second of every day, but it is truly amazing.

Most cats are very healthy throughout their lives and need little more than preventive care. They can get viruses, eat too much, or have allergies—just like we can. Knowing these things should make your life as an owner less worrisome.

Becoming familiar with some of the common diseases that affect certain body systems will help you to identify them, or at least understand them, when they are diagnosed by your veterinarian. Early disease detection and treatment is the key to keeping your cat healthy. You will be able to make better decisions about treatment options if you understand what is going on, and these chapters will help you do just that.

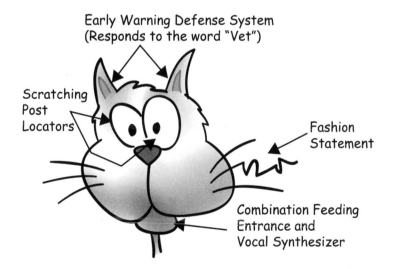

Early Warning Defense System
(Responds to the word "Vet")

Scratching Post Locators

Fashion Statement

Combination Feeding Entrance and Vocal Synthesizer

Chapter 13

The Cat's Need to Breathe

In This Chapter

➤ The various causes of sneezing in cats

➤ Kitty colds

➤ Asthma

➤ Pneumonia

Breathing is a bodily function that you usually do not think too much about. It is a process controlled by your brain and nervous system. In healthy, normal animals breathing is a subconscious action. Animals exchange oxygen and carbon dioxide by breathing.

The respiratory system of an animal is composed of two parts: upper and lower airways. The organs that comprise the upper respiratory tract are the nose and throat. The organs that comprise the lower respiratory tract are the trachea and lungs. Both parts of the respiratory tract must be functioning for a cat to breathe normally.

Oxygen is essential to maintaining life and body functions, so if an animal becomes starved of oxygen, it will die. Some of the diseases that affect the respiratory tract of cats are life-threatening, but others are more of a nuisance and discomfort for the animal. This chapter will introduce you to some of the most common disorders of the feline respiratory system.

It' Snot Funny

Cats cannot blow their noses, and unfortunately because of this they sneeze out a lot of junk. This sounds gross, and it is. Sneezing is a non-specific sign that occurs when the nasal passages become stimulated by secretions or an irritant.

Meow Wow

A cat's respiratory anatomy is very similar to ours. Although our noses are shaped differently, and theirs are more hairy, the functions are the same. Air enters into the body through the nostrils. Mucus and small hairs cover the lining of the nasal passages and trap small particles and bacteria from the air. The air is warmed and moisturized as it passes through the nasal cavity.

Worth a Paws

Although examining your cat's nasal discharge is not a pleasant task, the color and consistency hold clues. In general, if the discharge is clear and watery, it is nothing to worry about. If the discharge is green, yellow, or bloody, medical care is required.

How You Can Cure Your Cat's Sneezing

There is no "cure" for sneezing because there are so many different causes. Possible causes of sneezing include:

➤ Viral infections

➤ Bacterial infections

➤ Fungal infections

➤ Allergies

➤ Irritants

➤ Foreign objects

Antihistamines, decongestants, and nasal sprays for humans are usually not very useful against sneezing in cats. If you have a sneezing cat, the best thing to do is have it examined by a veterinarian, so that a potential cause can be determined and a specific treatment suggested.

Cats can get bloody noses from dry air and irritation just like we do, but a bloody nose can also be a sign of severe infection or even a nasal tumor.

Allergies

Although most cats with allergies have itchy skin, some do sneeze. Cats can be allergic to just about anything in the world, including pollen, house dust, and even kitty litter. Allergies usually produce a clear discharge when the animal sneezes, and they are a condition that is managed rather than cured.

It can be quite difficult to determine which specific allergen is causing the sneezing. Although it is impossible to test a cat for all possible allergens, your vet can test for common allergens. If specific allergens are identified, you can either remove them from the environment or try to hyposensitize the animal with allergy shots.

Irritants

Smoke, cleaning products, and even a cat's own hair can irritate the nasal passages and cause sneezing. To determine if an irritant is causing the sneezing, it must be removed from the environment and sneezing must cease.

Meow Wow

Cigarette smoke can be very irritating to cats, and cats are susceptible to all of the problems of secondhand smoke that humans are. These include sneezing, bronchitis, and even lung cancer. If you smoke, try to keep the fumes away from your cat.

Something Stuck Up Kitty's Nose?

Cats are like small children; they are subject to accidents, and objects can become lodged in their noses. The most common object to get stuck in a cat's nose is a blade of grass. If you have a cat that repeatedly sneezes 8 to 10 times in a row, it might be due to a foreign object stuck in the nose.

It can be difficult for a veterinarian to find something in a cat's nose without sedating the animal. Most cats are not thrilled with the idea of putting a scope up their nostril or keeping their mouth open while a veterinarian probes the back of the mouth. In some cases a special fiberoptic scope is needed to look into the rear nasal passages.

145

How You Can Help Alleviate Sneezing

Wiping a cat's nose and keeping it free of discharge will help improve the animal's comfort. If the animal sounds congested, you may try putting it in a steamy bathroom or with a vaporizer to help open up the airways. Seek veterinary advice if the sneezing persists or if the cat is showing signs of discomfort.

Use a moistened piece of cotton gauze to wipe the eyes and nose clean.

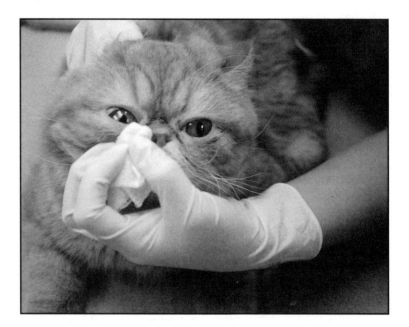

Your Cat Has a Cold

Upper respiratory infections (URIs) are common in cats, and they can be caused by viral, bacterial, or fungal infections. These "kitty colds" can range in severity from mild to severe, with kittens being the most susceptible to infection. Cats are routinely vaccinated against some of the agents that cause upper respiratory infections. However, vaccines only decrease the severity of the clinical signs and do not completely prevent infection.

URIs can last a few days to weeks, so it important to monitor your cat's clinical signs and work with a veterinarian if you are not seeing an improvement. They can be very annoying and frustrating infections to deal with.

Stress and crowding are two factors that increase the risk of a URI. It is very common for a cat that has been adopted from a shelter or foster home to start off healthy, only to develop a cold shortly after its arrival in its new home. The animal was likely exposed to a microorganism that caused the infection before it was adopted, but the stress of being in a new home weakened the immune system and triggered the infection.

Viral Infections

Viruses are the most common cause of kitty colds. The good news about viruses is that they will resolve over time, but the bad news is that there is not any specific treatment for their cure and it can take a long time. The clinical signs typical of a viral upper respiratory infection are:

➤ Sneezing

➤ Runny nose

➤ Runny eyes

➤ Mild lethargy

➤ Decreased appetite

➤ Fever

Avoid CATastrophe

Sick cats must eat and drink. Cats with URIs will often have decreased appetites because they cannot smell. If your cat is not eating, try offering it smellier canned cat food, baby food, or tuna. You can also try heating food in the microwave for a few seconds to increase its aroma. If the cat will not eat on its own, then it will need to be hand- or force-fed.

A veterinarian may treat a cat with a suspected viral URI with fluids, antibiotics, ophthalmic medication, pediatric nasal sprays, antihistamines, immunostimulants, or with nothing at all. Treatment depends on the clinical signs exhibited by the cat.

Most veterinarians will base diagnosis of a viral URI on their interpretation of the animal's clinical signs. Definitively diagnosing viral URIs is difficult because the lab tests that isolate viruses are expensive, can take weeks for results, and may only be 50 percent accurate. Don't get too frustrated if your veterinarian cannot make a positive call on the cause of infection. Continue to pursue treatment options if you think that your cat is uncomfortable.

Meow Wow

Feline rhinotracheitis is a very common cause of URI, and because it is a herpes virus, it can cause recurrent disease. Most cats can have colds and conjunctivitis off and on as kittens, but they tend to grow out of them by the time they are 2 years old.

Kitty Ditty

The terms **acute** and **chronic** are used to describe diseases. Acute means that a disease comes on suddenly. A chronic disease is one that lasts for a long time or that does not completely go away.

Bacterial Infections

Bacterial URIs can occur on their own or as secondary infections along with viruses. The clinical signs associated with bacterial infections are:

➤ Fever

➤ Enlarged lymph nodes

➤ Yellow to green discharge from the nose and/or eyes

➤ Sneezing

➤ Coughing

➤ Decrease in or loss of appetite

➤ Lethargy

➤ Dehydration

Treatment is aimed at killing the bacteria and supporting the cat and can include antibiotics, fluids, ophthalmic medications, antihistamines, pediatric nasal sprays, immunostimulants, and hand-feeding. Bacterial cultures are not routinely run on cats that develop *acute* URIs, but they may be performed if the infection does not resolve, worsens, or becomes *chronic*.

Meow Wow

Culturing the specific bacteria that are causing a URI is difficult because the nose is also the home of many normal bacteria that can contaminate a culture. To get a more reliable culture specimen the cat should be sedated, sterile saline flushed into a nostril, and a sample collected from the back of the nasal passages.

Fungal Infections

Fungal URIs occur occasionally, with Cryptococcus neoformans being the most common fungus. Cats with compromised immune systems, such as those infected with FeLV or FIV, are most at risk for developing fungal URIs. This fungus can be found in bird droppings and as unlikely as it seems, it can affect cats that are housed indoors.

Fungal URIs are usually slowly progressive and do not improve with antibiotic treatment. As fungal infections progress they can cause growths in the nostrils and bulging of the sinuses. Fungal URIs may be diagnosed by examining a smear of nasal discharge microscopically, by performing a blood test for Cryptococcus, or by a biopsy or needle aspirate of a nasal growth. Antifungal drugs are effective against this fungus, but the treatment may last months and the drugs are quite expensive.

If the URI Doesn't Go Away

If your veterinarian is performing treatments that are not helping, more aggressive care and hospitalization may be needed. Other diagnostic tests should be performed that will look for other diseases that can mimic URIs, including:

➤ Complete blood count and blood chemistries

➤ FeLV and FIV tests

➤ Microscopic evaluation of nasal discharge

➤ Bacterial culture

➤ Fungal blood titer and/or culture

➤ Skull x-rays

➤ Rhinoscopy (examination of the back of the nasal passages with a fiberoptic scope)

➤ Nasal biopsy

➤ Tracheal or bronchial wash

➤ Bronchoscopy

Other possible diagnoses are nasopharyngeal polyps, inflammatory conditions, sinus infections, and neoplasia. These other diseases will not respond to conventional URI treatments.

Could Your Cat Have Asthma?

Cats do get asthma. Asthma is a form of bronchitis—an inflammation of the large airways called the bronchi. Allergies or irritants can cause asthma, and since asthma affects the lungs, it is a lower respiratory disease with more serious implications. Diseases that affect the lower respiratory tract are potentially more dangerous because the lungs can be permanently damaged.

Signs of Asthma

The clinical signs associated with asthma include:

➤ Coughing

➤ Gagging

149

Worth a Paws

When cats cough and gag, owners can be quick to blame the problem on hairballs. Although initially an asthmatic cat may appear to be coughing up a hairball, nothing will come up and the problem will progress. Do not ignore this important clinical sign of asthma.

Avoid CATastrophe

Do not treat your cat for asthma unless it has had a chest x-ray. The clinical signs that are typical of asthma can also be present with heart disease or when fluid is present in the chest cavity, and these serious conditions have very different treatments.

➤ Increased respiratory rate

➤ Open-mouth breathing

➤ Wheezing

➤ Lethargy

➤ Difficulty breathing and distress

The number and severity of the clinical signs is usually proportionate to the severity of the asthma. Asthma can progress to a life-threatening situation. It can only be diagnosed definitively by an x-ray. A complete blood count could also be a helpful test because some cats with asthma have elevations of a type of white blood cell called an eosinophil.

Treating Asthma

There are various drugs veterinarians prescribe for the treatment of asthma, including cortisone, antihistamines, bronchodilators, antibiotics, oxygen, and even some asthma drugs designed for humans. Most of the time the cause of asthma is not found, but it is often linked to allergies. A condition linked to allergies is managed rather than cured, and thus a cat can have recurrent problems.

Observant owners can tune in to their cats and catch asthma, when it recurs, at an early stage. The early clinical signs are a non-productive cough or gag. Some cats need to be on long-term medication to control their problems, and medication can be injectable and/or oral.

Some cats can have life-long asthma that causes permanent damage to the lungs through scarring. Scarring prevents the lung tissue from expanding normally, and as it progresses can lead to respiratory collapse. Managing the inflammation helps to prevent scarring.

Pneumonia

Pneumonia is an infection in the lungs. Viruses, bacteria, and fungi can all cause pneumonia. Pneumonia is most common in young cats and infrequent in adults. It is a serious condition because if it progresses, it can lead to severe congestion within the lungs and respiratory collapse.

Why Would a Cat Get Pneumonia?

Young cats can get pneumonia by choking and aspirating fluid into their lungs. This might occur when a bottle-fed kitten does not suck normally and the milk is swallowed improperly. Pneumonia can then ensue. A cat might also get pneumonia when it has another disease that has weakened its immune system and allowed infection to travel down into the lower respiratory tract.

A third cause of pneumonia could be parasites. There is, for example, a species of worm known as *Aelurostrongylus abstrusus,* which like to live in the lungs and cause infections. These worms can be carried by the birds, frogs, or rodents that are eaten by cats. Sometimes gastrointestinal worms migrate in an abnormal manner and become lodged in the lungs. In addition, a protozoal parasite, *Toxoplasma gondii,* can occasionally cause pneumonia in cats.

Treating Pneumonia

Because a lower respiratory tract infection poses much graver consequences than a URI, aggressive therapy is needed. Pneumonia can only be definitively diagnosed by a chest x-ray. A cat with pneumonia usually requires hospitalization, intravenous antibiotics, fluids, diuretics, bronchodilators, oxygen, and *nebulization.*

The prognosis for a cat with pneumonia is uncertain. If infection responds to treatment and the lung does not become permanently damaged, recovery is possible. The longer the lung stays congested, the harder it is to treat.

Kitty Ditty

Nebulization is a process in which saline and antibiotics are mixed and turned into very small particles that are made into a mist. This mist can enter the lower airways when an animal breathes in.

The Least You Need to Know

➤ Sneezing is common in cats, but the color of the discharge and presence of associated clinical signs determine if treatment is needed.

➤ Colds (URIs), also common in cats, can last from days to weeks, and are caused by viral, bacterial, or fungal infections.

➤ Asthma is a serious disease in cats that can only be diagnosed by a chest x-ray.

➤ Pneumonia requires aggressive treatment and can potentially cause respiratory collapse.

Chapter 14

Look Out Stomach, Here It Comes

In This Chapter

➤ How dental disease can affect cats

➤ Vomiting—when it's normal, when it's not

➤ Feline diarrhea

➤ Constipated kitties

➤ Liver disease in cats

If your cat is anything like either of mine, eating is an important part of each day. The intake and processing of food sustains life for a cat, so disorders of the gastrointestinal (GI) tract can have serious implications. The gastrointestinal system includes many organs and extends from the mouth, to the esophagus, to the stomach, to the small intestine, to the large intestine, and finally to the rectum. Along the way the liver and the pancreas get into the act.

There are many diseases that can affect the GI tract. In this chapter, I will describe some of the common signs and some of the diseases. Diet, stress, infectious agents, parasites, and age all play a role in GI health.

It All Starts in the Mouth

Digestion begins in the mouth with food being taken in by the lips, chewed by the teeth, mixed with saliva, and pushed into the esophagus by the tongue. Many cat owners know that their cats do not always perform the second step of digestion, chewing the food. Cats that eat rapidly without chewing may regurgitate their meal within minutes of eating.

Don't Call Me Tuna Breath

I don't know if cats ever have good breath, but cats with disease in their mouths generally have noticeably bad breath. A veterinarian should perform a dental exam on your cat at least once a year and evaluate the teeth, tongue, and gums.

Bad breath can be an indicator of dental disease, gum disease, or problems with the tongue. Cats with significant infection or inflammation in their mouths may eat surprisingly normally. Decreased appetite or problems eating are not the hallmarks of oral disease.

Aching Teeth

Even if you perform routine dental care on your cat, dental disease can occur. Just as some people have bad teeth, some cats naturally have bad teeth. Others develop bad teeth because of diet and lack of care. Teeth can break, crack, develop erosions, abscess, and fall out on their own. Owners are sometimes shocked when I show them that their cat is missing teeth. They cannot believe how normally their cat is eating.

Infections from the mouth can get into the blood and spread to other organ systems, so regardless of age, cats with dental disease should be treated. Before performing any dental procedures, a cat's general health and metabolic state should first be assessed and stabilized.

Look at Those Gums

The signs of gingivitis or gum disease are:

➤ Red gums

➤ Swollen gums

➤ Gums growing up and over teeth

➤ Inflammation at the corners of the mouth, making it difficult to open

Similar to other disease processes, the longer gum disease persists, the harder it is to control or cure. Early intervention against gum disease is very helpful to a cat. When significant gum disease is present, causes to consider are:

➤ Feline Leukemia Virus (FeLV)

➤ Feline Immunodeficiency Virus (FIV)

➤ Tooth infection

➤ Inflammatory condition

➤ Neoplasia

A cat with bad gums should be tested for FeLV and FIV. If these tests are normal, the teeth should be cleaned and any affected teeth repaired or removed. A gum biopsy and treatment with antibiotics should be performed if there is significant gingivitis. The biopsy results would then guide any further treatment.

Meow Wow

There is a group of inflammatory conditions of unknown origin that can cause severe dental disease. An example is called lymphocytic-plasmacytic stomatitis. Treatment of this condition can include cortisone, antibiotics, immunostimulants, and full-mouth dental extractions. Some veterinarians treat this condition with lasers.

Kitty's Going to Be Sick

Cats frequently vomit, and owners hate to clean up after them. When cats live in the wild, vomiting is not a big deal, but when they live in our homes, it can create quite a mess. Sometimes vomiting is normal, but other times it is an indication of internal disease.

Some of the most common causes of vomiting in the cat are:

➤ Hairballs

➤ Sensitivity to a diet

➤ Eating too quickly

➤ Viral or bacterial infections

➤ Consumption of plants or other non-food items

➤ Inflammatory conditions

➤ Metabolic imbalances

➤ Gastrointestinal parasites

➤ Foreign body ingestion

➤ Intestinal obstruction

Spitting Up Hairballs

If you have a cat that grooms itself regularly, you are probably familiar with hairballs. Some cats spit up hairballs on a regular basis (once or twice a week), and others may only produce a hairball a few times a year. The first time you see a hairball, you may not be sure which end of the cat it came out of because hairballs can appear as long, tubular structures.

Many cats like the taste of lubricant hairball remedies and will readily lick them from your finger.

Hairball remedies do not cure hairballs; they merely help the hair to pass through the cat's GI tract (one way or the other), rather than causing an obstruction in the intestines. Commonly found hairball remedies include:

➤ Lubricant pastes

➤ Fiber supplements

➤ Special diets

If your cat spits up hairballs on a regular basis, one of these remedies may decrease the frequency. Note that mineral oil is not a safe or effective treatment for hairballs.

Is Your Cat Bulimic?

Many cat owners have seen their cat eat rapidly, regurgitate its food a few minutes later, then go back to eating. Cats may eat rapidly because they feel competition at the food bowl or because they like to overeat.

Cats that regurgitate tend to bring up piles of food that has not been chewed. These cats usually eat a dry (but sometimes canned) diet too quickly, which blows up and over-distends their stomachs, causing the regurgitation. Some suggestions for curbing this problem are:

➤ Feed a less palatable diet

➤ Feed a diet with a larger kibble size so that the cat will have to chew

➤ Add water to moisten the food before it is fed

➤ Mix canned food with the dry to slow down eating and add moisture

Avoid CATastrophe

It is common to blame a cat's coughing and gagging on hairballs, but there are some serious conditions that can mimic the same signs (see Chapter 13). If your cat is not spitting up a hairball when it goes through the motions, consult your veterinarian. Possible causes could be asthma, heart disease, and other gastrointestinal problems.

If you try these all of these suggestions and your cat continues to regurgitate, consult with your veterinarian.

Does Your Cat Have the Flu?

Cats can contract viral or bacterial infections that cause vomiting. Because routine blood tests may have normal results, it is not easy to diagnose a gastrointestinal infection. If fever and discomfort are present, an infection should be suspected. It is common for cats with infections to also have diarrhea.

Infections can be contagious to other cats, but are rarely transmissible to humans or other species. When possible, an exact cause for vomiting should be determined.

Other Causes of Vomiting

A cat that is vomiting and is unable to hold down food and water can get dehydrated and feel quite poorly. If you have a cat that is vomiting and cannot keep any nutrition down, you should have it checked out as soon as possible. A veterinarian may want to treat the cat with fluids to improve hydration and also use other injectable medications. Injecting medications will ensure that they get into the cat's system rather than being spit up and not absorbed.

Kitty Ditty

Any time a cat eats something other than its food, veterinarians call it **dietary indiscretion**. Cats may ingest plants, strings, cat toys, holiday decorations, and even pieces of shoes and clothing. A **foreign body** is an inanimate object that a cat swallows and cannot digest.

Although blood tests are not very specific when it comes to diagnosing gastrointestinal disease, your veterinarian should perform them nonetheless. Other diagnostic tests that may be needed are:

➤ X-rays

➤ Abdominal ultrasound

➤ Barium upper GI series

➤ Endoscopy

➤ Abdominal exploratory

➤ Biopsy of the stomach and intestines

➤ Hypoallergenic food trial

Veterinary medicine is quite advanced with diagnostic options. Depending on where you live, some of these tests are readily available. Tests that use high-tech equipment tend to cost more money, but are very effective at reaching a diagnosis.

What Is a Foreign Body?

We think of cats as being picky and extremely discriminating. So how can it be that they would willingly swallow inanimate objects that can lodge in their intestines? The answer to the question of *dietary indiscretion* is a mystery. It could be that their hunting and stalking behavior gets the best of them. They chase and pounce on the quick-moving object, and then ingest it as they would captured prey.

Worth a Paws

I have observed my own cats attempt to swallow the string on their "fishing pole" toys. I now keep the toys in a closed closet whenever they are not in use. To protect your cat from potentially dangerous objects such as toys with strings, sewing materials, ribbon, and newspaper ties, store them in a secure place.

Another possible explanation for the ingestion of foreign objects is boredom. Cats like to indulge in attention-seeking behaviors. Some cats seem to like being scolded and chased away from trouble. Playing with items that they fish out of trash cans can be a game. Unraveling balls of yarn or pulling apart a carpet or drape can be lots of fun. It is even more fun for the cat when you yell and run after it!

Early detection of *foreign bodies* allows successful removal from the stomach and intestines of cats. If not found in time, they can cause the intestines to become blocked or coiled, which can progress to a life-threatening situation. Some foreign objects can be easily found on an x-ray, while others cannot and may not be found without exploratory surgery.

Getting to the Box

Diarrhea is another common problem in cats. It can have many of the same causes as vomiting, and it requires the same diagnostic work-up. If your cat has diarrhea, a veterinarian will want to examine the cat and a fecal sample because parasites are a frequent cause of diarrhea. If a fecal check is negative, and the animal's physical exam is relatively normal, other diagnostic tests should be considered.

Diarrhea can be a sign of a mild problem, or it can indicate a serious condition. A cat can have one episode of diarrhea, which is not a big deal, or it can have chronic diarrhea and weight loss that need significant care.

Avoid CATastrophe

Although it may sound extreme, if you have a cat that is unable to hold down food or water, exploratory surgery can be the best way to find a foreign body that cannot be seen on an x-ray. The risk of waiting for other diagnostic tests that may (or may not) show the problem can outweigh the risk of doing surgery.

Bland Is Better

A diet change or dietary sensitivity can cause diarrhea. Any time a cat eats something new, there is the possibility of gastrointestinal upset. Cats can also develop intolerance to foods that they have handled previously. Feeding your cat a bland diet and with-holding table scraps is always a good idea if it has diarrhea.

Meow Wow

As contrary as it seems, feeding a cat that has diarrhea a high-fiber diet can firm the stool. Fiber helps to stimulate normal GI contractions, reduce bacteria in the bowel, and promote water reabsorption—all of which can improve diarrhea.

Check Out the Litterbox

Although you probably do not want to talk about the size, shape, and consistency of your cat's stool, these factors will help your veterinarian determine the cause of the problem. Helpful observations are:

➤ Is the stool formed?

➤ Is there mucus present?

159

➤ Is there blood in the stool?

➤ Is there an abnormal odor?

➤ Can the cat make it to the litterbox?

➤ When was the last normal stool?

Seeing blood in your cat's stool is scary, but it is unlikely to be a sign of grave illness. Cats that have irritated colons will pass bright red blood or clots. Cats that have bleeding in the stomach will pass dark to black stools because the blood goes through some digestion along the way. A one-time episode of blood in the stool may be insignificant, but if it continues, check with a veterinarian.

Inflammatory Bowel Disease (IBD)

Inflammatory bowel disease (IBD) is a condition in cats that can cause diarrhea and/or vomiting. A diagnosis can only be confirmed by a biopsy, which reveals an abnormal infiltration of inflammatory cells into the lining of the stomach and/or intestines. Biopsies can be obtained through endoscopy or surgery.

When other causes of GI disease have been eliminated, IBD becomes a more likely diagnosis. It is typically a disease of middle-aged to older cats, but it can affect young cats too. It is always best to make a definitive diagnosis of this disease through biopsy, but in some situations this may not be a possibility. Treatment for IBD may include special diets, antibiotics, cortisone, and other anti-inflammatory drugs. IBD is another feline condition that cannot be cured, but can be managed.

Meow Wow

Endoscopic biopsies are obtained by using a fiberoptic endoscope in the GI tract of an anesthetized cat. The scope enters the mouth, goes down the esophagus, enters the stomach, and then passes into the intestines. Along the way all of the tissues can be examined and pinch biopsies of the linings can be obtained. This diagnostic test is limited to the lining of the tubular GI tract, and it cannot tell you about the outer layers, lymph nodes, liver, or pancreas.

Intestinal Cancer

Cancer can only be definitively diagnosed by a biopsy. A type of intestinal cancer called intestinal lymphosarcoma (LSA) is common in cats. Intestinal lymphosarcoma can result from uncontrolled inflammatory bowel disease. The clinical signs associated with this disease are similar to IBD, but by the time it has progressed to neoplasia, the cat is usually in much worse physical condition. Cats with intestinal LSA can respond favorably to chemotherapy.

Intestinal adenocarcinoma is another type of neoplasia seen in cats. If this type of cancer has not metastasized, the treatment is surgical removal. The affected piece of intestine is surgically cut out, and the intestine is reconnected—similar to removing a bad piece of garden hose! Adenocarcinomas do recur, but surgery has the potential to buy a couple of good-quality years of life.

When Your Kitty Is Constipated

Cats normally have one bowel movement per day. When stools become less frequent or straining is observed, it is important to determine:

➤ Is the cat able to pass stool?

➤ Is the cat eating?

➤ Is the cat dehydrated?

➤ Could the cat be straining to urinate instead?

➤ Is the cat defecating somewhere else in the house?

Avoid CATastrophe

Cats have different postures for urinating and defecating, but if you are not sure and the animal is straining, you should take it to a veterinarian as soon as possible. Instead of being constipated, the cat may actually be unable to urinate. Urinary blockages can become life-threatening situations within a very short period of time—as little as 12 hours.

Help for Kitty Constipation

If your cat is constipated, there are a few things you can try at home. If you have any type of lubricant hairball remedy, these products also work as laxatives. Adding psyllium, which is the ingredient in Metamucil and other fiber remedies, to the food can also help the irregular cat. You may try feeding canned food and encouraging water consumption.

Don't let your kitty go more than two days without passing a stool. If you think an enema is needed, let your veterinarian administer it and then deal with cleaning up any mess. Never give a phosphate enema designed for a human to a cat—they are toxic to felines!

What Has Stopped Up Your Cat?

There are many reasons why a cat can become constipated, and it is a good idea to narrow down the possibilities in order to prevent recurrences. Causes of constipation include:

➤ Hairballs

➤ Dehydration

➤ Metabolic disease

➤ *Megacolon*

➤ Diet

If your cat has more than one episode of constipation, you should work with your veterinarian to determine a diagnostic and treatment plan. Treatment can involve fluids, stool softeners, motility-enhancing drugs that promote intestinal contractions, and even shaving a cat to reduce hair in the stool.

Kitty Ditty

Megacolon is a chronic condition that causes constipation. The colon becomes dilated and stops having normal contractions. It can be a progressive condition that needs long-term medication. Cats that do not respond to medical treatment need surgery to remove the inactive colon.

Kitty Ditty

Jaundice is a condition causing the eyes, skin, and gums of an animal to have a yellow discoloration. The color change is due to bile pigments in the blood that rise to abnormal levels in liver disease or gall bladder obstruction.

If Your Cat Is Turning Yellow

The liver is a vital organ with many functions, including:

➤ Digestion

➤ Vitamin and mineral storage

➤ Protein synthesis

➤ General metabolism

➤ Neutralizing toxins

A cat can become very sick when its liver function is impaired. Most of the signs of liver disease in cats are similar to those of other gastrointestinal problems, but one different sign seen in many cases is *jaundice*.

What Is a Fatty Liver?

Cats that do not eat begin to break down their body fat for energy. Even though many cats are overweight and have lots of energy stored, the liver becomes overwhelmed by the amount of fat it must convert, and a condition called hepatic lipidosis—fatty liver disease—can develop.

Sick cats will often eat small amounts of soft food, such as baby food, when hand-fed from a tongue depressor.

Cats that start off with other problems, such as viral infections, can develop hepatic lipidosis if they become anorexic. If the process continues, hepatic lipidosis can become life-threatening to the cat.

A diagnosis of hepatic lipidosis can only be confirmed by a liver biopsy, but can be suspected if a blood test shows elevated liver enzymes and a cat is not eating. Needle biopsies of the liver can be obtained with the aid of ultrasound, and wedge biopsies can be obtained through exploratory surgery.

Treatment for hepatic lipidosis may include:

➤ Force-feeding

➤ Treatment of an underlying medical condition

➤ Supplementation with essential amino acids

➤ Placement of a feeding tube

➤ Extended supportive care (weeks to months)

Worth a Paws

If your cat is not eating for more than a day, it is crucial to get food into it as soon as possible. If you are unable to entice the cat with tuna, consult with your veterinarian. Every day makes a difference when trying to prevent hepatic lipidosis.

Meow Wow

A feeding tube can be a lifeline for sick cats. Tubes can be placed through the nose or esophagus into the stomach, or they can be placed directly into the stomach or intestine. Nasogastric tubes (nose to stomach) can be irritating and are best used only in a short-term situation.

Other Causes of Liver Disease

Hepatic lipidosis is generally considered to be a secondary problem, occurring after another disease has caused anorexia. Some primary liver diseases are:

➤ Viral, bacterial, or parasitic hepatitis

➤ Cholangiohepatitis

➤ Exposure to toxins

➤ Congenital disease

➤ Liver shunts

➤ Hepatic neoplasia

Blood tests can indicate that inflammation of the liver is occurring, and they can indicate that liver function is significantly impaired, but they are not specific when it comes to determining cause. A liver biopsy is needed to make a conclusive diagnosis. Some types of liver disease are easier to treat than others, and the liver is an organ that can regenerate if it is not too severely damaged.

Meow Wow

Seventy to 80 percent of a liver can be impaired before functional problems are apparent. A cat's liver is comprised of four lobes and may fill up to one-fourth of the animal's abdominal cavity.

The Least You Need to Know

➤ Good dental health is essential to good general health in a cat.

➤ Although hairballs can cause vomiting in cats, vomiting can also be a sign of serious disease.

➤ Vomiting and diarrhea are signs of many different types of gastrointestinal disease, and a series of diagnostic tests may be needed to determine a specific cause.

➤ Chronic constipation is not a normal condition in cats, and medical intervention is likely to be needed.

➤ It is important that sick cats continue to eat so that they do not develop hepatic lipidosis.

Is Beauty Only Skin Deep?

In This Chapter

➤ Allergies in cats that manifest in dermatitis

➤ Ringworm fungus

➤ Different traumatic injuries to the skin

➤ The effects of insect and spider bites on cats

➤ The types of mange that can affect cats

➤ How to protect your cat against skin cancer

The skin is the largest organ of any animal's body, and it comprises 12 to 24 percent of a cat's body weight. It functions as protection and is responsible for much of an animal's external appearance. Changes in a cat's skin and haircoat can alert an owner to problems with the animal. Some feline skin conditions are contagious to humans and other animals, and others are exclusive to the individual cat.

There are numerous different dermatological conditions that can affect cats, and I'll discuss some of the most common in this chapter. Most skin disease looks the same regardless of the initial cause, so testing and response to therapy are important to making a proper diagnosis.

Itchy Cat

We treat itchy cats on a daily basis at my clinic. Some cats are mildly itchy, and others are miserable and scratch themselves until they are raw. Historically, fleas have been the most common cause of itchy cats, but with improvements in the flea-control products available today, flea infestations can be easily controlled. (Specifics for flea control are discussed in Chapter 4.)

Finding the Cause

When you bring your itchy cat to a veterinarian, the animal should initially have a full physical exam. The doctor should check the cat for fleas and note the distribution of the *lesions*. She should also take the cat's history from you. Many diagnoses can be made based on the animal's age, history, and location of problem.

If a diagnosis is not apparent at this time, the next steps would be to perform some diagnostic tests, such as:

Kitty Ditty

The term **lesion** is used to describe a change or injury to a body tissue that impairs or causes a loss of function.

1. Skin scraping

2. Wood's lamp evaluation

3. Fungal culture

4. Microscopic evaluation of an imprint of the lesion (impression smear)

5. Blood test

6. Allergy testing

7. Hypoallergenic diet

8. Skin biopsy

Allergies Cause Itchiness

An animal can be allergic to just about any substance in the world, so allergies are a difficult problem to diagnose. Most cats with allergies have itchy skin rather than respiratory signs. Allergies are suspected when infectious causes of itchy skin and *miliary dermatitis* are ruled out. The infectious causes are parasites, fungus, and bacteria.

Kitty Ditty

Miliary dermatitis is the term used by veterinarians to describe scabby, crusty skin.

There are four types of allergies:

➤ Inhaled allergies (atopy)

➤ Food allergies

➤ Flea allergies

➤ Contact allergies

Meow Wow

Eosinophilic granulomas are inflammatory lesions frequently seen on cats that may be caused by allergies. The three types of lesions are rodent ulcer of the lip, linear granuloma of the back legs, or eosinophilic plaque that can be found anywhere. Treatment for these lesions is similar to that of other allergies.

Atopy

Inhaled allergies are generally managed rather than cured. If a specific *allergen* can be identified and eliminated from the environment, a particular allergy can be stopped. In order to identify specific allergens, some type of allergy testing is needed.

Veterinary dermatologists feel that intradermal skin testing is the most reliable way to test for allergies in cats. This test involves sedating the patient, clipping the hair on one side of the chest, and then injecting tiny doses of *antigens* under the skin. The number of antigens injected can vary, but it would not be unusual for 60 different substances to be included in a test. The skin is then monitored for the formation of wheals—red, raised, skin reactions. Each site that forms a significant wheal is considered to be an allergen to that cat.

Kitty Ditty

Allergens are foreign substances that can cause an allergic response in some animals. **Antigens** are foreign substances that cause the body to produce an antibody that responds exclusively to that antigen.

Other allergy tests involve checking the blood for specific antibodies to different allergens. There is usually a correlation between antibody levels in the blood and allergic reactions, and specific antibodies pinpoint specific allergens. High antibody levels signify a high level of reaction.

If allergens are identified, a cat can receive allergy antigen injections that desensitize it to the substances. This hyposensitization therapy is about 70 percent effective, but it can take 6 to 12 months before results are seen. Most cats receive these "allergy shots" once a month, and owners can learn to give the injections themselves.

Treatment of atopy may include:

➤ Corticosteroids
➤ Antihistamines

169

➤ Fatty acids

➤ Antigen injections

➤ Antibiotics for secondary skin infections

Itchiness Caused by Diet

Cats with food allergies are usually itchy around their heads and ears. Although intradermal skin tests and antibody blood tests look at some food antigens, the best way to diagnose a food allergy is with a food trial. In a food trial, a cat is fed an entirely new protein source for four to six weeks. If improvement is seen, the animal can be challenged with its original food to see if it has problems again, or it can be maintained on the new diet.

Lamb used to be considered a hypoallergenic food and was used in food trials. Pet food companies all jumped on the bandwagon and started putting lamb in many commercially available products, thus it is no longer a unique protein source. A lamb diet may help some food-allergic cats, but other less widely used protein sources are probably needed instead.

Worth a Paws

A successful food trial involves eliminating all treats and table scraps, serving distilled water, and feeding the test diet exclusively. Some of the unique proteins currently being used are venison, duck, and rabbit. Lamb or ham baby food may also be used during a hypoallergenic food trial.

Flea Allergy

The most common allergy in cats is flea allergy dermatitis (FAD). It's not bad enough for the animal to just have fleas. One flea bite can cause a reaction equal to 100 fleas. Cats with FAD are very itchy and have hair loss and miliary dermatitis along their backs, bases of their tails, and behind their back legs. The hair loss is due to self-trauma—incessant chewing at the sites of flea bites.

To diagnose FAD, look for fleas or flea dirt on the cat and observe hair loss in the typical pattern. The best way to do this is by using a flea comb on the animal to hunt for evidence. Some cats are so sensitive to fleas that they bite off every flea that jumps on them and leave no trace of infestation. If a veterinarian does not observe fleas but still suspects FAD, he will treat it. Treatment involves flea control (the once-a-month topical adulticides work wonderfully) and usually cortisone to break the itch/scratch cycle.

Contact Allergies

These are the least frequent types of allergies in cats, but they can occur when a cat touches an allergen. The reaction is usually localized to the site of contact, but if the cat licks or rubs, the problem area can enlarge. Topical treatment can be attempted for these cases, but oral or injectable medications will be needed if the cat insists on licking.

One potentially common contact allergy is with flea collars. There are some cats that develop a rash or hair loss on their necks after having a flea collar placed on them. The dermatitis resolves when the collar is removed, but it can take weeks.

Zitty Kitty

Feline acne is a fairly common problem that affects cats of all ages. Owners often look at me incredulously when I diagnose their pet with this condition. "My cat is too old to have acne!" or, "All he eats is cat food. Wouldn't he have to eat junk food?" are typical owner replies. Just as in most cases of human acne, more than one cause contributes to feline acne. Diet, hormones, allergies, bacteria, and cleanliness can all play roles in the development of acne.

This cat has severe acne, and has had its chin clipped and medicated.

Diagnosing Acne

A diagnosis of feline acne is made during a physical exam. Sometimes the owner has noticed draining sores on the cat's chin and sometimes a veterinarian will discover acne lesions while performing a routine examination. Blackheads and/or whiteheads are observed around the lower lips or on the chin. These clogged pores can become infected by bacteria and develop into a pustule. Pustules can burst and drain or can enlarge and cause discomfort. Acne usually looks worse to the owner than it feels to the cat.

The onset of puberty does not trigger acne in cats as it does in humans, and cats do not grow out of acne. I have seen cats over 13 years of age with feline acne. Acne can occur as a one-time episode, or it can be chronic and recurrent. It is not contagious to other cats or humans. It is thought that acne may occur in older cats due to decreased grooming activity. The chin is one of the areas that a cat can have difficulty cleaning.

Food Bowl Reaction

A topical reaction to plastic food and water bowls has been implicated as a cause for acne. Changing to a more inert substance such as glass, ceramic, or stainless steel helps some cases. Food oil residues that build up on food and water bowls can also contribute to acne. Proper daily washing and drying of bowls is helpful in many cases, especially if canned food is being fed. If the animal's chin comes in continual contact with the dirty bowl edges, it makes sense that oily buildup could contribute to clogging pores.

Some cats immerse their chins in their food during eating. I have had owners inform me that simply feeding on disposable paper plates has cured their cat's acne.

Worth a Paws

Mucopurin (brand name—Bactoderm) is a product that is useful in some cases of feline acne. It is not currently approved for use in cats, but it is an accepted treatment. Each patient responds differently to topical treatments. In some cases, the treatment can cause severe dryness and irritation and should be discontinued.

Clearing the Lesions

In mild cases of acne, daily cleaning of the animal's chin with hydrogen peroxide is helpful. It will open up the pores, remove the blackheads, and clean out oils from the hair follicles. When more pronounced inflammation and infection are present, clipping of the hair and a veterinary benzoyl peroxide scrub or cream is recommended. Oral antibiotics may be needed for 10 to 30 days.

Corticosteroids are useful in relieving inflammation and decreasing fatty secretions in the skin in some cases of acne, but if deep infection is present, corticosteroids can exacerbate infection. In more advanced cases, vitamin A treatment may be necessary. Topical and oral preparations of vitamin A are available, but side effects are possible.

Ringworm Is Not a Worm

Ringworm is actually a fungal infection and has nothing to do with worms. The groups of fungi capable of causing ringworm are called dermatophytes. *Microsporum canis,* or *M. canis* for short, causes the most common type of feline ringworm. The fungus is transmitted by fungal spores in the environment that land on and grow on the skin. Typically cats with ringworm are itchy and have red, scaly patches on their skin along with areas of hair loss.

Diagnosing Ringworm

Ringworm is contagious to humans and other animals, but the good news is that just because you are exposed to it doesn't mean that you will get it. If your cat has some sort of dermatitis, wash your hands after you touch it and don't allow the animal to sleep on your bed until a diagnosis has been made. Ringworm is tentatively diagnosed by a positive Wood's lamp test. A Wood's lamp is a black light that causes shafts of hair infected with the fungus to glow an apple-green color.

To definitively diagnose ringworm, a dermatophtye test medium (DTM) culture should be performed. Ringworm fungus will grow a colony on the DTM, and the specific type of fungus can be isolated and identified.

Treating Ringworm

It can take four to eight weeks to cure a ringworm infection. There are various ways that an infection can be treated, but recent studies in cats show that using oral anti-fungal medication is best. Shampoos and lime sulfur dips can make the skin more comfortable and decrease the amount of contagious spores on the cat.

Some cats have side effects from the medications used to treat ringworm, so a veterinarian should monitor the animal's response to treatment. Repeat DTM cultures should be performed, and the cat should continue to be treated for two weeks after the last negative culture. If an animal is not treated completely, ringworm can quickly flare up again. In multi-cat households it is usually necessary to treat all the cats so that the infection is not passed back and forth between them.

Worth a Paws

Human ringworm looks like red, circular patches on the skin. These areas are very itchy. Humans with isolated lesions respond well to topical anti-fungal creams. Creams are not particularly effective on cats because the cats often have multiple lesions, they lick it off, and it is hard for the medication to get through the hair onto all the affected skin.

Previous infection with ringworm does not confer immunity, so it is possible to have multiple episodes of infection within an animal's lifetime. It can be a frustrating condition to treat, but if you stick with it, the fungus can be controlled.

Looking Mangy

Mange is due to small bugs called mites. The two most common mites that can affect cats are *Otodectes cynotis* and *Notoedres cati*. Cats can also be affected by a type of fur mite called *Cheyletiella*. Mite infestations typically make a cat very itchy. These parasites can be diagnosed by finding their presence on an ear swab, skin scraping, or tape impression examined microscopically.

Meow Wow

Although it is not licensed for use in cats, a drug frequently used by veterinarians to treat mites is actually a cattle dewormer! Used at the proper dose, this drug can be given every two weeks for two to three treatments. Treatment is easy and especially practical for multi-cat households.

Does Your Cat Have Ear Mites?

Otodectes cyanotis is the common ear mite of cats. These mites can also infect dogs, but they are not transmissible to humans. Although ear mites are frequently found in cats, they are not the only type of ear disease in cats. Bacteria, yeast, allergies, and polyps can also affect the ears of cats.

The classic signs of an ear mite infection are:

➤ Head shaking

➤ Brown crusty discharge from the ears

➤ Ear scratching

Ear mites can live for periods in the environment, but they must feed off a dog or cat. If you have indoor animals that do not come into contact with others, it is easy to cure an infection. If you have animals that go outside, they have the potential for re-exposure.

There are effective over-the-counter treatments for ear mites, but I recommend that if your cat has an ear infection, you have it properly diagnosed by your veterinarian. If you treat for ear mites and there is another problem, your pet has to be uncomfortable for a longer period of time. Some of the prescription medications used for ear mites can relieve itchiness and treat other secondary infections.

A positive diagnosis of ear mites is made by using an otoscope and observing the mites crawling in the ear canal or by examining an ear swab under a microscope and observing live mites and/or mite eggs. Cats with chronic ear mite infections can develop inflammatory polyps in their ear canals. They can also develop blood blisters on their earflaps secondary to constant rubbing.

A veterinarian looks into a cat's ear with an otoscope.

Can Your Cat Get Scabies?

Scabies is a type of mite infection caused by a *Sarcoptes scabei*. This mite is rarely found in cats, but a similar mite, *Notoedres cati,* is common. *Notoedres* can jump on humans and cause temporary itchiness, but they cannot live on our skin. On cats the mites tend to live around the face and ears, and the cat develops a very crusty appearance. Affected animals are very itchy.

A veterinarian will perform a skin scraping to diagnose this type of mange and will be able to tell you within minutes if the parasite is observed. A skin scraping involves using a scalpel blade to scrape small amounts of hair and skin onto a slide with a drop of mineral oil. Mites or mite eggs are then observed on the slide. Medicated baths, dips, or even a cattle dewormer can effectively treat this mite.

Cheyletiella

This fur mite is more difficult to isolate and identify than other types of mites. It is typically found on the trunk of a cat, and it causes hair loss, scaling, and itchiness. When *Cheyletiella* is suspected, an impression of a lesion is made on a piece of transparent tape and then examined microscopically. Treatment for this mite is similar to that of other types of mange, except that this mite can live in the environment for up to three weeks. Using some type of premise treatment effective against fleas will also kill these mites.

Demodex

Demodex is a type of mange more frequently found on dogs, but it is occasionally found on cats. This mite does not cause the intense itching characteristic of other types of mange. It can cause patches of hair loss and redness. Your vet can diagnose the infection by observing the mite on a skin scraping.

Worth a Paws

Cats usually receive bites and stings on their noses and paws. They like to nose and bat at little creatures. If you notice swelling on these areas, it may be due to an insect bite.

Insect and Spider Bites

Cats have a fascination with bugs, and even if you live indoors, it is likely that your cat will find every creepy crawly in your house. Many of these creatures are harmless and may be eaten by your cat, but others will bite and sting when threatened.

Some beetles and bugs taste bad and will cause drooling. Others will cause some minor gastrointestinal upset that passes within a few hours.

Bee Stings

Bee stings are painful and cause swelling on any animal. They are uncomfortable and look bad, but are only dangerous if the animal has an anaphylactic reaction. In anaphylaxis, the allergic reaction that occurs causes fever, redness, and difficulty with breathing.

Antihistamines and/or cortisone can be used to decrease the swelling and itchiness associated with any sting or bite. The earlier these medications are used, the less swelling will develop.

The Itsy-Bitsy-Spider Bite

I always know when there is a spider in my house because my cats go wild. They jump up the walls and cry in their desperate attempts to catch it. Most spider bites are not a big deal, but cats are not very discriminating, and will hunt harmless and dangerous spiders alike. Depending on where you live, brown recluse and black widow spiders may exist, and these spiders can be quite dangerous.

With their bite, poisonous spiders inject venom that can seriously damage tissue. Initially, a bite wound may not be detected, but within a day or so, an oozing wound with skin sloughing can be seen. These types of wounds can take weeks to heal and should be treated by a veterinarian.

Cats Can Get Skin Cancer

There are a few different types of cancer that can affect the skin of cats, and *squamous cell carcinoma* (SCC) is the most common. Other types are malignant melanoma, mast cell tumors, and cutaneous lymphosarcoma. Some can be cured by surgical excision, while others cannot.

In general, cats do not get many lumps and bumps on their skin, but benign growths called sebaceous cysts are sometimes found. Any time you notice a growth on the cat's skin, you should monitor it and have it checked out by a veterinarian. Increasing size, change in consistency, spread to other locations, or pain associated with a growth are all reasons to have it examined.

Kitty Ditty

Squamous cell carcinoma (SCC) *is a type of cancer that affects skin. It can be caused by excessive exposure to sunlight, but it can also occur for no known reason. Aside from the ears and face, SCC can occur in the mouth, on the body, and on the feet.*

If You See a Lump

When your veterinarian examines a growth on the skin, he will likely part the hair, assess the size, and squeeze the tissue. Different types of growths have different characteristics. To make a definitive diagnosis of any skin growth, some type of biopsy is needed.

Some veterinarians are able to perform needle biopsies and *cytology* in their clinics. They will aspirate a few cells from the growth, place them on a slide, and examine them microscopically. Inflammation, infection, and fatty tissue are easily diagnosed this way. Other types of cells may be sent to a lab for a clinical pathologist to review.

Kitty Ditty

Cytology *is a term used to describe the evaluation of cells under a microscope. It is typically performed on a needle biopsy or impression smear. This is different than a full biopsy, which involves a piece of tissue. The larger the sample, the more cells there are available for making an accurate diagnosis.*

If your veterinarian recommends a biopsy, the entire growth or just a piece may be removed. In general, it is a good idea to take as much tissue as possible the first time, so that if a problem is found, the animal may not need another surgical procedure.

Early detection and surgical excision can potentially cure some types of skin cancer. Cryosurgery and laser surgery are other methods for removing skin growths.

Avoid CATastrophe

If you notice red, inflamed skin or scabs on your cat that seem to go away and then come back, you should have the area examined by a veterinarian. It is not common for a cat to injure itself recurrently in the same area. Non-healing sores may be indicative of skin cancer.

Sun Exposure and Cancer

We have all heard about the damage that the sun can do to our skin, but do we think about what it is doing to our pets? Fair-skinned people are more sensitive to the effects of sunlight, and the same is true for cats. Protruding white-haired areas and pink, unpigmented skin (such as the ear tips and the end of the nose) are the most affected parts on cats. Cats first become sunburned, the skin becomes damaged, and then squamous cell carcinoma can develop.

Indoor cats are not at as much risk for SCC as outdoor cats, but many cats like to lay in pools of sunlight coming through windows. If the ultraviolet rays are not decreased by shades or tinting, indoor sunlight is still harmful. Waterproof sunblock can be applied to white ear tips and pink noses to help protect skin against the sun. Keeping an at-risk cat inside between 10 a.m. and 2 p.m., when the sun is strongest, will decrease exposure to the most direct and damaging rays of sunlight.

The Least You Need to Know

➤ Most types of dermatitis look very similar regardless of the cause.

➤ Many allergic cats develop dermatitis, and allergies are managed rather than cured.

➤ Ringworm is due to a fungal infection on the skin.

➤ Mange is caused by tiny parasites called mites.

➤ Cats that receive insect and spider bites and stings may need medical treatment.

➤ White-haired and pink-skinned areas on cats are the most susceptible areas to damage from the sun.

Chapter 16

Grooving to a Perfect Beat

In This Chapter

➤ What to do if your cat is bleeding

➤ What causes anemia and what can be done about it

➤ The heart defects a cat can be born with

➤ The different types of heart muscle disease

➤ Find out about high blood pressure

➤ Should you be concerned about heartworms in your cat?

A heart is an amazing organ that will continuously pump throughout the entire life of an animal. This adds up to more than 350 million beats during a 13-year feline lifetime! This powerful organ weighs less than one-tenth of an ounce in an average cat.

The cardiovascular system in a cat is comprised of blood, blood vessels, and the heart. All three components work in harmony to supply oxygen and nutrients throughout the body and drain away carbon dioxide and metabolic waste products. Humans are concerned about their hearts because heart disease is a common problem, but fortunately cats do not develop arteriosclerosis, (hardening of the arteries), the leading cause of heart attack. However, cats can develop hypertension and other cardiovascular diseases.

How the Heart and Circulatory System Work

Blood leaves the heart through arteries and returns to the heart through veins. Arteries and veins channel into smaller and smaller blood vessels that meet at capillaries. Blood leaving the heart is full of oxygen, but blood returning to the heart is full of carbon dioxide. Nutrients from digested food are absorbed by blood vessels in the intestines and liver and enter the blood stream. Waste products are produced by all cells, are filtered out of the blood by the kidneys, and then made into urine.

Kitty Ditty

Oxygenation is the process through which red blood cells become saturated with oxygen in the lungs.

The path that blood takes as it is pumped through the heart is complicated. The heart has four chambers with valves that regulate flow. The major veins bringing blood to the heart are called the vena cavas. Blood first enters the right atrium of the heart. It flows into the right ventricle of the heart as it passes through the tricuspid valve. The right ventricle contracts and sends blood into the pulmonic artery through the pulmonic valve. Blood then goes to the lungs and becomes *oxygenated*.

Oxygenated blood from the pulmonic vein enters the left atrium. It then passes into the left ventricle via the mitral valve. When the left ventricle contracts, blood is sent out of the heart through the aorta and circulates throughout the rest of the body. This entire cycle continues without pause, regulated by the pacemaker. Cats only very rarely have problems with the pacemakers of their hearts. The pacemaker is the sinoatrial node, tissue that sends out electrical impulses triggering the heart muscle to contract.

Meow Wow

The heart is covered by a sac called the pericardium. The pericardium is not essential for life, but serves the important role of protecting the heart against friction and inflammation. It stabilizes the heart's position in the chest cavity and maintains its shape.

Blood and Bleeding

Blood is the fluid that supports any animal's body. It is composed of three different types of cells:

1. Red blood cells, which carry oxygen
2. White blood cells, which fight infection
3. Platelets, which are needed for clotting

All of these cells must be present in certain numbers to keep an animal healthy.

Bleeding occurs when a blood vessel becomes damaged, and this can happen inside or outside of the body. Under normal circumstances, platelets and clotting factors in the blood help to control bleeding, but if a large blood vessel is damaged, these components may not be able to form an adequate clot.

How to Stop Bleeding

Cats are not any different from humans when it comes to bleeding, so one of the first steps that should be taken if a cat is bleeding is to apply pressure. Adhesive bandage strips are not very useful on cats because of all of their hair, so applying a more secure bandage is necessary. Care must be taken when applying a bandage so that the proper amount of pressure is applied to the wound but not enough to impair surrounding circulation.

Applying ice or cold water to a bleeding wound is also useful. Cold temperatures trigger vasoconstriction, so the blood vessels actually get smaller, and less blood is lost. Another helpful hint is to keep the cat calm and stay calm yourself. Cats are very attuned to their owner's body language, and they will be upset if you are. In turn, their blood pressure will rise and make the bleeding worse.

Meow Wow

Cats have about 30 milliliters of blood per pound of their body weight. This means that a 10-pound cat has about 1¼ cups of blood in its body.

Worth a Paws

Cats have veins in their toenails, so if a nail is cut too short or broken accidentally, bleeding can occur. You can apply ice, cornstarch, pet cautery powder, or a styptic pencil (if you have one) at home, but if bleeding continues or recurs, seek help from your veterinarian.

Avoid CATastrophe

Bruising is due to bleeding under the skin. It can be difficult to find bruising on a cat because hair covers most of the skin. If you notice bruising and your cat has not sustained any known trauma, check with your veterinarian. It could be a sign of a clotting disorder.

Don't Let It Bleed

If the application of ice and a bandage does not stop bleeding, stitches are probably needed to close the blood vessel and surrounding skin. A veterinarian should perform any suturing. Cautery (using chemicals or electricity to seal a blood vessel) can be used in some bleeding situations, such as with a broken toenail, because it is safe and easy.

Generally, if you see a few drops of blood come from your cat in an isolated incident, there is no need for alarm. Often it is difficult to even determine where the bleeding is coming from. Common sources of bleeding are:

➤ Broken toenail

➤ Broken tooth

➤ Loss of a baby tooth in a young animal

➤ Rectum

➤ Any external wound

➤ Biting of tongue

➤ Bladder inflammation

➤ Ingestion of rat poison (it contains a chemical that prevents blood clotting)

If you cannot isolate the source of the blood, or if there is more than one episode of bleeding, consult your veterinarian. Bleeding can be a sign of other diseases, and uncontrolled bleeding can lead to anemia.

If Your Cat Is Anemic

Anemia is a low red blood cell count. Most owners would not know if their cat was anemic unless they knew that their pet had lost a significant amount of blood. There are two major classifications of anemia:

1. Lack of red blood cell production

2. Loss of red blood cells

A veterinarian may suspect that your cat is anemic if the animal's gums look pale upon inspection. A relatively simple test called a packed cell volume (PCV) can be performed in a veterinary office in about five minutes, and will tell the doctor the percentage of red blood cells in the sample. A feline PCV should be around 37 percent. Once the value drops below 20 percent, the situation is serious.

Meow Wow

A cat can die suddenly if its PCV drops below 15 percent. At this percentage, its body could become starved for oxygen, and a blood transfusion needs to be considered.

Cats that are anemic will often breathe in rapid, shallow breaths. This is because their bodies are trying to get more oxygen, but there are not enough cells with which to transport it. Anemic cats are generally weak and have poor appetites because it is too much work to eat.

Causes for Low Red Blood Cell Production

Red blood cells come from the bone marrow. The marrow is the tissue at the center of bones where immature blood cells live and then become stimulated to mature. Diseases that affect the bone marrow will impair red blood cell production. Examples of these are:

➤ Cancer

➤ Lack of iron

➤ Toxins

➤ Hormonal imbalances

➤ Kidney disease

➤ Other metabolic diseases

➤ Drugs

Avoid CATastrophe

While fleas can cause dangerous anemia in cats of all ages, they are especially dangerous to young kittens with small blood volumes. Cats and kittens can die from flea anemia, but they can easily recover if flea control and supportive measures are performed in time.

Causes for Red Blood Cell Loss

Bleeding due to trauma can cause an obvious red blood cell loss, but red blood cells can be lost in other ways. One common and unfortunate cause of anemia is an overwhelming flea infestation. Fleas feed on the blood of cats, and if enough fleas are present, the animal can be drained of blood, and severe anemia can result.

Another parasite that can cause anemia is called *Hemobartonella*. This parasite gets into a cat's blood and causes destruction of red blood cells within the animal's body.

183

Hemobartonellosis is also called Feline Infectious Anemia. This condition can be effectively treated with oral medications if diagnosed in time.

Autoimmune hemolytic anemia is a disease in which the cat's body no longer recognizes its own red blood cells. The immune system actually causes its own red blood cell destruction. This type of anemia can be life-threatening if the process is not reversed. Jaundice is a clinical sign that is often observed in cats with hemolytic anemia.

Kitty Ditty

Cats have two main blood types: "A" and "B." Fortunately, almost all mixed-breed cats and most pure-bred cats have A-type blood. British Shorthairs and Devon Rexes are examples of breeds that may have B-type blood.

Diagnosing Anemia

The different types of anemia are diagnosed based on history, exam, blood tests, and testing of the bone marrow. Once a specific cause or type of anemia is determined, steps are taken to correct the underlying problem and support the animal.

Severely anemic cats need blood transfusions or blood extenders to live. If the cause of anemia is not a problem with the bone marrow, the animal will usually be able to regenerate new cells.

Blood typing can be performed on cats. There are in-clinic test kits or samples that can be sent to a reference laboratory for blood typing. Most veterinary hospitals have a blood donor cat on the premises to use for transfusions, but modern technology has led to the production of blood replacers that may make transfusions obsolete.

Born with a Bad Heart

Congenital diseases of the heart do occur in cats but are not as common as they are in dogs. Any component of the heart can cause disease if defective. The important components of the heart are:

➤ Blood vessels leading into and out of the heart

➤ The four main chambers of the heart

➤ The valves between the chambers of the heart

Cats born with bad hearts may not show any signs of problems. Signs of heart disease are weakness, rapid or difficult breathing, and exercise intolerance. A veterinarian may suspect heart disease in a cat after listening to the animal's chest with a stethoscope and evaluating the rate, rhythm, and heart sounds.

Leaky Valves

The tricuspid and mitral valves are important mechanisms in regulating blood flow through the heart. In cats, deformities of these valves are the most common congenital cardiac malformations. Problems with the valves can often be detected by cardiac *auscultation*. A murmur—a "squishing" noise that represents blood leaking out of the valves during heart contraction—can be detected during cardiac auscultation. Instead of forming a tight seal, blood escapes around the valve.

Kitty Ditty

Auscultation is the term used to describe listening to the heart and lungs with a stethoscope.

A veterinarian auscults a kitten's heart and lungs.

The intensity or loudness of a heart murmur does not correlate to severity of damage to the valves. Some kittens are born with murmurs that they outgrow, much like human children. Other cats have murmurs their entire lives that never progress or cause heart disease. Unfortunately, some murmurs progress and lead to congestive heart failure. Murmurs are also extremely common in older cats. Over time, the seal that a valve forms may begin to leak. Leaky valves causing congestive heart failure are uncommon in the cat compared to the dog, where this disorder is frequently observed.

How the Heart Is Evaluated

Hormones and other chemicals within the body affect heart output. Every cat owner has felt the pounding of his pet's heart when it becomes fearful. Adrenaline stimulates the heart to pump faster so the animal can react more quickly to fear. I meet many fearful animals at my veterinary clinic. Gentle stroking and calm words are often needed to relax the animal so that heart auscultation can be properly performed. But I have to be careful not to relax the animal too much—if it *really* relaxes, I can't hear its heart over the purring!

The tests that are performed to check the heart are:

➤ Auscultation

➤ Chest x-ray

➤ ECG (electrocardiogram)

➤ Heart sonogram-echocardiogram

If a veterinarian suspects heart disease because of examination and auscultation findings, the next diagnostic step taken will likely be a chest x-ray. X-rays show the size, shape, and location of the heart. They also show if fluid or other problems exist in the lungs or chest cavity.

The feline heart is relatively small, which makes diagnostic testing difficult. An ECG may or may not be performed. This test measures the electrical activity of the heart and can localize some types of heart disease. Electrocardiograph measurement in cats produces small tracings that can be a challenge to interpret.

Cardiac ultrasonography, or sonogram, is the most useful diagnostic tool available to assess heart function and appearance. X-rays of the heart tell veterinarians about the size and shape of the heart, but not how the blood is being pushed through. Ultrasound allows the veterinarian to visualize and measure the individual heart chambers, valves, and major blood vessels. It can also document cardiac output and blood-flow patterns. This information is crucial when diagnosis of a cardiomyopathy is needed. It can also be used to measure response to drug therapy.

Treatment for Congenital Heart Disease

About 2 percent of cats are born with congenital heart defects. Aside from valvular defects, holes in different chambers of the heart can be found as well as strictures in veins leaving the heart. Some types of congenital heart diseases can be surgically corrected, and the cat can live a normal life. Other types may be monitored throughout a cat's life but never cause any clinical signs, and still others may be life-threatening.

Heart surgery is tricky in any animal, but due to the small size of kittens, it can be risky and expensive. Most congenital disease involves defects in the structures of the heart, and these problems generally do not respond to medication.

Heart Muscle Disease

The pumping action of the heart is achieved through contraction of different heart muscles in a specific sequence. The heart itself is primarily composed of muscle tissue, and diseases can affect these tissues. The medical term for heart muscle disease is cardiomyopathy. There are three main types:

1. Dilated cardiomyopathy (DCM)
2. Hypertrophic cardiomyopathy (HCM)
3. Restrictive cardiomyopathy (RCM)

Meow Wow

Cardiomyopathy should be suspected in the sudden death of an otherwise young, healthy animal. Obvious clinical signs of heart muscle disease often do not exist, so the problem may not be detected or suspected before heart failure occurs.

Dilated Cardiomyopathy

This disease is no longer very common due to the finding that it was commonly caused by a dietary deficiency of the amino acid taurine. This discovery led pet food manufacturers to add more taurine to cat foods, and virtually eliminate the problem.

In dilated cardiomyopathy (DCM), the heart muscle stretches out and becomes a thin, flaccid sack that is unable to contract properly. Blood is not effectively pumped between the chambers or out of the heart.

Hypertrophic Cardiomyopathy

Hypertrophic cardiomyopathy (HCM) is currently the most common type of heart muscle disease. The cause is unknown, but the disease may be due to a congenital defect or acquired during a cat's

Worth a Paws

A heart murmur may or may not be a sign of significant heart disease, and the intensity of a murmur is not directly proportional to the problem creating it. Murmurs occur when blood does not flow smoothly between different parts of the heart.

Avoid CATastrophe

If a cat is suddenly unable to use its rear legs, the problem may be due to a thrombus rather than trauma or damage to a nerve. Have your veterinarian examine an acutely weak cat as soon as possible so that the cause can be isolated.

lifetime. A cat with hypertrophic cardiomyopathy has thickened walls of its left ventricle. This in turn can lead to thickening of other heart chamber walls.

As the wall thickens, the size of the chamber decreases, and less blood is pumped through the heart. Turbulence and pressures build within the heart, aggravate the condition, and make the thickening worse.

There are some drugs that can be used to reduce the stresses and improve the function of a heart with HCM, but the disease cannot be cured. Cats with HCM have shorter life spans because at some point the heart fails.

A complication of HCM in cats is aortic thrombosis or saddle thrombus. This is a blood clot that forms in the heart and then becomes trapped at the splitting of the aorta, where this large blood vessel supplies blood to the rear legs. The prognosis for a cat with an aortic thrombus is not good. Treatment to dissolve the clot can be used, but the underlying heart disease cannot be stopped and will progress.

Cats with aortic thrombosis will suddenly become weak or paralyzed in their back legs due to the discontinued blood supply. This loss of circulation is very painful to the animal. Less commonly, thrombi can lodge and obstruct circulation to the front legs. A cat with a thrombus will have cold, dark footpads and its toenails will not bleed where circulation is lost.

Restrictive Cardiomyopathy

There are cats with heart muscle disease that does not classically fall into either DCM or HCM. These animals are usually put in the category of restrictive cardiomyopathy. Medications can be used to help make the heart pump more effectively, but this disease will also progress.

Echocardiography is needed to definitively diagnose any type of cardiomyopathy. It is also used to monitor progression or response to therapy. If your veterinarian does not have an ultrasound machine, a specialist with a mobile unit may be asked to come to the hospital or you may be referred to a specialty center that has this equipment.

High Blood Pressure

Blood pressure measurement in cats is now becoming a more routine practice because of equipment that can fairly reliably be used. For a long time, most veterinarians didn't know that feline hypertension existed because they didn't know how to check for it. *Systolic* values are considered the most sensitive indicator of feline hypertension, and values over 180 mm Hg are considered too high.

Kitty Ditty

The highest blood pressure occurs when the heart contracts. This is called **systole**. The lowest blood pressure occurs when the heart relaxes. This is called **diastole**.

Hypertension is usually found in older cats affected with kidney disease and/or hyperthyroidism, but it can also be a primary disease. If the heart sustains long periods of high pressure, it can weaken. Hyperthyroidism can lead to over-stimulation of the heart muscle, which also wears the muscle out prematurely and leads to failure. To control blood pressure in cats, the underlying disease must first be controlled. If no underlying disease is found, drugs are available to control blood pressure.

Feline Heartworm Disease

If you have a dog, you may be familiar with heartworm disease. These parasites are transmitted by mosquito bites, which inject the immature stage of the worm into an animal's blood. These larvae develop into adult worms that like to live in the heart or pulmonary blood vessels. Without exposure to infected mosquitoes, cats cannot get heartworms. Heartworm disease can cause breathing problems and damage to the heart.

How Common Are Heartworms?

Cats have natural resistance to heartworms, but they can still become infected. Higher risk of infection exists in areas where there are more mosquitoes carrying heartworm larvae.

Preventive treatment is available to protect cats that are at risk for heartworms. Ask your veterinarian about the risk of heartworm in your area, and then decide if preventive care is needed.

Discuss the risks of heartworm disease with your veterinarian.

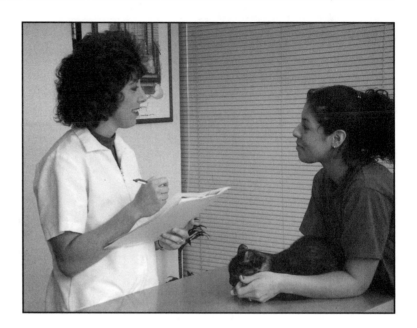

Diagnosing Heartworms

Heartworms should be considered as a possible diagnosis for cats that have signs of heart disease or asthma and live in a high-risk area where mosquitos are present. Blood tests that look for antigens to the parasite and antibodies that the cat produces against the parasite are useful in making a diagnosis. Heartworms can be observed on an ultrasonic evaluation of the heart.

Meow Wow

Dogs infected with heartworms have many adult worms in their bodies, whereas cats may only have one to three worms. Smaller worm loads in cats make diagnosis more difficult.

Treating Heartworms

The toxicity and side effects of treatments that kill adult heartworms (adulticides) in cats are considered more of a risk than living with the parasites. Adult worms usually only live for about two years in cats, so if the clinical signs that they are creating can be controlled medically, adulticides are not used.

190

The Least You Need to Know

➤ The cardiovascular system is the pump and fluid that run an animal's body.

➤ Anemia is a low red blood cell count, and if the count gets low enough, it can be life-threatening.

➤ Cats can be born with bad hearts.

➤ Cardiomyopathy can lead to serious consequences and even sudden death in a cat.

➤ Kidney disease or hyperthyroidism can cause hypertension in cats.

➤ Heartworm disease is more common in dogs, but it can occur in cats.

Chapter 17

The Musculoskeletal System

In This Chapter

➤ How arthritis can affect cats

➤ Find out about fractures

➤ What can you do about sprains and strains?

➤ Does your cat have extra toes?

A cat's body is shaped the way it is because of its musculoskeletal system, which is comprised of the bones, muscles, and the tissues that connect them. The bony skeleton is responsible for supporting the structure of the body and protecting some internal organs. The muscles are responsible for allowing movement of the body by controlling direction and range of motion. Cartilage, tendons, and ligaments hold it all together.

House cats are fairly sedentary animals, but they have bodies that are designed for hunting and stalking. Cats are extremely flexible and quick, unless they are over-weight, and they are able to perform some very athletic feats. It is not uncommon to find cats perched on top of dressers in the home or even climbing up on roofs of houses. This chapter will address some of the more common problems of the bones and muscles of cats.

It's Hard to Get Up in the Morning

"Fluffy doesn't jump up on my bed the way she used to. Could she have arthritis?" "Sly has a hard time walking after he's been asleep. What could this mean?" Questions such as these are commonly asked at my clinic. I tell owners that just like humans, cats can develop arthritis.

Classic osteoarthritis can develop in cats—the medical term is degenerative joint disease (DJD). Arthritic animals have bony changes in their joints that cause discomfort and can decrease range of motion. Your vet may suspect arthritis based on a cat's physical examination and pain in the joints, but it can only be confirmed by taking an x-ray and observing the characteristic changes.

The earliest clinical sign detected in cats with DJD is lameness. This progresses to reluctance of the animal to perform certain movements or activities without apparent stiffness or pain. As the disease progresses, stiffness may become more pronounced after periods of rest. Affected joints may look and feel enlarged and swollen, and the range of motion becomes restricted as DJD progresses. There are some uncommon types of arthritis where inflammation of joints occurs but bony changes do not. This can occur with joint infection, trauma, and immune mediated conditions.

A cat's skeleton supports the structure of its body.

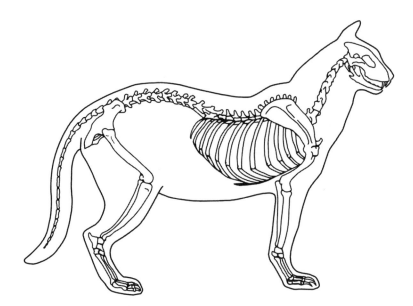

Can You Prevent DJD?

Once DJD has developed it cannot be cured, although small amounts do occur as a normal part of aging. Signs of DJD include:

➤ Stiffness after sleeping

➤ An inability to jump up on things

➤ Lameness

➤ Problems getting into and out of a litterbox

Joints are made up of bones that have cartilage on their ends. The cartilage cushions the bones and decreases friction. Each joint has a small amount of fluid in it called synovial fluid that lubricates the cartilage and adds more cushioning. When DJD occurs, the cartilage becomes rough, the joint fluid becomes thick, and abnormal calcium deposits are formed at the ends of the bones.

Meow Wow

Hip dysplasia is a type of DJD most commonly seen in dogs, but is also seen in cats. It is a disease of young animals born with poor conformation of their hip joints. Rubbing occurs between the bones in the hip joint and arthritis follows.

Cat owners can decrease the risk of DJD in their cat by feeding a good diet that ensures proper bone growth and development. Controlling a cat's weight is very important because the heavier a cat is, the more stress is placed on its joints. Keeping a cat indoors will lower the risk of trauma to bones and joints, which in turn can lead to DJD. Cold temperatures make joints ache more, so allowing an older animal with DJD to sleep on a padded, warm surface can help improve comfort.

Don't Take Two Aspirin and Call in the Morning

Cats are very stoic animals, so it is difficult to assess how much pain they are experiencing with DJD. The worst thing an owner can do is try to treat pain without consulting a veterinarian. Over-the-counter anti-inflammatory and pain medications for human should *never* be given to a cat. If you think that your cat has DJD and discomfort, consult your veterinarian to find out what safe medical treatments exist.

Worth a Paws

If a veterinarian suspects DJD but x-rays don't support the diagnosis, it is likely that nerve pain rather than bone or muscle pain is the problem. Referral to a veterinary neurologist and/or a special x-ray of the spine, called a myelogram, may be needed.

Medications used to treat DJD may include children's aspirin, cortisone, and nutritional supplements. One 83-mg children's aspirin can be safely given once every three days. Cortisone is frequently used in cats to reduce pain and inflammation. Owners are sometimes reluctant to use corticosteroids because they have heard of the problems that these drugs cause in humans. Cats are much less sensitive to the effects of these drugs and most show no side effects. Corticosteroids can be given orally or by injection. Whenever this class of drugs is used, the lowest dose that controls the symptoms is best.

Glycosaminoglycans (GAGS) have also been used in the management of arthritis. They are available as an injectable drug or as an oral supplement. Various manufacturers make glucosamine nutritional supplements containing slightly different forms of the chemical. GAGS do not provide immediate relief from pain or inflammation; rather, GAGS improve the consistency of the cartilage and joint fluid so that joint friction is reduced. This process takes from three to six weeks because that's how long it takes to remodel the tissue. In many cases cats can be managed with these products alone.

Helping a cat with DJD jump up or down is beneficial. It is also helpful to be sure that food and water bowls are easily accessible, and that the animal is able to get in and out of its litterbox.

It's Broken

Any bone in the body can fracture if enough force is applied to it. Fractures can occur if a cat is hit by a car, falls from a height, gets shaken by a dog or larger animal, gets caught in a garage door, or even gets stepped on by its owner. The bad news is that fractures are painful injuries, but the good news is that cats generally heal well.

Assessing the Injury

There is significant pain and swelling associated with a fracture. During examination, a veterinarian may be able to feel the ends of the broken bone or hear abnormal cracking sounds, but an x-ray is always needed. At least two views of the bone are necessary to properly evaluate the fracture and assess options for fixation.

Some fractures heal adequately without surgery or casting, such as pelvic fractures that don't involve the hip joints. Aside from diagnosing the fracture, it is necessary to evaluate the surrounding tissues to see if other damage is present.

Meow Wow

If no damage has occurred to nerves, hip joints, or other organs, cats with pelvic fractures can be confined and treated with supportive care, and up walking and functioning on their own within two weeks. This is quite a feat, considering that humans with the same injury can be bedridden for months.

Putting the Puzzle Together

The location of the fracture and the number of pieces of bone involved will determine how easy or difficult the repair will be. Many veterinarians do basic orthopedic procedures in their hospitals, but complicated injuries may need to be referred to a board-certified veterinary surgeon. Surgeons usually have more experience and equipment available for good repair.

The equipment used to repair bones includes:

➤ Surgical wires

➤ Stainless steel pins

➤ Bone plates

➤ Bone screws

➤ External fixation apparatus

➤ Casts

➤ Splints

Is Amputation an Option?

There is an art to fixing leg fractures, but sometimes the damage is so severe or costly that amputation may have to be considered. It is an idea that may be hard to accept, but cats with three legs can do extremely well and lead normal lives. It may take cats a few weeks to figure out how to make the remaining limbs work together, but after a while you may even forget that the animal is handicapped.

The Healing Process

The younger the animal, the quicker the bones will heal. Complete fracture healing can take 6 to 12 weeks, depending on severity. During this period the cat should be kept indoors and its activity restricted. It's hard to restrict a cat, but lifting it up and down and carrying it up steps is helpful. Confinement to one room may be needed if you are unable to get the cat to rest.

Follow-up x-rays will show how the bone has healed. Even if healing is not perfect, pet cats will do well since they don't have to hunt to feed themselves and they can stay indoors and be protected. Sometimes when orthopedic hardware is used in the fixation process, it needs to be removed once the bone has healed. This may involve tranquilization or sedation.

Sprains and Strains

Sometimes cats that sustain trauma do not break bones but experience soft-tissue injuries. Soft-tissue injury involves tissue other than bone and includes sprains and strains. Sprains are twisting or pulling of ligaments, which are the tissues that connect bones. Strains are twisting or pulling of tendons, which are the tissues that connect muscles to bones.

Assessing Soft-Tissue Injuries

Soft-tissue injuries can be just as painful and swollen as fractures. To diagnose a sprain or strain, a veterinarian will first examine the cat and manipulate the affected limb joint by joint in an attempt to isolate the injury. If pain and/or swelling can be isolated, and a joint is involved, the stability of the joint will next be evaluated.

An x-ray of a sprain or strain may show swelling, but it won't show the specific tissues involved or the amount of damage. This is because x-rays don't show much contrast between different soft-tissue structures. If a significant number of ligaments around a joint are seriously damaged, bones may not line up as expected and this will show on an x-ray.

The Healing Process

Cats don't know when they need to rest, so keeping an animal confined so that healing can occur can be difficult. Pain relievers can be used, but there may be a trade-off between pain control and activity. Cats may need to feel some discomfort so that they will take it easy.

You can sling or place a support wrap on a soft-tissue injury, but often the cat is more bothered by the wrap than the injury. Cats are free spirits that hate having their movement restricted in any way, so it may be better to do nothing.

It usually takes from two to six weeks for a sprain or strain to heal, and once a joint has been damaged, it is never the same again. It is easy for injuries to recur after a sprain or strain because the scar tissue that forms during healing is not as strong as the original tissue.

Kitty Ditty

A veterinarian can determine if a cruciate injury is present by performing an **anterior drawer test**, which involves measuring the amount of laxity present when moving the knee forward and back. The more movement present, the more damage the ligament has sustained.

Could Your Cat Tear Its Cruciate?

Sports fans may be familiar with the term anterior cruciate ligament (ACL). This is one of the main ligaments that work to hold an animal's knee together, and it is a common injury of football players.

Even though most house cats are agile athletes, they can get their leg stuck or land on it in an awkward position and sprain or tear their anterior cruciate ligament. Depending on the severity of the injury, a cat may or may not walk on a leg with cruciate damage. An *anterior drawer test* confirms ACL involvement in an injury.

Most ACL injuries in cats will heal if the animal is put on injured reserve for two to four weeks. If during this time adequate healing does not occur, surgery may be needed to stabilize the knee.

Meow Wow

Cats carry 60 percent of their weight on their front legs, so during normal activity less stress is placed on the back legs. Jumping up initially puts all the stress on the back legs, and jumping down puts all the stress on the front legs.

Born with Strange Bones

Kittens can be born with a variety of different skeletal problems. Some give them a unique appearance, and others affect the way that they function. In the latter situation, surgical correction is necessary. Some breeds of cats developed from conformational differences of certain bones.

Beauty Is in the Eye of the Beholder

There are some well-known breeds of cats that have unique bone structures, the most popular of which is the Persian cat with its round skull and flattened, *brachycephalic* face.

Kitty Ditty

The flattened facial structure of Persians, Himalayans, and Burmese cats is called **brachycephalic**.

Differing numbers of tail bones characterize some breeds. Most cats have between 18 and 20 caudal vertebrae that make up their tails. Manx cats have far fewer, and are considered "rumpys" or "stumpys" based on how much of a tail they have. Their lack of tail is due to an inherited dominant trait. Japanese Bobtails and Pixie Bobs are other breeds that have a shorter-than-average tail length.

Another tail defect is a congenital kink. Many cats are born with kinks in their tails, and this is considered a recessive trait. The kink can come from trauma at birth (or immediately following), or it can just be the way the kitten turned out. Most owners think the kinky tail gives their cat character.

Persian cats are deliberately bred to have a flat face. (Photograph by Eric Ilasenko)

Meow Wow

You may think of the skull as one unique bone, but this is not the case. Cats are considered to have 29 different bones composing their skulls.

Kitty Ditty

Domestic cats have 19 pairs of chromosomes. Eighteen pairs are **autosomal**, meaning non-sex determining chromosomes, while the last pair are the sex-determining sex chromosomes.

Kitty Has Extra Toes

A polydactyl cat is one that has extra toes, and this trait results from an *autosomal* dominant gene. Some cats have extra toes on their front feet, and some have extras on all four feet. Most people think that the extra toes are cute, but they would be considered a defect if they were found on a purebred that is supposed to have the normal number of toes. Any trait not in the breed standard is not cute to cat-show judges.

Polydactyl cats need more help with keeping their toenails short because the extra nails usually do not get worn down during normal activity. Nails that continue to grow will actually penetrate into the footpads, causing pain and infection.

Meow Wow

Humans can also be born polydactyl. Throughout history, people with extra fingers were considered to be witches. Anne Boleyn, one of Henry VIII's wives, had six fingers on one hand. She was decapitated on accusations of adultery before a strong witchcraft case could be made against her.

Surgery for Bone Deformities

Hip dysplasia can occur in cats, but because most cats, unlike dogs, don't do a lot of running, they live fairly comfortably with this condition. If pain or problems progress, a surgical procedure called a femoral head osteotomy can help keep the hip bones from rubbing and worsening the condition.

Pectus excavatum is a congenital deformity of the rib cage. Kittens with pectus have a flattened chest cavity and their breathing can be impaired. Some cats grow out of this condition, but in others breathing worsens, and a surgical procedure that pulls out the ribs is needed to correct the defect. This defect can be seen in any cat, but certain lines of Bengal cats seem to have a higher incidence.

Some cats are born with luxating patellas. Luxating patellas are kneecaps that pop out of joint. This condition is usually due to an abnormally shallow groove in the femur, the long bone that the kneecap sits on. Cats with luxating patellas may have an intermittently collapsing rear leg. They may hop temporarily until the kneecap pops back into place. A surgical procedure that deepens the groove and tightens the knee joint can successfully correct this problem.

The Least You Need to Know

➤ Older cats can develop osteoarthritis, also known as degenerative joint disease.

➤ An x-ray is needed to diagnose a broken bone and determine how it can be fixed.

➤ Cats can get sprains and strains, and these injuries do not specifically show up on an x-ray.

➤ Variations in appearance of certain breeds of cats are due to the conformation of their bones.

➤ Some congenital skeletal defects can affect a cat's functioning, but they can be surgically repaired.

Chapter 18

It's All Got to Do with Hormones

In This Chapter

➤ Overactive thyroid glands in cats

➤ Cats can be diabetics

➤ Uterine infection in unspayed cats

➤ Cats can get breast cancer

When you hear the word "hormone," do you think about chemicals in your body that make you feel a certain way? The system of glands that secrete hormones is the endocrine system. Hormones are chemicals that produce an effect on another part of the body, and some hormones have very specific functions, while others affect many other body systems in a subtle manner.

There are many different hormones produced throughout a cat's body, but there are only a few that cause common imbalances or problems. Hormones are usually transported through the blood to their target tissues. The main endocrine glands of the cat's body are the pituitary, thyroid, parathyroid, pancreas, adrenals, ovaries, and testes.

If Your Cat Has a "Hyper" Thyroid

Cats have two thyroid glands located on their lower necks. A normal thyroid gland is difficult to palpate during a physical exam but may be detected if enlarged. Hyperthyroidism is the most common endocrine abnormality seen in cats. This condition is usually caused by a benign growth known as a thyroid adenoma that overproduces thyroid hormone. Cats 9 years old and up are most affected by hyperthyroidism.

The Function of the Thyroid

The thyroid gland produces hormones that have many different functions. Their main purpose is to regulate metabolism. Thyroid hormone affects every part of the body to some degree, but its major effects are on the heart, skin, and gastrointestinal tract.

Meow Wow

While it is common for cats to be hyperthyroid, it is common for dogs to be hypothyroid and have underactive thyroid glands. Humans can have thyroid imbalances either way.

Signs of Hyperthyroidism

The common clinical signs associated with hyperthyroidism are:

➤ Weight loss

➤ Increased appetite

➤ Increased thirst

➤ Increased urination

➤ Increased heart rates and possibly heart arrhythmias

Owners might notice these changes in their cat, but often they are discovered during a routine physical examination and discussion with a veterinarian. If a veterinarian suspects that your cat is hyperthyroid, she will want to perform some blood tests.

Blood tests are good at pinpointing hyperthyroidism, and for differentiating the disease from other metabolic imbalances. If the thyroid hormone level is not out of the normal range on the basic test, but clinical signs suggest a problem, the veterinarian may want to perform another test called a T3 suppression test. Finally, another test called a technicium scan may be required. This test highlights the thyroid gland and shows if there is overactive tissue.

Treating Hyperthyroidism

Uncontrolled thyroid disease will lead to many problems in a cat. Aside from poor general condition and a slow wasting process, a hyperthyroid cat can develop serious heart disease. Heart disease occurs because the heart is under too much continual stimulation, and the muscle begins to weaken. Hypertension can also result from hyperthyroidism.

There are three accepted treatments for hyperthyroidism:

1. Drug therapy
2. Surgery
3. Radioisotope treatment

Each treatment has its pros and cons with respect to owner involvement, cost, side effects, and efficacy. A veterinarian should discuss all the options and help an owner decide on the most appropriate course based on the individual situation. Once a cat becomes hyperthyroid, it will always be hyperthyroid unless the overactive tissue is removed.

Drug Therapy

Medical therapy is initially the least expensive option for treating hyperthyroidism and usually involves twice-daily dosing with a drug called methimazole. Most cats tolerate this drug extremely well, but others can have side effects such as vomiting, bone marrow suppression, and dermatitis.

To monitor for side effects and efficacy of treatment, a cat is started on a low dose of medication and then evaluated two weeks later. At that time it is advisable to perform a blood cell count to look for bone marrow suppression. Based on the results, the cat may stay on the same dose or the dosage could be modified. Cats are generally checked every two weeks until the thyroid level is regulated in the normal range.

Medical treatment will last the rest of the cat's lifetime. It is not the end of the world if an owner misses giving a dose every now and then, but to be properly regulated, constant treatment is needed.

Take 'Em Out

Surgical removal of the thyroid glands can be a successful treatment. Both glands are usually removed because it is difficult to tell if one or both glands are affected without looking at the tissue microscopically. The surgery involves the tissues of the neck, and no body cavities are opened.

Once the thyroid is removed, it will not grow back. Some glands have malignant tumors called thyroid carcinomas, which are discovered when a biopsy is performed. A risk of surgery is that the closely associated parathyroid glands can be accidentally removed at the same time as the thyroid glands, and these glands are responsible for calcium balance in the body. Other risks of surgery are that a cat's thyroid level can become too low if both glands are removed, and if overactive thyroid tissue is located outside of the gland itself, it will remain in the body and continue to cause problems.

If an owner does not want to medicate his cat, surgery is a reasonable option. There is not a long recovery period, but hormone and calcium levels should be checked post-operatively, and supplementation given if needed.

Nuke Them Out

Radioisotope therapy involves treating the cat with radioactive iodine (I 131). The thyroid gland naturally uptakes iodine from the blood and concentrates it, so the radioisotope gets to its target tissue easily.

Meow Wow

Iodine is an essential mineral for animals, including humans. People used to become iodine deficient and develop goiters (swollen thyroids) because they did not get enough in their diets, but today good old table salt is iodized and provides iodine to the body.

I 131 therapy is considered state of the art and superior to surgical removal and medical treatment because:

➤ A one-time treatment is performed

➤ The overactive tissue is selectively destroyed rather than the entire gland removed

➤ There is no risk of anesthesia

➤ The parathyroid glands are untouched

The disadvantages to I 131 therapy are:

➤ Significant expense

➤ Hospitalization for approximately 10 to 14 days while the radiation is eliminated from the cat's body

➤ Some cats develop kidney disease when their thyroid level is dropped too low too quickly

Radioactive iodine treatment is only available at special veterinary hospitals with the proper facilities. Depending on where you live, this mode of treatment may be readily available. If you have a hyperthyroid cat, discuss all of the options with your veterinarian.

Cats Can Be Diabetics Too

Diabetes mellitus is a disease in which sugar in the blood cannot be properly taken up and used by the cells of the body. This is usually due to a lack of insulin, a hormone responsible for transporting sugar into cells. The pancreas is the organ that produces insulin.

Diabetic cats eat but are essentially starving because the sugar in their blood cannot be used for energy. As this process continues, the animal's body condition declines. Muscle and fat are broken down because the body is not obtaining sugar from food.

Meow Wow

There are actually two major types of diabetes in animals. Diabetes mellitus (DM) is the disease with which most people are familiar. Diabetes insipidus (DI) is a less common disease involving water balance in the body.

Signs of Diabetes

The classic signs of diabetes are:

➤ Increased thirst

➤ Increased urination

➤ Weight loss

Other signs that can be associated with the disease are bladder infection (caused by too much sugar in the urine), abnormal posture (cats get a nerve disorder that makes them walk on their heels), and shock.

Overweight, older cats are at greater risk for developing diabetes than others. The disease is diagnosed by finding high levels of sugar in the blood and urine of the affected animal. If the disease has been present but undetected for a while, other metabolic imbalances may concurrently exist.

Worth a Paws

There are some drugs that can cause diabetes mellitus as a side effect. Megestrol acetate is the most common culprit, but some cats are sensitive to even routinely used corticosteroids. Drug-induced diabetes is usually a temporary condition, but it may need treatment for months.

Hyperglycemia is the medical term used to describe higher-than-normal levels of sugar in the blood. Although this situation is usually attributed to diabetes, cats that are stressed will have high blood sugar levels. Truly diabetic cats will have significantly higher blood sugar levels than stressed cats. If there is any question, a blood test that measures serum fructosamine can determine actual diabetes.

Avoid CATastrophe

If there is ever any doubt as to how a diabetic cat is doing, or if the animal is not eating, it is always better to skip an injection rather than to keep giving insulin. Too much insulin, or insulin given without food, can cause hypoglycemia, which can be a life-threatening condition.

Treating Diabetes

If left uncontrolled, diabetic cats will starve to death, but the progression may take years. Each veterinarian has his own way of treating diabetic cats. The choices for treatment are insulin supplementation by injection or oral hypoglycemic agents (drugs that lower blood sugar). The problem with the disease in cats is that cats metabolize some drugs very rapidly, and insulin's effects are variable.

My personal experience using hypoglycemic agents has been poor, and effective results have only been obtained by using insulin. Most cats need twice-daily insulin injections, ideally 12 hours apart. Giving insulin injections is relatively easy if you are willing to learn.

Diet can play a role in the management of diabetes, because research indicates that fiber added to a diet helps control blood sugar. If cats are eating well and are not in poor body condition, it can be helpful to put them on low-fat, high-fiber diets.

Insulin is easily given by subcutaneous injection.

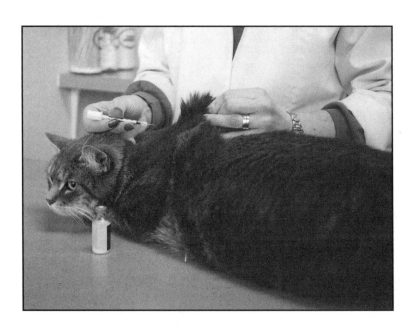

Although most diabetic cats will require insulin for their entire lives, some are "transient" or temporary diabetics, and their need for insulin will come and go. Even when regulated, diabetic cats should be examined and have their blood sugar monitored at least every six months.

Uterine Infections

One of the reasons that spaying is recommended in cats is because intact female cats are at risk for pyometra, a uterine infection. Pyometra is a serious condition in which the uterus becomes distended and filled with pus. If the infected organ ruptures, pus can spread all over the abdominal cavity and in turn create peritonitis—a potentially fatal infection of the abdomen.

Signs of Pyometra

Fortunately, most pet owners spay their cats at an early age and do not have to worry about this problem. Experienced cat breeders are aware of the condition and monitor their queens for the telltale sign of creamy-colored vaginal discharge.

Cats with pyometra can have fevers, lethargy, and poor appetites. If a veterinarian suspects pyometra, he may confirm the diagnosis by palpitating the abdominal cavity and finding an enlarged, fluid-filled uterus. If this is not found, he may do a blood test to look for a high white blood cell count. Other useful tests are vaginal smears to look for white blood cells (the components of pus) and bacteria, x-rays, or ultrasound, which can be more sensitive at identifying uterine enlargement.

Treating Pyometra

Unless there is a very good reason to keep a female cat intact, the best treatment option is spaying a cat with pyometra. The surgical procedure is more complicated than routine spay surgery because the infected uterus is fragile and must be carefully handled to prevent problems. A cat with pyometra is usually not in prime health, as it has been fighting an internal infection. Under these circumstances, close monitoring and strong supportive care is needed.

If an owner does not want to have the cat's uterus and ovaries removed, medical treatment can be performed. Antibiotics and drugs called prostaglandins are used to treat infection and shrink the uterus. Prostaglandins stimulate uterine contraction, but they can also cause general cramping and discomfort.

Cats that have experienced pyometra have a high chance of recurrence. If you want to breed the cat, you should do so at its next heat cycle and then sterilize it as soon as you are done with breeding.

Cats Can Get Breast Cancer

We're all quite aware of breast cancer, and most women do their best to routinely screen themselves for problems. Cats can get breast cancer too, and the type they get is usually malignant. Cats most at risk for developing breast cancer are unspayed older females, cats that had litters earlier in their lives, and cats that were spayed later on in life.

Prevention

The risk of breast cancer in a cat that has never experienced a heat cycle is about zero, so again this is another reason to spay a young animal. There are no other specific steps that will prevent breast cancer, and monitoring the mammary glands for lumps, in hopes of early detection, is a good idea.

During a routine annual physical exam, a veterinarian should palpate all eight mammary glands on a cat and search for lumps. Occasionally cats will develop cysts or benign growths, but a biopsy is the only way to know the exact status of a lump.

Avoid CATastrophe

Mammary cancer is not strictly a disease of female cats; male cats can be affected too. Even though they have not been in heat or had female hormonal stimulation, male cats have nipples. If you have a male cat with a growth near a nipple, have it examined by a veterinarian.

If You Feel a Lump

There are astute owners who feel the lumps on their cats. Initially, a malignant growth will feel like a hard BB near one or more of the nipples. The smaller the growth and the earlier it is removed, the better the cat's chances for survival.

Most often a veterinarian will remove the entire growth rather than take a small biopsy. Mammary cancer tends to run down the mammary chain first on one side, then the other, so a radical mastectomy may be recommended.

Treating Breast Cancer

As with most cancers, it's important to begin treatment right away. Surgical excision of the affected tissue and even unilateral or bilateral radical mastectomy may be needed. The tissue should definitely be sent for biopsy.

Your veterinarian may recommend additional chemotherapy, or you may want to consult with a veterinary oncologist. Chemotherapy is an aggressive approach, but it is well tolerated by most cats and may help to preserve a good quality of life.

The conservative approach would be to monitor the cat for recurrences, and surgically remove any other lumps that develop. Taking chest x-rays every six months or so will monitor for metastasis of cancer to the lungs. If a cat that has been previously diagnosed with breast cancer and starts to have problems with coughing or breathing, there is a good chance that metastasis has occurred.

Meow Wow

It is uncommon for male cats to develop any type of reproductive tract disease. In contrast, prostate disease and cancer are fairly common in humans and dogs.

The Least You Need to Know

➤ Older cats should be monitored for hyperthyroidism.

➤ A cat that is drinking and urinating more than usual and is losing weight should be checked for diabetes mellitus.

➤ Life-threatening uterine infections can occur in female cats.

➤ The mammary glands of cats should be monitored for lumps that could be malignant.

Chapter 19

Kitty's Got a Lot of Nerve

In This Chapter

➤ Diseases of the eyes

➤ The causes of seizures in cats

➤ Neurologic diseases a cat can be born with

➤ Spinal disease in the cat

What makes a cat want to hunt birds? Why does a cat recognize the sound of the can opener? How does a cat think? How do reflexes work? These and many other questions are answered by the intricate feline nervous system. It is the control panel for every sense and body system. The brain is the computer that commands the other parts of the body. The central nervous system (CNS) is composed of the brain and spinal cord. Cerebral spinal fluid (CSF) surrounds the brain and spinal cord and acts as a shock absorber. It helps to prevent concussions when the head is traumatized.

There are five primary senses: vision, hearing, touch, smell, and taste. There are additional body-monitoring sensors for balance, temperature, muscle tension, and blood oxygen level. You are probably thinking, who cares? How does it relate to me and my cat? Well, there are millions of stimuli bombarding the nervous system every second. The able CNS makes sense of it all and preserves and protects each animal, so it is important for it to be functioning properly. Damage or disease affecting the nervous system can have far-reaching implications.

Avoid CATastrophe

Many veterinary prescription eye drops and ointments contain a combination of antibiotic and cortisone. Drops containing cortisone should never be used on cats with corneal ulcers, as cortisone retards corneal healing.

Worth a Paws

Persian and Himalayan cats have very prominent eyes that are easily injured. These cats can develop a condition called corneal sequestrum, in which part of the cornea actually dies and turns black. A veterinary ophthalmologist can perform a procedure called a keratectomy to remove this damaged corneal tissue. A corneal sequestrum is not painful, but it will block vision through that part of the cornea.

Eyes See You

The eye can be compared to a computerized camera. The pupil is the camera's aperture. The iris works as the shutter, regulating the amount of light entering the eye. The lens is the focusing mechanism. The retina is the film; it is where photoreceptors process the image into electrochemical signals. Nerves to the brain are the computer lines that transmit the signal. The brain is the site of the finished photo. There are 193,000 optic nerve fibers (wow!) that transmit information to the cat's visual cortex.

Ouch! A Scratch on the Eye

A common cause of a squinting, red eye in a cat is a corneal ulcer. Corneal ulcers are irregularities on the surface of the eye, and they can be detected by placing a drop of a fluorescent dye on the eye surface and then rinsing it off. A normal cornea is smooth, and the dye will flush off. If any abrasion, scratch, or other lesion is present that has affected the integrity of the cornea, the dye will stick to it. Ulcerated corneas are quite uncomfortable to an animal, so you may see a decreased activity level in a cat with an ulcer.

In the springtime when plants and weeds are growing, it is common for cats to get foxtails in their eyes (not on purpose, of course). Foxtails are pointy grass awns that are quite sharp and can get stuck under the eyelids of cats that go outdoors. If you live in an area where these annoying plant seeds are present, be on the lookout for them. They can also get stuck in between toes, in ear canals, and be found throughout a cat's coat. They can penetrate into the skin and cause more serious problems.

An antibiotic drop or ointment is typically prescribed to treat a corneal ulcer. A protective Elizabethan collar may be recommended as well. An Elizabethan collar is the protective "lampshade" that animals wear to prevent them from rubbing their eyes or faces or to stop licking. Lesions can resolve in about a week if properly treated.

Kitty Pinkeye

The most common problem directly affecting the eyes of cats is conjunctivitis. Inflammation of the tissue around the eye can result from viral or bacterial infection, allergies, trauma, and immune-related diseases. Conjunctivitis does not directly affect vision, but it can do so indirectly if a cat is squinting due to discomfort or if the cornea is secondarily affected.

A red, puffy eye or an eye that is tearing is a clinical sign of conjunctivitis. Cultures and conjunctival scrapings are not routinely reliable diagnostic tools, so it can be difficult for a veterinarian to determine an exact cause of a case of conjunctivitis.

Avoid CATastrophe

Feline chlamydia can be transmitted to humans and cause conjunctivitis. To prevent the spread of infection, wash your hands before touching your own eyes after handling a cat with conjunctivitis.

Kittens can be commonly infected with feline herpes virus or chlamydia, which can cause conjunctivitis. Both can be difficult to treat, and the herpes can cause recurrent draining of the eye and conjunctivitis throughout the cat's life.

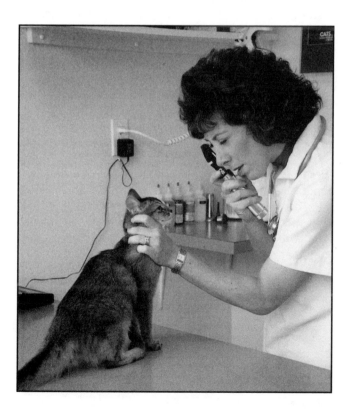

A veterinarian uses an ophthalmoscope to evaluate a kitten's eyes.

Kitty Ditty

The **nasolacrimal** duct provides drainage from the eye out through the nose.

Worth a Paws

Regarding ocular discharge, the general rule is that clear is good, and yellow or green is bad. A dark crusty material in the corners of the eyes can also be normal. Tears contain pigments that turn dark when exposed to light. This coloration is not due to blood or infection.

Stop Crying

Many cats have eyes that tear on a regular basis. The most common cause of chronic tearing is a flare-up of a feline herpes virus infection, or scarring of the *nasolacrimal* drainage duct that resulted from a previous herpes virus infection.

Chronic tearing can also be the result of facial conformation and breed predisposition. Owners of Persian and other brachycephalic breeds of cats are familiar with this occurrence. The normal drainage system for the tears does not function in these cats due to the size and shape of the eyes and nose. They may also lack drainage ducts.

Allergies can trigger conjunctivitis or mild chronic tearing. Intermittent use of an eye treatment containing cortisone can help cats with eye problems due to allergies.

Just like many people have "sleep" in their eyes each morning, so do many cats. Wiping with a moist tissue or cotton ball should be adequate for cleaning most cats' eyes. Short-nosed cats, such as Persians, may need their eyes cleaned two to three times daily to prevent buildup. If the discharge is allowed to accumulate, it can cause hair loss and dermatitis in the skin folds around the eyes.

Should You Worry About Blindness?

It is normal for a cat's eye lenses to thicken with aging and for clarity of vision to diminish. Very few felines go blind from cataracts; blindness is usually the result of another condition or trauma. If a cat loses vision in one eye, an owner may not even realize it because the animal will still be able to function fairly normally. Even when both eyes are blind, a cat can get around in surroundings with which it is familiar, and it will use its other senses to compensate for its lack of sight.

Kitties and Convulsions

A seizure is an uncontrolled release of electrical activity from the neurons of the brain. When you observe a seizure, it may seem as though it lasts for a long time, but in reality they rarely last more than 30 to 60 seconds. Seizures are scary episodes to observe because your normally responsive pet will not recognize you and may even bite you if you try to hold it down.

There is nothing that an owner can do to stop a seizure in progress. The best thing to do is to be sure that the animal cannot fall off something and hurt itself and then leave it alone. Why do cats have seizures? There are many possible causes. Epilepsy, a disorder triggering recurrent seizures with no underlying disease process occurring in the brain, is not as common in cats as in dogs or humans. Most feline seizures are triggered by specific causes.

Diagnosing Seizures

A diagnostic work-up for seizures and other brain-localized diseases will initially include a history, physical and neurologic exam, a complete blood count and chemistry panel, and urinalysis. If the veterinarian is unable to make a specific diagnosis based on this information, and the cat is continuing to have seizures, further diagnostic testing should be pursued.

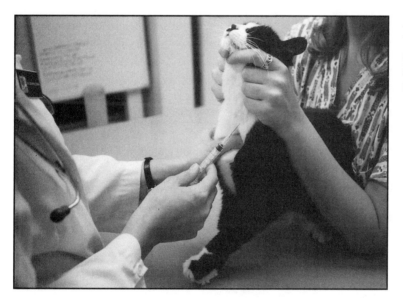

Part of the diagnostic work-up for a seizure disorder is drawing a blood sample and having it analyzed.

Such tests might include:

➤ Blood pressure measurement

➤ Skull x-rays

➤ CSF tap and analysis

➤ EEG (electroencephalogram)

➤ CT (computerized tomography) scan

➤ MRI (magnetic resonance imaging)

➤ Radioisotope brain scan

As you might imagine, it can be expensive to pursue a definitive diagnosis, and referral to a veterinary neurologist may be needed to provide access to diagnostic equipment and interpretation.

There are many possible causes for seizures, including:

➤ Congenital disease

➤ Metabolic disease

➤ Neoplasia

➤ Nutritional imbalances

➤ Infections with viruses, bacteria, protozoa, or fungi

➤ Trauma

➤ Toxins

➤ Parasites

➤ Vascular disorder

Treating Seizures

If a specific trigger for the seizures is identified, treatment for the underlying problem may be successful in controlling future neurological events. Some of these conditions are more responsive to treatment than others.

Idiopathic epilepsy is a seizure condition with no known cause. If a seizure is an isolated incident, no treatment may be recommended. If seizures occur at least once a month, oral anticonvulsant therapy is instituted. The most commonly used drug to treat seizures is phenobarbital, but diazepam and potassium bromide are also prescribed.

Meow Wow

Some cats almost appear to be having seizures when exposed to catnip. Catnip, *Nepata cataria,* is a member of the mint family. The active chemical in catnip is called nepetalactone, which is a hallucinogenic compound that induces a pleasure response in cats. A cat's genetic makeup is a factor affecting the animal's responsiveness to catnip. Apparently catnip is an acquired taste, as young kittens usually do not respond to it.

Born with Neurologic Problems

Three congenital abnormalities are somewhat prevalent in cats. The first is hydrocephalus, otherwise known as "water on the brain." In a hydrocephalic animal, cerebral spinal fluid (not water) abnormally pools in certain parts of the brain. The classic appearance of a cat with hydrocephalus is a dome-shaped skull. Siamese are the most commonly affected breed. This condition is noticed in young kittens. Abnormal physical appearance, behaviors, and seizures may be seen, and there is no treatment.

Siamese cats are more often born with hydrocephalus than other breeds. (Photograph by Andy Jones)

The second congenital abnormality can be found in some Manx cats. Manx cats do not have normal tails, and some are born with malformations of nerves and spinal cord segments. One condition is called spina bifida, which is a defect in the closure of the vertebrae. This condition leads to a protrusion of the spinal cord and nerves. The clinical signs observed are loss of urinary and fecal control, otherwise known as incontinence. Even if a Manx cat does not have spina bifida, it may have minor spinal cord defects.

The last congenital abnormality is cerebellar hypoplasia. This is another condition seen in young kittens. The signs observed are tremors, imbalance, and an exaggerated gait. No treatment exists for this condition. Owners need to decide if they can live with a pet that does not function normally. Cats with cerebellar hypoplasia need help eating, eliminating, and getting around, although their external physical appearance is normal.

Meow Wow

Most Manx cats "bunny hop" when they run, a significantly different movement from that of other cats. This change of gait is related to their short tails and possible vertebral malformations. Bunny hopping, without incontinence, does not create any management problems for Manx owners.

Cats with Bad Backs

Compared with dogs, cats have quite flexible backs and so infrequently sustain back injuries. If injury or disease affects a cat's spine, possible clinical signs would be:

➤ Limb weakness or paralysis

➤ Instability

➤ Stiff or painful muscles

➤ Loss of normal reflexes

➤ Urinary or fecal incontinence

Tests for the Spine

The diagnostic work-up options for cats with suspected spinal problems are similar to those for brain disease. Additional tests that might be performed are a myelogram (an x-ray taken after dye is injected around the spinal cord) and an electromyelogram (which measures the electrical activity of muscle). Some diseases of muscles have clinical signs similar to those caused by nerves.

Traumatic Experience

Examples of trauma causing damage to the spine are when a cat is hit by a car or becomes stuck under a garage door. The back end of the animal is affected most often in these situations. The tail can be damaged, back end nerves can be torn, and the spinal cord can be damaged. Cats are amazing creatures with an unbelievable capacity to heal. Many cats with severe damage will regain normal function with treatment, tender loving care, and time.

Generally, the more severe the signs, the less optimistic the prognosis with spinal disease. Once a nerve is cut, it will not reconnect, but it can regenerate at a very slow rate. It is not particularly hard to control pain and inflammation in cats that have sustained trauma, but managing the inability to eliminate is difficult. If control of these processes has not returned within a couple of weeks, it most likely will not return. Owners can be faced with making a decision about euthanasia if the animal is unable to regulate its bodily functions.

Cats with broken, limp tails can do very well, if no other signs exist, by amputating their tails. When the tail loses feeling and motor control, it is not doing the cat any good anyway, so it is best to surgically remove it.

Kitties with Slipped Disks

Intervertebral disk disease is occasionally seen in cats. A veterinarian might suspect a disk problem in a cat as he pinches down the spine from the neck to the tail and localizes a sensitive spot, and the cat presents with pain, instability, weakness, or paralysis. Disks in the neck are more commonly affected than those further down the spine. Disks can degenerate with aging, be pushed out of place by trauma or tumors, become infected, or be pinched by arthritic changes.

If intervertebral disk disease is diagnosed, the cat should be confined so that it can rest, and anti-inflammatory doses of cortisone used to help with pain and swelling. If the condition progresses to paralysis, surgical decompression of the spinal cord is needed immediately.

Cauda Equina Syndrome

This condition has clinical signs that are very similar to intervertebral disk disease, although it affects only those nerves at the end of the spinal cord. Cauda equina syndrome occurs most frequently in senior cats. Signs observed in cats with cauda equina syndrome include:

➤ Difficulty in rising

➤ Rear-limb lameness that progresses with use

➤ Dragging of the rear toes

➤ Rear-limb and tail weakness

➤ Urinary or fecal incontinence

➤ Pain at the lumbosacral junction of the spine

Worth a Paws

If your cat requires surgery on any part of its spinal cord, consider consulting with a board-certified veterinary surgeon. Spinal surgery is a delicate and risky procedure that is best left to experts.

If treatment with rest and corticosteroids does not give the cat significant relief of pain or return to function, you should discuss decompression surgery with your veterinarian.

The Least You Need to Know

➤ If your cat has a red, puffy eye and is squinting, you should have it examined by your veterinarian.

➤ Seizures in the cat are usually triggered by an underlying problem.

➤ There are some congenital defects that affect the neurological system of cats.

➤ If trauma causes damage to the spinal cord, monitoring the cat's ability to eliminate is important.

➤ If a cat develops paralysis because of pressure on its spinal cord, decompression surgery is needed.

Chapter 20

It's All About Pee

In This Chapter

➤ Lower Urinary Tract Disease (LUTD) in cats

➤ Life-threatening urinary blockages

➤ Bladder stones

➤ Kidney disease and what to watch out for

The popularity of cats has flourished over the last decade because of their ability to thrive with minimal human care. Their urinary elimination behavior is a big part of this, since owners do not need to rush home to take their cats out for a "potty" walk. Cats are born with the idea of burying their urine in dirt or sand. Proper litterbox usage can ensure a comfortable indoor life for a pet cat. The urinary tract is the body system that most cat owners are aware of. Aside from monitoring it for disease, cat owners are always concerned about where their cats are urinating and hoping that it is in the litterbox.

The urinary tract is composed of the kidneys, which are responsible for filtering blood and producing urine; the ureters, which transport urine from the kidneys to the bladder; the bladder, which stores urine; and the urethra, which is the passageway from the bladder to the penis or vulva. All parts of the urinary tract play a role in proper fluid waste product elimination from the body.

Lower Urinary Tract Disease

Lower Urinary Tract Disease (LUTD) is a broad term involving many different syndromes. The lower urinary tract of cats involves the bladder and urethra. You may hear your veterinarian use the acronym "FUS" when referring to urinary tract problems. FUS stands for Feline Urologic Syndrome. Medical personnel may use the terms LUTD and FUS interchangeably, but the former is more accurate and that is the acronym that I will use here.

Worth a Paws

One recommendation that has stayed fairly consistent is trying to avoid feeding seafood products to cats with a history of urinary tract problems. Seafood tends to have a high mineral content, especially a high level of magnesium.

Theories Are Changing

Theories regarding what causes bladder problems in cats have changed over the past 20 years. Historically, owners were concerned about the "ash" content of their cat's food, but the controversial component du jour is magnesium.

There has been a see-sawing of recommendations with regards to feeding canned versus dry foods to cats with bladder problems, and the pendulum has swung back to recommending more canned food. Canned food increases a cat's water intake, which can lead to more dilute urine with fewer crystals forming.

The urinary tract is an area constantly being researched in academia and the pet food industry, so expect new information to be available each year. Litterbox usage and diet are important issues to discuss with your veterinarian at each annual visit.

Blood in the Urine

Bloody urine is a frequent finding in cats with LUTD. Owners notice blood in the litterbox or on other objects that the cat has decided to eliminate on. Blood is a sign of inflammation of the bladder (cystitis) but it does not necessarily mean that a bacterial infection is present.

A veterinarian should examine cats with blood in their urine. The veterinarian will want to perform a urinalysis to help reach a diagnosis. A proper urinalysis will:

➤ Check the cat's ability to concentrate urine

➤ Show if red blood cells are present

➤ Show the pH of the urine

➤ Show if sugar is present

➤ Evaluate protein levels in the urine

➤ Check for the presence of other metabolic chemicals, crystals, or cells

Urine can be cultured for bacteria, and antibiotic sensitivities can then be determined.

There are a host of reasons for blood in a cat's urine, including:

➤ Bacterial infections

➤ Viral infections

➤ Trauma to the kidneys or bladder

➤ Stress

➤ Bladder stones

➤ Crystal buildup

➤ Tumors

➤ Blood clotting disorders

➤ Idiopathic (no known cause) *interstitial cystitis*

Kitty Ditty

Interstitial cystitis (IC) is a benign inflammatory condition that can affect the bladders of cats. It is one of the LUTD syndromes. Although there are no conclusively effective treatments, veterinarians can prescribe a mild human anti-anxiety drug called amitriptyline. It is effective in cases of human IC.

How to Make Your Cat More Comfortable

Cats with LUTD can strain to urinate and pass only a few drops of urine at a time. The most important factor is that they are able to pass some urine, differentiating them from cats with urinary blockages.

The results of a physical exam and urinalysis will give a veterinarian a good idea about what is causing LUTD. Controlling bacterial infections is fairly easily achieved with antibiotics, but decreasing the straining and increased frequency of urination can be more difficult. A host of medications can be tried, and time can also heal. It usually takes three to five days for a case of LUTD to improve.

Avoid CATastrophe

Cats that urinate outside of their litterboxes may be trying to get your attention and let you know that they are not well. Don't automatically blame the problem on bad behavior. Have the cat examined by a veterinarian so that if an underlying medical problem exists, such as LUTD, it can be treated.

When cats have recurrent bouts of LUTD, further diagnostic testing is needed. Tests that are helpful are:

➤ Plain x-rays

➤ Contrast x-rays (for better evaluation of the lining of the bladder and certain stone types)

➤ Ultrasound

➤ Urine culture

➤ Bladder biopsy

225

What About Diet?

It is normal to have some crystals in the urine. To determine whether crystals are a problem or not, the number of crystals, the presence of other cells, and the pH of the urine should all be taken into consideration. Your veterinarian may recommend a special diet if she feels the crystals are a problem.

There are prescription brands and grocery store cat foods that are formulated to improve urinary tract health. If your cat has a history of urinary tract problems, the urine should be monitored after the diet is changed to be sure that the correct balance is being achieved. I would not recommend feeding a special diet without first consulting with your veterinarian. Special diets may be harmful to young, growing kittens or older cats with other medical conditions.

As I've mentioned, feeding more canned food is recommended for cats with urinary tract problems. Special diets are usually available in canned and dry forms. Ultimately, your cat may be the decision-maker and choose what it is willing to eat.

Kitty Can't Pee!

If an owner calls my clinic and tells my receptionist that his cat can't urinate, she becomes alarmed especially if a male cat is involved. Due to the length and shape of their urethras, male cats are more susceptible to developing life-threatening urethral obstructions. The narrow exit passageway from the bladder can become clogged with mucus, crystals, and even small stones.

A cat that cannot urinate should be examined immediately because if he is truly obstructed, he could die within hours due to toxins building up in the blood and pressure on the kidneys. If the animal's bladder is small and soft, there is no problem. If the bladder is hard and large, an emergency is present.

It's Gonna Cost How Much?

It is good to know ahead of time that effectively treating a urinary blockage is expensive. Expenses will be even higher if you are forced to visit an emergency veterinary clinic, but you really have no choice. Factors that affect the amount of treatment a cat will need are:

➤ Duration of the obstruction

➤ Whether kidney damage is present

➤ Degree of difficulty in unblocking the urethra

➤ The cause of the obstruction

➤ Whether the cat blocks up again

Each veterinarian will probably handle treatment of a blocked cat a little differently, but the basic steps are:

1. Pass a urinary catheter into the bladder.
2. Drain out the retained urine.
3. Determine what other metabolic imbalances exist.
4. Treat for infection and shock (if necessary).
5. Maintain the cat's hydration.
6. Flush debris out of the bladder.
7. Evaluate the cat's ability to urinate once the catheter has been removed.

A blocked cat may require one to five days of hospitalization and nursing care. Home care will likely involve treatment with antibiotics and possibly a diet change. Some cats need medication to relax their bladders and urethras to ease elimination.

Three Strikes and You're Out

For some reason, there are cats that will become re-obstructed. Medication and diet are just not enough to keep things flowing out smoothly. Again, each veterinarian will have his own approach to the problem, but my rule is that if a cat obstructs three times, he needs a procedure called a perineal urethrotomy (PU).

We call the PU surgery our "kitty sex-change operation" because afterward, the urinary tract and genitalia look more like those of a female than a male. Males are more prone to obstruct because of their narrow, twisting urethra that ends at their penis. Females have a short, wide urethra that ends in the vulva. Cats that have perineal urethrotomies lose their penis, and are given a new opening from which to urinate.

This surgery successfully opens up the urethra, but it is not without risk. If not performed carefully or if trauma or excessive scarring occur, a cat may not be able to control his urination and dribbling will occur. Scarring can also cause another obstruction. The shortened urethra may increase the likelihood of bacteria entering the urinary tract.

Is This Cat Stoned?

Stones can form throughout the urinary tract, but are most often seen in the bladder. The medical term for stones of the urinary tract is uroliths. Kidney stones are the second-most frequent type of urolith, but unless they cause a blockage of the ureter, they are usually left alone.

The Origin of Stones

When dissolved minerals are present in high concentrations, they can reach a saturation point and begin to precipitate out of the urine as crystals. Bladder stones are created in this manner, which is similar to the formation of rock candy. Some debris comes together to form a small center, then other crystals join on and make a stone.

Worth a Paws

In order to compete with prescription urinary tract diets, many of the commercial foods on the market today are over-acidified. Some cats fed diets that are too acidic will develop a different type of stone called calcium oxalate.

Struvite is the name used to describe magnesium ammonium phosphate crystals or stones. High levels of magnesium combined with a high urine pH create an environment that allows struvite to precipitate in the urine. Commercially available urinary tract diets for cats have been created to decrease this compound from forming in the urine by reducing magnesium and pH. These foods are labeled "pH control" or "urinary formula."

In addition to struvite, calcium oxalate, ammonium, and urate stones can develop in cats when certain metabolic conditions exist. Each type of stone requires different conditions to form. Some can be controlled by diet, but others can be difficult to prevent.

Struvite stones are the only types that can be dissolved by feeding a special prescription diet, which is only available through veterinarians. After a stone-dissolving diet is fed for about two months, a preventive diet is fed to prevent recurrence.

How Stones Are Diagnosed

It is uncommon to feel stones in a cat's bladder because they are relatively small. Stones should be suspected any time a cat has more than one episode of LUTD or develops a urinary blockage. Most feline uroliths are visible on plain x-rays if they are large enough.

To make stones more visible, a special x-ray called a pneumocystogram is performed. The procedure involves catheterizing the bladder and injecting air as a contrast agent. Ultrasound is also able to detect small stones and piles of crystalline sand on the bladder floor.

Urine pH, appearance on x-ray, and blood work can give clues as to the type of stone present. A definitive identification of the stone is performed at a lab where its chemical components are analyzed.

Treatment for Stones

If the veterinarian is unsure whether the stones will dissolve with a change in diet, or if you want to get them out and get your cat comfortable as soon as possible, surgical removal is recommended. The procedure is called a cystotomy and involves abdominal surgery and incision into the bladder. Stones are removed, and the bladder and urethra are flushed out. In certain situations, *urohydropropulsion* can be used to remove stones.

Kitty Ditty

Urohydropropulsion *is a technique that forces small uroliths out of the body. It is an option for female cats with small stones.*

Can Stones Recur?

If your cat is found to have stones that cannot be prevented with diet, there is a good chance that they will recur. There are usually some steps that can be taken to decrease risk, but the cat should be monitored about every six months for recurrence.

The bladder is an organ that heals incredibly well, so although it seems traumatic at the time, cats have excellent recoveries from cystotomies. The key to success with the surgery is thorough removal of all stones and follow-up with an x-ray.

Kitty's Kidneys

The kidneys are the organs responsible for filtering out waste products from the blood, conserving water in the body, and producing urine. A cat's body is a great machine, and even though it works best with two kidneys, it can do well with one kidney or 50 percent kidney function.

Kitty Ditty

Your veterinarian (or your physician) might use the term **renal** *to describe things having to do with the kidneys. For example, renal insufficiency means loss of kidney function.*

There are many different diseases that can affect the kidneys, but regardless of the cause, most *renal* diseases are treated similarly. The prognosis for cats with kidney disease depends on whether the disease is acute or chronic—long-standing problems tend to have a less favorable outcome. Unlike other vital organs, the kidneys are not capable of regenerating themselves.

Signs of Dysfunctional Kidneys

Clinical signs associated with kidney disease are similar to those of other diseases and can include:

Avoid CATastrophe

Antifreeze is a potent toxin when ingested by cats. A chemical in antifreeze, ethylene glycol, irreversibly destroys kidney cells. If you have any reason to suspect that your cat has consumed antifreeze, get it to a veterinarian *immediately*.

➤ Increased thirst

➤ Increased urination

➤ Weight loss

➤ Dehydration

➤ Dental disease

➤ Vomiting

Blood tests and urinalysis results will not indicate that kidney function is compromised until more than 50 percent function is lost. In fact, they may not show abnormal results until more than two-thirds of kidney function has been affected.

Cats with kidney disease tend to become dehydrated. A skin turgor test is a simple procedure that cat owners can do at home to check on their cat's hydration. If neck skin is pinched up and does not bounce back into place within a second or two, the cat is significantly dehydrated. In this situation, injectable fluid supplementation is probably needed.

A skin turgor test is performed by pinching the skin between the cat's shoulder blades and observing how quickly it bounces back into shape.

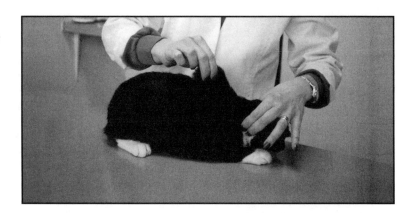

Kidney Infection

Pyelonephritis and glomerulonephritis are terms used to describe infection and inflammation involving different cells within the kidneys. Because the kidneys filter all of the body's blood, any infectious agent in the blood is transported to the kidneys.

The clinical signs of pyelonephritis are the same as other types of kidney disease, but fever and pain on palpation of the kidneys may be present. White blood cells can also be present in the urine.

Kidney infections are very serious, and are usually treated by giving intravenous antibiotics. After initial treatment, oral antibiotics can be used, but a course of three to six weeks of medication may be needed. When pyelonephritis is suspected, a urine culture and antibiotic sensitivity should be started before treatment begins and afterward as follow-ups to treatment.

Breed-Specific Kidney Disease

Particular kidney diseases are seen in certain lines of purebred cats. The two most common types are renal amyloidosis in Abyssinians and Somalis and polycystic kidney disease in Persians and Himalayans.

There is no specific test for renal amyloidosis, but it is suspected in young to middle-aged purebreds that develop kidney disease of no other known cause. A kidney biopsy can be performed that may show the particular protein deposits that are the characteristic lesions of this disease.

Polycystic kidney disease (PKD) is found in purebreds and in related longhaired cats. This disease can be diagnosed by feeling lumpy, bumpy kidneys on palpation and by seeing the cysts on ultrasound. The presence of cysts will not necessarily cause significant kidney disease, and some affected animals live normal lives. Others develop kidney dysfunction at a young age as the cysts grow and destroy the normal kidney tissue.

Old Kidneys

The kidneys tend to wear out faster in cats than other organs. Chronic interstitial nephritis is the medical term for the slowly progressive loss of kidney function found in older cats. It is the most common disease of cats over the age of 10 years.

As a cat ages, the kidneys scar and become smaller and less efficient at filtering the blood and preserving water in the body. The progression of chronic interstitial nephritis can vary depending on the individual animal and the amount of nursing care that an owner is willing to do.

The goals of treatment are:

➤ Maintain hydration

➤ Keep blood waste product levels down

➤ Prevent anemia

➤ Control secondary infections

Although veterinary diets have been developed for use in cats with kidney disease, the restriction of protein levels in these diets is controversial. Cats are carnivores, so when their physical condition is diminished, adequate protein is needed more than ever.

Meow Wow

Kidney transplants are available for cats. The surgery is performed at a few specialty clinics and universities around the country. It is a costly procedure with risks of organ rejection, but a successful transplant may buy a cat a few more years of life.

Kitty Ditty

A dialysis machine removes the blood from the body and cleans it when the kidneys are unable to do the job. Dialysis is only available at a few specialty centers for cats, but **diuresis**—flushing the body with fluids and diuretics—is easily performed in most veterinary hospitals.

Specific Treatments

Fluid therapy is the cornerstone of helping cats with kidney disease. The fluids given to affected cats are balanced electrolyte solutions. Cats who have high waste product levels in their blood should be initially *diuresed* with intravenous fluids. They also may be given diuretics to help flush waste products.

In cases of chronic kidney disease, owners can be instructed on injecting fluids under the skin of their pets. This procedure can be done at home on a long-term basis. We have owners that have happily given their cats subcutaneous fluid injections for years.

Maintaining proper levels of minerals in the blood is important in controlling kidney disease. The two minerals that need to be closely watched are potassium and phosphorus. Cats with kidney dysfunction tend to have insufficient levels of potassium but an overabundance of phosphorus. Potassium supplements and phosphate binding agents can be used to create the right balance.

Cats suffering from chronic kidney disease can become anemic because their kidneys stop producing enough erythropoietin, a hormone that stimulates the bone marrow to produce red blood cells. Erythropoietin can be supplemented by injection if the red blood cell count gets too low.

Some cats with kidney disease become anorexic and can be treated with appetite stimulants, anabolic steroids, and by hand-feeding. If there is concern of nausea or upset stomach, oral antacids can be used. Antibiotic treatment may be required if infection is a secondary problem.

Is the Clock Ticking?

Even if a cat is being well maintained on fluid therapy and other treatments, kidney disease will invariably progress past a treatable stage. Cats with kidney disease should be monitored at least every six months.

Worth a Paws

Even though it may sound beyond the call of duty, learning how to inject your cat with subcutaneous fluids is fairly easy and can make a significant difference in the way the animal will feel, improving its quality of life but not curing the problem.

The Least You Need to Know

➤ LUTD can have many causes and may not be related to diet at all.

➤ Male cats that develop urethral blockages should be treated as soon as possible since this condition is life-threatening.

➤ Cats can develop uroliths, especially in their bladders.

➤ Kidney disease is the most common medical condition in cats over the age of 10 years.

Chapter 21

The Dreaded Viruses

In This Chapter

➤ All about Feline Leukemia Virus

➤ Feline Immunodeficiency Virus

➤ The difficult-to-diagnose Feline Infectious Peritonitis

➤ Why you should care about rabies

Viruses are microorganisms that are composed of protein chains (DNA or RNA). They are considered living organisms, although they can not reproduce unless they attach themselves to other live cells. They cause infection but they do not respond to antibiotics because antibiotics fight bacterial infections. Most viruses are species-specific, which means cat viruses affect cats and human viruses affect humans.

Viruses mutate and change, and that is why people are subject to so many "flu bugs." There are numerous viruses that affect cats, but some are more dangerous than others. Viruses are destroyed in the body by the host animal's immune system, but some viruses hide out and cannot be totally removed. Some viruses can be fought through vaccination, which stimulates an animal's immune system to fight the infection.

Feline Leukemia Virus

Feline Leukemia Virus (FeLV) is a serious virus in cats because at this time it has no cure. Unlike some of the other deadly viruses that affect cats, there are reliable screening tests for FeLV. This makes it possible to identify sick cats and healthy cats carrying the virus.

FeLV is contagious and is passed by direct, cat-to-cat contact, such as fighting and biting, mutual grooming, and reproduction. Not all cats that contract FeLV die from the disease, but any cat that tests positively should be monitored closely.

Worth a Paws

The results of different FeLV tests can be confusing if they are not all positive or all negative. If this situation occurs, a veterinarian should follow the AAFP/AFM FeLV testing guidelines and consider re-testing before making a final diagnosis.

Can You Test You Cat for FeLV?

Most veterinary clinics have the capacity to test for Feline Leukemia in the office in a 5- to 10-minute period. The most reliable tests use small amounts of blood, but saliva and tears can be used in some test kits. Most of the tests used in clinics are very reliable. However, when a positive test occurs, it should be verified, as there are sometimes false positive tests for FeLV.

The in-house tests for FeLV check for antibodies to a specific FeLV protein in the blood (or body secretions). If this type of test is positive, a secondary, verifying test should be performed. Secondary tests, which check for antibodies to FeLV antigens within blood cells, are available through an outside lab. There also is a test for FeLV that looks for viral DNA in the blood.

One problem with testing for FeLV is that if an animal was exposed to the virus within a few weeks of being tested, the test could be negative because antibodies and the virus would not yet be present in the blood. If there is any question as to the status of a cat, it should be re-tested one to three months later.

What Does FeLV Do?

Feline Leukemia Virus can suppress a cat's immune system so that other diseases make the animal extremely sick. It can also cause lymphatic cancer and suppress a cat's bone marrow and blood cell production. Once a cat has developed clinical signs and tests positively for FeLV, the animal usually only lives a few months at best.

A small number of cats contract FeLV, never get sick, and live normal life spans. This is because their immune systems are able to fight off active infection. Some animals carry FeLV and are healthy for years before any signs of illness develop.

Protection Against the Virus

There are steps that can be taken to prevent your cat from contracting FeLV. These include:

➤ Test any cats for FeLV before introducing them into your household.

➤ Keep your cats indoors.

➤ If your cats go outdoors, vaccinate them against FeLV.

➤ Spay and neuter your cats so that they are less likely to fight and come in contact with FeLV.

➤ Lock any pet doors to prevent unknown cats from entering your home.

Kittens are most at risk for exposure to FeLV because of their immature immune systems. A queen can pass FeLV to her kittens. Even if you don't plan on letting your kitten go outside, it is a good idea to test it and initially vaccinate it against FeLV. If your kitten's lifestyle changes and it is no longer a housecat, you would want to protect it. If after a year the cat never goes outside, vaccination for FeLV can be discontinued.

Avoid CATastrophe

You should test any new feline addition for FeLV and FIV before introducing it into your household. Since both viruses are contagious, your best intentions could bring in a deadly disease, and risk the health of your existing cats.

Coping with FeLV

If all tests and clinical signs point to a diagnosis of FeLV and the animal is sick, the prognosis is poor. At this time there are no effective treatments or cures for FeLV. There has been experimentation with some drugs that stimulate the immune system, but none has been conclusively shown to have any effect.

Treatment of FeLV-positive cats is aimed at making the cat as comfortable as possible and controlling secondary problems. An owner is usually faced with deciding whether to continue to support the cat as its condition declines, or humanely put it to sleep.

Humans cannot transmit FeLV from one cat to another. FeLV does not live outside of infected cats, but it is always a good idea to wash your hands and clean thoroughly if an infected cat has been around.

Feline Immunodeficiency Virus

Feline Immunodeficiency Virus (FIV) is in the same family as HIV, but it is not transmissible to humans. Although drug cocktails are currently helping humans with HIV from developing full-blown AIDS, we have not yet made the same strides in veterinary medicine. The good news is that FIV in cats usually does not progress to a debilitating, life-threatening condition.

How Cats Get Infected

FIV is another virus that is passed by direct cat-to-cat contact. It is most commonly transmitted during cat fights when cats bite one another. Not surprisingly, the highest incidence of FIV is found in stray, intact male cats.

It is rare for kittens to be infected with FIV, but it has been documented. Most veterinarians are not worried about FIV in kittens under the age of 6 months.

Diagnosing FIV

Good tests are available for detecting FIV in cats. In-house tests can be completed in about 10 minutes, and the incidence of false positives is less than that of FeLV. One of the most popular in clinic tests checks for FeLV and FIV at the same time. To confirm a positive test, a test called a Western Blot can be sent out to a lab.

If a cat fits the demographic profile—outdoor and male—then a positive test is most likely truly positive. Whereas FeLV makes cats very sick, FIV is comparatively subtle. Cats are diagnosed with FIV when they are tested as new additions to a home or if a general blood panel is run that includes viral tests. FIV is not typically suspected as a primary diagnosis.

Even though this cat looks normal, it should be tested for FeLV and FIV before being introduced into a new home.

The Impact of FIV

FIV does not cause cancer like FeLV can, but it does suppress a cat's immune system. It usually is not a fatal disease, and there are few external clinical signs. I have been surprised when doing blood tests on cats as old as 18 years and finding a positive FIV test.

Cats infected with FIV will have a harder time when they are fighting other infections. They need more supportive care and a longer course of antibiotics when they have bacterial infections. They can handle anesthesia if needed, and they can tolerate other routine health care. It is important to extend treatments beyond normal durations when dealing with FIV positive cats.

One clinical sign commonly seen with FIV-positive cats is gum disease. They can have red, inflamed, malodorous gums that do not respond to brushing. If your cat has bad gums, FIV status should be checked because it will affect how well the cat will respond to treatment.

Care for FIV-Positive Cats

Currently no vaccine is available to protect a cat against FIV. Some pharmaceutical companies are working on developing vaccines, so these may be an option in the future.

There is a controversy in veterinary medicine over what should be done with stray cats that test positively for FIV. These animals can live relatively normal lives, but they are a potential source of viral spread. It is not recommended to bring an FIV-positive cat into a household with FIV-negative cats, but the animal could be a good pet in a single-cat home or in a home with other positive cats. If no one wants the cat, and it will be returned to an outdoor life, euthanasia may be considered.

Avoid CATastrophe

The most important thing an owner of an FIV-positive cat can do is to keep the cat indoors. Indoor living fulfills two purposes—it decreases the cat's exposure to infectious agents, and it prevents the cat from spreading the disease to other cats.

Feline Infectious Peritonitis

Feline Infectious Peritonitis (FIP) is one of the most frustrating and scary diseases in veterinary medicine. It is frustrating because of the difficulty in making a definitive diagnosis, and it is scary because there is no cure. I hate to mention FIP to owners of a sick cat, even if it is to tell them that their cat *doesn't* have it. I know explaining it will be hard and proving it may be even harder.

So What Is FIP?

FIP is a coronavirus. Feline coronaviruses are common and usually don't cause many problems in affected cats. The current theory is that FIP is a mutation of a common virus called Feline Enteric Corona Virus (FECV). Why this virus mutates to become deadly FIP in some cats is not known. It is possible that stress, genetics, a poor immune system, and concurrent diseases may predispose a cat to developing FIP.

The clinical signs associated with FIP can include:

➤ Fever

➤ Failure to gain weight or weight loss

➤ Lethargy

➤ Poor appetite

➤ Vomiting

➤ Diarrhea

➤ Fluid buildup in the abdominal or chest cavities

➤ Neurological disorders

There are two forms of FIP: wet and dry. The wet form is the "classic" disease, in which fluid builds up in a cat's abdominal and/or chest cavity, making the animal uncomfortable and giving a potbellied appearance. In the dry form, the virus is present but does not create fluid.

Cats with FIP have a waxing-to-waning illness. This means that they have good days and bad days, so an owner may not be able to tell how sick the cat really is. Progression of signs is slow, and cats with FIP can have undiagnosed illness for months.

A kitten can be exposed to FECV by its mother, start off fairly normally, and then develop full-blown FIP at even 2 years of age. Fortunately, the mutation to FIP usually occurs in only a small percentage of cats, and in a litter of four kittens, one could become infected and die and the others could grow up normally.

Building a Diagnosis of FIP

Diagnosing FIP is like putting a puzzle together. The only test that conclusively diagnoses the disease is a tissue biopsy with the classic "pyogranulomatous" lesions. Performing exploratory surgery to obtain a biopsy is not what most owners, with a gravely sick cat and a poor prognosis, want to do.

Avoid CATastrophe

Although it may be called an FIP titer, the commonly run corona virus titer present on many blood panels is *not* diagnostic for FIP. Cats truly infected with FIP can have positive or negative tests, and normal cats that have been exposed to FECV can actually have positive tests. An FIP titer alone means nothing.

Instead, the diagnosis is presumptively based on other tests and typical clinical signs. The tests that can be performed are:

➤ Complete blood count (CBC)

➤ Blood chemistries

➤ Corona virus titer (KIP titer)

➤ 7B ELISA for FIP

➤ X-rays

➤ Fluid analysis

➤ FIP PCR

A lack of response to supportive therapy and not being able to pinpoint any other disease, along with suspicious test results, can lead to a presumption of FIP. In a multi-cat household it is not necessary to isolate an FIP suspect because all of the cats will have undergone the same coronavirus exposure, and odds are that no one else will get sick.

Dealing with FIP

Owners of cats suspected of having FIP are faced with the tragic decision of ending their cat's life as body condition and quality of life diminishes. Veterinarians can help support the sick animals with fluids, antibiotics, anti-inflammatories, and immunostimulants, but the ultimate outcome will be the same. Veterinarians are researching ways to effectively treat FIP, so there is hope for the future.

What About the FIP Vaccine?

A vaccine is available that claims to protect cats against FIP, but the veterinary community has questioned its effectiveness. Independent studies on this vaccine have not clinically proven that it protects significantly under normal conditions.

The vaccine is considered to be safe and is likely most useful for cats that have not had any previous exposure to FECV. Figuring out who those cats are is the question.

Decreasing Risk

FIP occurs most frequently in purebred cats that come from catteries, and in cats that have come from shelters. This is because exposure to FIP is higher in environments with many cats, and larger multi-cat facilities have more stresses and less ability to isolate sick cats.

Purebred cats may also be more at risk due to genetics and weaker immune systems. The more closely related cats are, the fewer different genes there are to make their systems stronger.

To try to decrease the risk of FIP, take these steps:

Worth a Paws

If a purebred cat breeder tells you he has never had a case of FIP in his cattery, don't believe him. Odds are that if a breeder has been in business for a few years and has bred multiple litters, FIP has occurred at one time or another.

1. If you go to a cattery or shelter, pick a big, healthy-looking kitten and have it examined by a veterinarian.

2. Isolate the new kitten from other cats for at least a week to monitor its health.

3. Allow the kitten to adjust to its new environment before performing any elective procedures.

4. Decrease environmental stresses on the animal.

5. Keep litterboxes and food bowls clean.

6. Feed the kitten a good-quality diet and be sure that it is eating.

Even if you follow these suggestions, there is no guarantee you will prevent FIP. FIP occurs in only a small percentage of the cat population, but it is devastating if it affects your cat.

Filling the Loss

If you have had the sad and tragic experience of losing a cat to FIP, you may wonder when and if you should get a new cat. Veterinarians disagree on this issue. Research shows that FIP can live in the environment for months, but, in reality, if you throw away disposable items that the sick cat used and clean any other inanimate objects with a solution of 1 part bleach to 10 parts water, the risks of transmission are slim.

I think that the best replacement is an unrelated kitten or cat that is at least 16 weeks old and appears hearty and healthy. But unfortunately there are no guarantees with FIP.

Could Your Cat Be Rabid?

Rabies is a virus that can affect any warm-blooded animal. In certain parts of the country, rabies is present in a large number of wild animals, so the risk of exposure to outdoor cats is high. Depending on where you live, laws may mandate that your cat be vaccinated against rabies.

Animals infected with rabies usually die within weeks because the virus attacks cells in their brains. Skunks and bats can carry rabies but not develop outward signs of disease.

Vaccinating Against Rabies

The recommended protocol for immunizing a cat against rabies is to give the first vaccine at 3 to 4 months of age, repeat the vaccine one year later, and then re-vaccinate every three years. Some states require a different schedule by law, but your veterinarian will know the rules. If a rabies vaccine is not legally required in your state and your cat does not go outdoors, it can be an optional vaccine. But if your cat *does* go outdoors, you should consider vaccination whether or not it's legally required in your state.

You might also consider vaccinating your cat against rabies if the cat is aggressive and ever bites humans. If a bite wound requires medical attention, the doctor performing the treatment is required to report the bite to local animal control authorities. Any animal that bites a human is placed under some type of quarantine, but unvaccinated animals are placed under stricter rules.

Signs of Rabies

People occasionally joke about "looking like a rabid dog"—this expression is used to describe somebody or something with wide-open eyes and drool on their lips! However, these are actual clinical signs seen in cases of rabies.

Because rabies affects the brain, seizures, blindness, clumsiness, drooling, and behavioral changes are seen in afflicted animals. I hope that none of you ever come in contact with a rabid animal because if there is any risk that exposure has occurred, humans have to go through a battery of multiple, painful injections.

Meow Wow

As gruesome as it sounds, the suspicious animal must be dead to definitively diagnose rabies. The diagnosis is made by observing characteristic changes in the animal's brain.

"Parvo" for Cats

Feline panleukopenia is actually feline parvovirus. The incidence of this disease is extremely low because of the effectiveness of the currently available vaccines. Today the infrequent cases that are seen are in stray cats or cats in animal shelters that have never been vaccinated. Panleukopenia is a component of kitten vaccines and the basic booster that most adult cats receive.

Signs of Panleukopenia

Cats infected with this virus can have fevers and diarrhea that do not respond to treatment. It takes a few weeks after an animal is vaccinated for protective immunity to be conferred, so a kitten that was recently vaccinated could still be at risk.

Testing for Panleukopenia

The definitive diagnostic test for panleukopenia is an extremely low white blood cell count. The term "panleukopenia" actually breaks down as "pan" ("all"), "leuko" ("white cells"), "penia" ("low count"). Another way that this virus can be diagnosed is by doing a canine parvovirus test on an affected cat's stool or blood. The viruses are so similar that the test can diagnose both.

What's the Prognosis?

Most cats with panleukopenia die from the virus, but if the disease is diagnosed early and the animal receives enough supportive care, there is a chance of recovery. The virus attacks the rapidly growing cells in the body so the stomach, intestines, heart, and brain are the organs most affected.

The Least You Need to Know

➤ Viruses are microorganisms that have no specific treatment.

➤ Vaccines are available to protect cats against some types of viral infections.

➤ Cats that are FeLV-positive and are sick have a grave prognosis.

➤ FIV-infected cats can have normal life spans, but can be contagious their entire lives.

➤ FIP is a complicated disease without any cure.

➤ Rabies is passed by animal bites.

➤ Feline "parvo" is called panleukopenia.

Part 5
Problems with Cats

We would love to think that our cats are perfectly adjusted creatures, but, unfortunately, this is not always the case. Cats are basically asocial, and they are forced to conform to the environment that we place them in. Not only do cats have to worry about getting along with us, but they are often forced to interact with other animals.

Most cats are able to cope without problems, but cats that are unhappy about their home environments can let us know about their displeasure through undesirable behaviors. Owners need to be aware of these behaviors so that they can keep an upper hand on the situation.

Although they are easy to care for, cats are a long-term responsibility, and their needs must be considered whenever our lives change. We also need to be concerned about how cat ownership can affect our health and lifestyle.

All of these issues are addressed in the following chapters.

Chapter 22

Sssss!

Does Your Cat Play Nicely with Its Friends?

In This Chapter

➤ What it takes to handle a multi-cat home

➤ Learn what you can do about strays

➤ How can you keep strange cats out of your yard?

➤ How to prevent cat fights

The average cat-owning home in the United States has 2.1 cats, so chances are that if you are a cat owner, you will have more than one. Although we may force them to live in pairs or groups, is that really what a cat wants? Cats are usually described as being "asocial"—able to cohabit with others, but preferring to be alone.

Behaviorists who have studied feline social interaction note that cats set up their own territories, and their interaction may be based more on avoidance than direct contact. Cats communicate through vision and marking behaviors and do not distribute themselves randomly in an environment. Even if your cat doesn't spray urine to mark territory, face-rubbing and scratching leave scents behind. Creating a harmonious environment for both cats and humans is the goal. Benefits of having two or more cats are that they are company for each other and their play interaction keeps them fit and trim.

How Many Is Too Many?

Just how many cats belong in one home? This is a hard question to answer and I always feel like I'm shooting myself in the foot when I discourage owners from adding to their menageries. I am in the business of helping cats, so the more the merrier; but, in reality, more cats can mean more problems.

If you want to have more than one cat in a household, you need to think about:

➤ How much space you have

➤ How much time you have for cleaning and care

➤ How much money you have for food and health costs

➤ How to cope if your cats do not get along

The Top Cat

Experienced cat owners know that cats like to rule a home. As much as you think you are making the cat conform to your rules, the cat is just as much putting you in your place. The same is true with other cats because cats do have a social order, and one cat will usually be dominant.

Meow Wow

Selective breeding of purebred cats has created some behavioral characteristics. Siamese cats are generally regarded as a social breed of cat, but some lines can be aggressive or shy. When choosing a cat, try to evaluate its relatives for sociability. It will give you a better idea about what the cat will act like.

In feral cat colonies, a male cat is usually the dominant individual, and the other cats have the same social position. This can create confusion for the cats when food conflict arises, so instead of fighting or retreating, equal-status cats may share. In a home setting, my experience is that a female is usually the dominant cat, and even if she is not the biggest cat, she will have the last word in a conflict.

To a cat, space is important, and each cat has its personal distance and its social distance. The animal will decide who it will allow in its intimate personal space without becoming upset. Unfamiliar people or other animals may only be tolerated in its larger social space.

Young or Old?

You know your own cat best, and you know if the animal has had good relationships with other cats in its life or if it has never been exposed to other cats. You need to give this some thought when deciding on adding another cat.

Most of the time I will suggest that if an owner already has an adult, the new addition should be a kitten. A kitten will not know that it can claim territory in the home, and at least (at first), should submit to the established cat. On the other hand, a senior cat may be quite intolerant of a young kitten jumping and biting it all the time. Be sure to confine the kitten enough so that the other cat is not overwhelmed.

By introducing two kittens to the home at the same time, you have a very good chance for success. The kittens will develop socially alongside each other and concurrently determine their spaces and preferences. One will likely become dominant as it matures, but they will both understand the situation.

These two kittens arrived as a "package deal" that worked out well for them and for their owners. (Photograph by Andy Jones)

Male or Female?

Personalities of male and female cats do differ, and I suggest that you choose a cat that appears to be well socialized. Some people recommend getting a cat of the opposite sex of the one that you have. I don't know how much it really matters, except that hormones can trigger conflicts between cats of the same sex; so to have a harmonious home, be sure to spay and neuter all cats before the onset of puberty.

The Transition

Cats that feel like their territory has been invaded will show their displeasure through behaviors. These behaviors can include:

➤ Aggression

➤ Hiding

249

➤ House-soiling

➤ Excessive or insufficient grooming

➤ Overeating or undereating

➤ Failure to bury feces

There is no set time period for acceptance between cats to occur. Some cats will tolerate a new cat right away, some will take weeks, and others merely co-habitate with minimal interaction. The real issue is what you can handle.

And the Answer Is...

It is impossible to make a firm recommendation on how many cats is too many. A general rule is that in an indoor environment, two cats will usually do fine, but once there are three or more, conflicts can arise. There are many happy households with three or more cats, and the keys are providing enough litterboxes (one per cat), scooping boxes at least once daily, spacing out food bowls, and setting aside enough time to give each individual cat plenty of attention.

If you have not had problems introducing several cats, you are lucky, but you will find that behavioral changes do occur. If cats are slowly familiarized with one another and not just tossed together, the effects of overcrowding can be minimized.

The Problem with Strays

The disturbing number of unwanted cats in the United States makes any animal lover sad. Unfortunately, because many cats are able to survive on their own, people think that they can just be dumped and will turn out okay. This is not the case.

Cats can usually live on their own as strays, and they can form feral colonies in which the intact cats continue to reproduce. The best way to manage feral cat colonies and individual strays is controversial. Some people want to eradicate them and euthanize all of the animals. Others want to vaccinate, sterilize, and release the cats back to the wild.

Meow Wow

"Moggie" is a British term used to describe a stray tomcat. We don't have any equivalent term in the United States. If you hear an Englishman call a cat "an old tom mog," you'll know what he means.

Really Lost, or Just Cruisin'?

Cats that are allowed outdoors will often wander down the street and through the neighborhood. Because many of these cats are not wearing collars or any other type of visible identification, their ownership is uncertain. If you leave food outside or have a pet door into your house, a bold outdoor cat might visit you.

If a cat is frequenting your yard, and you are able to approach it, you should look for identification. If none is found, you should look at the overall health and condition of the animal and see if it looks like it needs help. Some cats that are owned by neighbors are very good at looking pathetic and begging for food, but they are usually in good shape.

Consider asking neighbors and posting signs to locate the cat's owner. If an owner is not found, you will have to decide whether you want to take in the cat, take it to the animal shelter, or leave it alone. You might also take the cat to a veterinarian who can scan it for a microchip, a type of ID that is injected under the skin.

All in the Family

If you want to bring a stray cat into your household, you should keep it isolated from other cats until you have it examined by a veterinarian. A veterinarian will want to give the animal a clean bill of health and make sure that it is not carrying FeLV or FIV (see Chapter 21) before you introduce it into your home. He will also want to be sure that the stray is not bringing any fleas or other parasites into your household.

Introducing a stray is the same as bringing in any new kitten or cat, so you need to be prepared. You will want to isolate the cat when it is not supervised so that you can feel comfortable about litterbox use, eating, and scratching behavior.

If the stray was used to being an outdoor cat, the transition to indoor living may be rough. If you do allow the animal to go outside, be sure that you place some type of identification on it. Options for identification are:

➤ Collar and tag

➤ Ear-tag

➤ Microchip

➤ Tattoo

If you need to wait for an ID tag to be engraved, use a ballpoint pen or permanent marker to write the cat's name and your telephone number on the collar.

Can a Stray Fit In?

A stray cat can become a loving member of your home, but if the animal was born wild and not socialized to humans during the critical 5- to 8-week age period, things may be very difficult. Don't expect too much even if it seems like the cat has lived with people before. You have to earn a cat's trust; it is not something that you can force.

The best approach is to go slowly. Cats have to feel comfortable with a situation before they will be calm and relaxed. Use praise and food rewards when the cat behaves in a manner that you want to reinforce.

No Trespassing

You may do your best to keep your cat inside and protected, but other cats in the neighborhood that go outside or strays may decide that your yard in is their territory. This may or may not be a problem, depending on the behavior of all of the cats involved.

In most areas there are no leash laws for cats. It is up to an owner to decide whether or not he wants to let his cat outside. Sometimes a cat will insist on going out, and the owner permits it to do so for the sake of his sanity.

Worth a Paws

If you have a bird feeder or bird-bath, you may actually be inviting neighborhood cats into your yard. How can they pass up the opportunity to have their own bird-hunting ground? You will have to decide how far you are willing to go to rid or repel the intruders.

An Uninvited Guest

Your indoor cat could actually feel threatened by an outdoor intruder. In this situation your cat might hide, spray, or even become aggressive toward you or other animals in the house. On the other hand, your cat may not care and might even like playing through the window with an outdoor cat.

The outdoor cat may just like cruising its territory and stopping by at your house to see how things are going, or it may want to exert dominance over its claimed territory and mark your house with urine. The outdoor animal may like to use your lawn or garden as its personal bathroom, which you may find unpleasant.

Discouraging Trespassers

If you want to keep a cat out of your yard, here are a few steps that can help:

1. Don't leave any food or water outside.
2. Cover any outdoor sandboxes.
3. Squirt the intruder with a hose when it enters your yard.

4. Place pet repellants around your house and garden (mothballs can do the job).

5. Wash down, neutralize, and deodorize any areas where urine spraying has occurred.

6. Get a dog (but not *just* for this purpose—dogs need attention and training!).

7. Modify a fence to make jumping over it more difficult.

Local animal control officials will not trap cats, but they will pick them up from your home if you have them confined. I do not recommend doing this unless you know that the cat is not owned. If you know who owns the cat, consider having a friendly conversation and expressing your concerns. If the person is not sympathetic to your wishes, you do have rights to protect your property within reason.

Kitty-to-Kitty Conflicts

In a perfect world all cats would get along. Unfortunately, the world is not perfect. Just like people, cats can be jealous, dominant, and territorial. When conflicts between cats erupt, the parties may back off or they may fight. Cats that live together usually develop a "comfort level" with each other and the fighting that does occur does not get out of hand. Cats that do not live together may go to war.

Fortunately these two housemates get along well and even groom each other.

War Wounds and Battle Scars

If your cat goes outdoors and you go to work, you may have no idea what happens to it during the day. Most cats sun themselves or patrol their territory, but others are very protective and will challenge intruders or try to take over new territory themselves.

You may see a scab here and there or hair strewn across the yard as indications that kitties have not been playing nicely. If so, take some time and check your cat over carefully. Because of their hair, wounds and punctures on cats may not be readily visible.

Often the signs of injuries are not apparent for one to two days after a fight. This is when swelling, pain, and infection take over. Undetected wounds that are allowed to fester can turn into abscesses. Abscesses are pockets of infection, characterized by pus, under the skin.

Dealing with Abscesses

Once a wound has abscessed, a veterinarian should care for it. Even if you think you have got the infection licked, chances are that it is still there and will blow up again. Abscesses are painful wounds. Cats with abscesses usually have fevers and are depressed.

Treating abscesses usually involves these steps:

1. Anesthetizing or sedating the cat
2. Clipping the affected area
3. Cleaning and surgically prepping the area
4. Lancing the abscess
5. Flushing out the pus
6. Cutting away infected and damaged tissues
7. Placing a drain
8. Suturing the wound closed
9. Treating with antibiotics
10. Placing an Elizabethan collar on the animal to protect the surgery site

Worth a Paws

To try to prevent infection, clean any wounds as soon as possible with hydrogen peroxide, which won't sting like alcohol. (If you use alcohol your kitty may never forgive you!) Clean wounds one to two times daily and apply warm compresses if swelling starts to build. If you start to notice a bad smell or discharge, turn the care over to your veterinarian.

Reducing the Likelihood of Abscesses

There are many steps involved to properly care for an abscess, and as you might expect, treating an abscess can be expensive. The best way to prevent an abscess is to prevent their cause—cat fights. Steps you can take to reduce the incidence of fighting are:

➤ Keep your cat indoors.

➤ Spay or neuter your cat before it reaches puberty (less roaming and aggression).

➤ Discourage intruding cats from entering your yard.

If you are home and hear cats fighting, be careful. You don't want to get injured while breaking up a cat fight. Make loud noises or squirt the animals with water to break things up. If your cat has been in a fight, examine it right away. Sites of punctures may be moist from saliva—clean them with hydrogen peroxide. If you are concerned about the severity of the wounds, take the cat to your veterinarian and get it started on antibiotics. Early treatment with drugs can prevent abscesses from forming.

Bigger than a Cat

If your cat goes outside, cat fights may be the least of your worries. Bigger creatures (and cars) may be more of a threat. Sometimes a cat will roam and end up face to face with an unfriendly dog. If you live in an area with coyotes, these animals will consider your cat a meal. Other wild animals such as opossums and raccoons will only fight with a cat over food. You cannot train your cat to watch out for these other dangers, so you must be prepared to deal with the consequences.

Dog attacks can cause serious injuries to cats. Dogs like to bite and then shake their adversaries, and this can cause trauma to the neck, spine, and legs of the cat. X-rays are needed to check for fractures, luxations, and internal injuries.

Most cats do not survive being attacked by a coyote. Dogs fight to protect territory, but coyotes want lunch. Coyotes tend to hunt from dusk to dawn, so these are especially important times to keep your cat inside. However, coyotes have become "urbanized" in many communities and are not afraid to walk down the street during the day. If you live in an area like this, your cat is at risk at all times.

You can decrease the risk of opossum and raccoons in your yard by never leaving any food out for pets. Putting secure lids on trash cans will also discourage these animals from coming into your yard, finding an easy meal, and coming in contact with your cat.

Avoid CATstrophe

If your cat goes outside and is at risk for fighting with other cats, vaccinate it against FeLV and rabies. If a vaccine for FIV becomes available, consider protecting against that virus as well. All three viruses can be passed by cat bites.

Worth a Paws

Coyotes tend to hunt more aggressively during the spring when they are feeding their young. They will also take more risks for food when their wild habitat is invaded and decreased by human developers.

The Least You Need to Know

➤ If you choose to create a multi-cat household, you need to be prepared to deal with some possible problems.

➤ Stray cats can become good pets.

➤ There are safe ways of keeping trespassing cats out of your yard.

➤ Cat-fight wounds can progress to more serious abscesses.

➤ Outdoor cats are in danger of being attacked by other animals.

Chapter 23

Keeping Kitty Problems from Getting Out of Hand

In This Chapter

➤ What you can do about undesirable kitty behaviors

➤ The best methods for flea control

➤ How to protect your cat from seasonal and holiday dangers

Domestication of the cat has taken thousands of years. Because cats can live on their own in the wild, some people question whether we can even call the cat domesticated. The process of feline domestication did not take the typical course of selective breeding to produce gentleness as occurred with other species. Instead, cat breeding has gone through periods in history when it has been selective and random, depending on whether cats have fallen in or out of favor.

Purebred cats of today are the result of selected breeding, but random breeding produces the more common domestic shorthaired cat. Selective breeding has not necessarily been focused on creating a cat that can live perfectly in a human world. Because of this we must find a balance between natural cat instincts and what we can tolerate in our homes.

When Your Good Kitty Does Bad Things

In Part 1 of this book I focused on getting a kitten off to a good start and training it so that undesirable behaviors would be eliminated. The behaviors we discussed were biting, scratching, improper litterbox use, and jumping up on things. In this chapter we will cover other problems, including excessive grooming, aggression, house-soiling, and excessive vocalization.

Worth a Paws

If you notice a sudden increase in frequency and size of hairballs, check out your cat's grooming habits. Cats that groom excessively ingest more hair and are therefore more likely to produce hairballs.

Licking

Some cats don't know when to quit when it comes to grooming themselves. The cause of excessive grooming may be itchiness related to a form of dermatitis, or it can be strictly due to a nervous behavior. A veterinarian should examine a cat that is pulling out its hair in order to determine the cause.

The cause of excessive grooming is deemed behavioral if physical reasons are ruled out. We wish that we could ask cats why they are doing what they are doing, but this is not possible. I like to compare excessive grooming in the cat to humans who bite their fingernails. Both are habits that become subconscious and can be difficult to control.

Cats may excessively groom due to nervousness, boredom, or to get more attention. Possible treatments for this condition include deterrents such as bad-tasting sprays and Elizabethan collars, behavior modification, and anti-anxiety medication. It can take weeks to reverse this behavior.

Avoid CATastrophe

Cats are not dogs, so if you see a cat wagging or thumping its tail, don't mistake the behavior for happiness. Cats swish their tails when they are mad! Watch out!

Kitty's Being Mean!

Cats may bite or scratch humans as a defensive mechanism—such as when a child pulls on a cat's tail—but aggression is not acceptable. Some cats give warning signs that they are about to blow their fuse by hissing or growling, but others just strike out. You need to use caution any time you are handling a cat that has previously shown aggressive tendencies.

One confusing type of aggression that some cats demonstrate is petting-induced aggression. Unfortunately my hospital cat, Henry, is afflicted with this unwanted condition. Cats with this behavior will sit contentedly on your lap and act like they are enjoying being petted, then suddenly they will turn and bite. This syndrome is seen more commonly in male cats, but the cause is not known. Two theories are:

1. Cats don't know how to tell you to quit when they are tired of your petting, so they bite.

2. Cats find the petting so pleasurable that they fall into a light sleep, but then startle and feel confined, so they strike out.

You can decrease the chances of being bitten in this situation if you refrain from petting the cat, even if it jumps on your lap. Become more aware of the subtle signs the cat may exhibit right before biting and back off. You can also consider treating the cat with anti-anxiety medications or female hormones.

Cats can exhibit aggression because they are fearful. I personally am very familiar with this situation because it happens daily in my veterinary clinic. Owners are shocked when their little sweetheart turns into a woman-eating lion during its examination. Speaking in a quiet voice and moving slowly will calm some cats, but others already have their minds made up and are not going to submit to examination quietly.

Using protective clothing and gloves helps my staff to protect themselves in these situations. We hate to see our patients get so upset. It's hard on the animal and makes it hard for us to do a thorough job. We prescribe a mild tranquilizer to be administered before the next visit, if possible.

Just like people, some cats will redirect their aggression. Your cat may be stressed or upset by something else, but it takes it out on you. For example, your cat might hear or smell another cat outside, feel threatened, and respond by biting or growling at you. Trying to eliminate the source of stress and squirting a cat with water if it attacks are ways to manage the problem.

A final cause for cats becoming aggressive toward their owners is if they are sick or suffering neurological disease. If your cat has a sudden behavior change and becomes aggressive, you should have it examined for medical problems.

Meow Wow

Cats with feline hyperesthesia syndrome will bite at the air when you touch the end of their spine or tail base. This syndrome is most commonly found in overweight cats that have difficulty grooming and have fleas. Treatment may involve flea control, grooming, anti-inflammatories, and even anticonvulsants. These animals can look like they are having a minor seizure.

House-soiling

House-soiling is a very frustrating problem for cat owners because the cat they know and love is destroying their house. An entire book could be written about all the options and treatments for this condition, but the bottom line is that no one can

Kitty Ditty

House-soiling and inappropriate elimination are two terms used interchangeably to describe urination and/or defecation outside of the litterbox on a horizontal surface. They are not the same as spraying, which is directed onto a vertical surface.

Avoid CATastrophe

Never use ammonia containing products to clean up urine or feces, especially if a cat eliminates outside of the litterbox. Ammonia will actually intensify the odors of the waste products you are trying to eliminate. Your best bet is to use specially formulated pet-odor neutralizers.

promise a cure. In almost every case the problem can be solved, but it takes a committed owner and early intervention. The longer the problem has existed, the longer it will take to extinguish.

I get frustrated myself when owners bring in a cat that they have allowed to eliminate outside of its litterbox for years and then want the problem quickly fixed because they are getting new carpet. I wish it could be that simple.

The keys to eliminating house-soiling are:

➤ Early intervention to stop the behavior

➤ Keeping the litterbox immaculately clean

➤ Making sure the box is in a convenient location

➤ Providing a litterbox for every cat in the home

➤ Giving the cat a type of litter it likes

➤ Ruling out any medical problems with the cat

➤ Using drug intervention when behavior modification fails

There are so many factors that can trigger a cat to stop or only intermittently use its litterbox that I use a questionnaire with owners when they bring a house-soiler in for an examination. An owner may not detect problems or stresses that the cat is experiencing, and the situation needs to be evaluated from the cat's perspective.

Multiple steps may be needed to get inappropriate elimination under control. Proper cleaning of the litterbox and environment are always the first step in treatment. Behavior modification is next. If all else fails, drug therapy should be considered.

There are a handful of drugs that can be used to try to control inappropriate elimination. Most of them are safe, even with long-term use, but the cat should be monitored regularly for side effects. In some situations a short course of medication stops the problem. In others the cat may be on medication indefinitely. Most of the anti-anxiety drugs available take one to two weeks to evaluate effectiveness. Initially they may make a cat sleepy or dopey, but this effect usually resolves within four to five days.

Turn It Down!

Excessive vocalization can be an annoying behavior of a cat. Some breeds, such as Siamese, are known for being talkative, but others may vocalize excessively and demand constant attention. A move, trauma, or some other significant change in the cat's schedule can trigger this behavior. It can occur in older cats that lose hearing and vision and become disoriented. High blood pressure, pain, or neurological disease can also trigger excessive vocalization.

If you have a young, healthy cat, establishing a routine where you give the cat your undivided attention for a few minutes twice a day can help. This is a good time to involve the animal in interactive play.

If you have an older animal, a veterinarian should examine it so that any medical triggers for the behavior can be treated. If no medical problems are found and the cat's senses of vision and hearing are normal, a senile syndrome called "cognitive dysfunction" should be considered. Medication is available that can improve this condition, although it is not currently approved for use in cats.

If you have tried everything and the cat won't stop howling, tranquilizers or anti-anxiety medications may be needed to manage the problem.

The War on Fleas

Even though I see fleas almost every day in practice, I still want to itch when I see a cat covered in fleas. Flea control was revolutionized in the mid-'90s by once-a-month flea products that are safe and effective.

The flea is a very hearty little creature, and it has been able to survive every attack aimed to destroy it throughout time by mutating and becoming resistant to chemicals. Although some of the current products are extremely effective at eliminating fleas, chances are that resistant fleas will evolve at some point and we'll have to find new products.

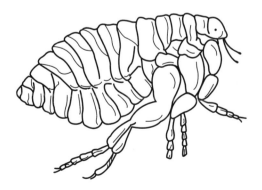

Fleas have been the bane of our pets for years, but new developments in flea control are quite effective.

Avoid CATastrophe

Many flea control products are not specifically formulated for cats and kittens. To protect your pet from poisoning, read the labels carefully. If you have questions regarding flea control, get advice from your veterinarian or his staff. With all due respect for pet store clerks, this is an area where professional guidance is a must.

Available Ammunition

There are many products that can be used in the war on fleas, including:

➤ Shampoos

➤ Dips

➤ Sprays

➤ Powders

➤ Collars

➤ Foams

➤ Foggers

➤ House sprays

➤ Dehydrating compounds

➤ Oral and injectable insect developmental inhibitors

➤ Spot-on adulticides

One of the cheapest and easiest items to have in your arsenal is a flea comb. Flea combs are excellent grooming tools even if fleas are not present. If fleas *are* present, the flea comb will let you know by trapping flea dirt and live fleas in its teeth. The flea comb can be a gauge of the effectiveness of your total flea control.

Getting the Best Guns

The once-a-month products that are available through veterinarians are among the best products you can use on your cat. The only disadvantage to these products is their cost, and if you have a large, multi-cat household, they may be cost-prohibitive. If you have a small household, ease and effectiveness justify the expense.

Some manufacturers have tried to copy the packaging and marketing of the prescription products, but don't be fooled. For spot-on products that kill adult fleas, fipronil and imidacloprid (the generic names for Frontline and Advantage) are recommended; products containing permethrin are *not* recommended. For oral or injectable inhibitor treatment, lufenuron (Program) is recommended.

Imidacloprid and fipronil are applied to the back of a cat's head, move over the skin's surface, and kill fleas that jump on the animal within a few hours. These chemicals are insecticides that were originally developed for use on the crops that we eat, and do not enter the cat's body.

Lufenuron is ingested or injected into a cat, and the chemical enters the cat's blood. The chemical is a *chitin* inhibitor. Because chitin is a protein only found in insects, it has no effect on the cat. Fleas that suck on a cat treated with lufenuron will not die, but the eggs they lay will not be able to hatch and immature stages of fleas exposed to the chemical will not be able to develop into adults. This is why lufenuron is considered a developmental inhibitor.

To achieve the highest level of flea control, a combination of a development inhibitor and an adulticide can be used. This combination has the best chance of preventing resistant fleas from developing because the products work in different ways. Imidocloprid and lufenuron or fipronil and lufenuron can be safely used together.

Kitty Ditty

Chitin is the component of a flea's external skeleton that makes it hard. If you have ever tried to squash a flea with the fleshy part of your finger, you know that the skeleton protects the flea and you have to use your nail.

Other Casualties to Consider

Fleas can bite humans but they can only live off of the blood of dogs and cats. If fleas are biting you, it is because they are desperately hungry. Immature stages of fleas can live for long periods of time in your carpet, so if you come back from vacation and get attacked by fleas, you'll know why.

Aside from being a nuisance and discomfort to your cat, fleas can:

➤ Cause anemia

➤ Transmit tapeworms

➤ Spread disease

➤ Trigger allergic reactions

With so many effective flea control products around, fleas are no longer a fact of life for a cat. Even though fleas will jump on cats that go outdoors, they will die if they choose animals treated with imidacloprid and fipronil. If a cat has been treated with lufenuron, the flea will not be able to produce live offspring, so the life cycle is halted.

'Tis the Season

You should be aware of seasonal dangers that face your cat so that you can plan ahead to prevent accidents. Springtime seems to be a good time for cats, but summer, fall, and winter bring hazardous conditions.

Worth a Paws

Normal body temperature for a cat is 100.5 degrees to 102.5 degrees F; values above 106 degrees F can be life-threatening.

Summertime

Heat can be a threat to your cat, especially if it is confined in an area without air-conditioning or proper ventilation. Cars and garages can become heat traps, and if an animal is not found in time, it can die. If you find an animal that is suffering heatstroke, immerse it in cold water as soon as possible to try to bring the temperature down, then contact your veterinarian right away.

Aside from heat, another summertime danger is air-conditioning coolant solutions. The chemical found in coolant/antifreeze products is typically ethylene glycol, a potent toxin to the kidneys. Cats may drink coolant if it leaks from a car radiator because it has an appealing taste, and if they do, the prognosis is poor. Check your car for leaks and use safer propylene glycol coolants if your cat spends time in the garage.

Fireworks on the fourth of July can frighten your cat, so if the noise can be heard near your home, keep your cat inside so that it does not run away. Keeping your cat in will also protect it from people who think firecrackers and cats make a funny combination.

Trick or Treat

Black cats are a familiar symbol of Halloween, but some people take the bad luck associated with them too far. To protect them from possible abuse, most animal shelters will not adopt out black cats during the weeks before Halloween. If you have a black cat, keep it safely indoors around Halloween.

Christmas and Chanukah

The year-end holidays pose many potential risks to cats, such as the lure of decorations, plants, and food. Party guests might let your cat out by accident, or it may slip unnoticed out an open door. Your cat might be smart enough to stay away from things that could harm it, but unfortunately curiosity can be dangerous.

Candles can be intriguing to cats, so if you light them during any celebration, be sure that kitty leaves them alone. Putting them up high is not a sufficient deterrent. Flickering flames are almost irresistible to some cats.

Chocolate is toxic to cats. Many people leave out candy during the holiday season so that it is readily available for guests. Cats do not naturally have a sweet tooth, so if they are not encouraged, they will probably leave candy alone. If a cat shows any interest in chocolate, the safest response is to put it away.

Ribbons are very enticing to cats. We all know how much cats like to play with things on strings, so when you are wrapping presents, be sure kitty is not left alone with the ribbon. Don't give your cat unsupervised access to packages wrapped with ribbons. String-like objects can be deadly to cats if they are ingested and coil up the animal's intestines.

Holiday decorations made with tinsel are also a tease to cats. Many cat toys are made with tinsel on the ends because cats are so attracted to the material. If you use tinsel, place it in areas that you are sure your cat cannot reach, or better yet, decorate with something else.

Cats like to eat plants, and some cats think that a Christmas tree is a giant plant for them to chew on. There is nothing dangerous about pine needles except that they can be an intestinal irritant and may cause your cat to vomit. Holly, mistletoe, and poinsettias should be kept away from cats because they can be severe irritants if ingested.

Worth a Paws

The holidays can be a safe and happy time for cats if owners are aware of potential dangers and keep them to a minimum. If you notice any signs of illness and you suspect that your cat may have ingested something that it shouldn't have, take it to your veterinarian immediately.

This cat doesn't like to chomp on poinsettias—but why take chances? After the holiday photo is taken, move the plants out of harm's reach.

The Least You Need to Know

➤ Early intervention to stop undesirable behaviors is one of the most important keys to success.

➤ Understanding why a cat behaves in a certain way can help you control the problem.

➤ Safe and effective products are available to help your cat win the war against fleas.

➤ If a cat is left in an area without proper ventilation, dangerous heatstroke can occur.

➤ Many of the festive aspects of the holidays are attractive to cats, so try to monitor your cat's behavior and keep it from getting into trouble.

Chapter 24

Special Considerations for Your Cat

In This Chapter

➤ Options for vacationing with or without your cat

➤ Ensuring a safe move with your cat

➤ What you can do if your cat becomes lost

➤ What happens if your cat outlives you?

Our cats play important roles in our lives, but they cannot always be included in our activities. Things come up, changes occur, or we just need a change of pace. We need to know how to accommodate our cats in these situations.

The unexpected also occurs when a cat gets lost or an owner dies. Having some ideas of how to deal with out of the ordinary circumstances could help you in the future.

The Suitcases Are Out; You Know What That Means

Every owner deserves to take a vacation at some time or another, but figuring out what to do with your cat can be a dilemma. It is difficult to decide what is best for the animal, what is best for you, and if these options can work for both.

Owners often feel guilty about their cats when they travel, but the fact is that cats are homebodies, and their idea of a vacation is not the same as yours. When planning a trip, you should know your options for including your cat or leaving the animal behind. Even if you leave your cat at home, it will have an impact on your travel logistics and possibly on your total travel budget.

This cat is not waiting for a vacation, but he is ready for Take Your Cat to Work Day!

For cats that get worked up when traveling, mild tranquilizers can be used. These drugs take the edge off of a cat and make it more quiet and sleepy but able to stand and function. Not every cat will need medication for travel; you will have to be the judge. Ask your veterinarian if you think medication would be useful.

Worth a Paws

Any time a cat needs to travel outside of the home, it should be placed in a secure cat carrier. Another safety option is to use a leash and collar or harness. Even if your cat stays calmly in your arms during transport, a sudden unexpected noise or accident could send the animal out of your control.

Safe and Secure

Just seeing the cat carrier come out can be enough to send a cat under the bed, so you might need a few tricks to get kitty under control. Leaving a carrier out in the open for a day or two before it is needed can decrease the anxiety associated with it. You can use a food treat to lure a cat into a carrier. If all else fails, tip the carrier on its side so that gravity will help you lower your kitty into it. If you have no cat carrier, try a box with a tight-fitting lid. Be sure there are air holes.

If you need to round up multiple kitties, get them confined before you start putting anyone in a carrier. If you don't, you may spend the rest of the day looking for dodgers. Another hint for catching a cat is to use a towel. Wrap the cat up before placing it in a carrier. If you must, use a pillowcase as a temporary carrier. As long as the fabric is not too thick and air can pass through easily, pillowcases can double for short-term cat carriers.

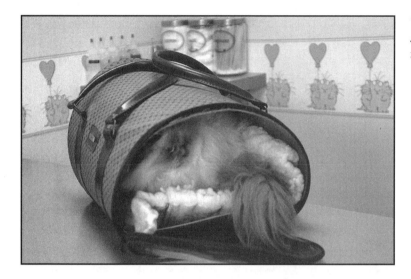

There are different types of safe carriers that can be used for your cat.

Cars, Ick!

There may be some rare exceptions, but most cats hate riding in the car. A car ride usually means one thing—a trip to the veterinarian. You can desensitize your cat by getting it used to travel by driving it other places, or you can ask your veterinarian about using tranquilizers to calm the animal.

Avoid CATastrophe

Cats can quickly face heat stroke if they are left in an unventilated car, or if their carrier is left baking in the sun without good air circulation. Be sure to monitor the temperature in your vehicle, park in the shade when needed, and do not leave your cat unattended for more than a few minutes.

If you are going on a long ride, you probably have concerns about where and when your cat will need to use a litterbox. The reality is that most cats do not eat, drink, or eliminate when they are confined in their carriers. Instead they sit inside and pray for the trip to be over. You can put something absorbent like a towel or newspaper at the bottom of the carrier in case there is an accident, or if you have a large enough carrier, provide a small litterbox.

I would not suggest letting a cat out of its carrier (even inside of your car) at rest stops, unless you have it leashed or harnessed. Cat behavior can be unpredictable in unfamiliar surroundings. My recommendation is to give the cat food and water at night, pick up the bowls at bedtime, travel on an empty stomach, and then give food and water at the end of the next day. Eating and drinking stimulate urination and defecation, so your cat will probably do its business before and after the car ride.

Some owners like to take long trips in motor homes, and cats can become used to this mode of travel. At first the cat may need to acclimate, but most cats can get used to having a home on wheels. Caution would still be needed when exiting the motor home so that the cat stays in, and identification for the cat is a good idea.

Worth a Paws

Some foreign countries have stringent rules for pet entry. If you are thinking of bringing your cat along on a trip abroad, contact the consulate for the destination country so that you can plan accordingly.

Flying the Friendly Skies

It is necessary to do some information-gathering before flying with your cat. Each airline has different rules regarding carrier size and shape, times of day the animal can fly, and the number of pets allowed on each trip. This information will help you coordinate a smooth trip.

Animals traveling interstate or internationally will need a health certificate. This verifies that the animal is in good condition for travel, is not carrying any contagious diseases, and is properly vaccinated for rabies. Health certificates are usually valid for 10 days after they have been written, and they need to be completed by a veterinarian.

If you are taking your cat to Hawaii, contact state officials and plan far ahead of time so that proper arrangements can be made. Animals entering Hawaii must be quarantined for six months unless you prearrange for a shorter quarantine period and follow specific procedures.

Depending on the size of the carrier and whether there is room, some airlines allow cats to be carried on into the passenger cabin rather than traveling as cargo. It is much more desirable to have your cat with you in the cabin, and it is worth the extra effort to pursue this option.

A Room with a View

The policy of some hotels is to allow pets, and most of the time cats are permitted—but you have to decide whether you want to inquire! Unless you put the "Do Not Disturb" sign on the door or keep the animal caged, you should not leave your cat alone in a hotel room. The pet could scurry out when a housekeeper or other staff member opens the door. It is also possible that the housekeeper simply wouldn't know about the cat's presence and would leave the door open.

If you frequently travel with your cat, you can buy a fold-up kitty teepee that zips closed and is large enough to hold food and water bowls and a litterbox. Breeders who travel around the country with their show cats frequently use this item.

Kitty Needs to Stay Home

If your cat does not travel with you, suitable arrangements need to be made for its care. Your options are to board the animal, have a friend or relative come in to provide care, or hire a professional pet sitter. Each cat is different as far as its personal needs and the amount of time that its care requires.

Boarding's Not That Bad

Boarding your cat is not the end of the world. There is no question that a cat would rather stay at home, but being sure it is safe and healthy are assurances that an owner needs when he is away from home. Being confined to a cage is not the most exciting way to spend time, but in reality most cats sleep almost all day anyway.

Before boarding your cat you should check out any facilities that you are considering. It is a good idea to find out what services are provided as part of the regular boarding "package" and what services are available if you are willing to pay for them.

Take along a pad of paper and make notes about:

➤ The cleanliness of the facilities

➤ The size of the cages

➤ Whether veterinary care is available if needed

➤ Whether a record is kept of how the cat is doing while boarded

➤ Whether your cat will be housed near dogs or other animals

➤ What food is provided

➤ Whether the staff will administer medications if needed

➤ The playtime and individual attention given to each animal

➤ Who will take care of the animals

➤ Whether anyone is on the premises after hours

➤ Whether you can bring any food or toys with the cat

Each boarding facility will have its own requirements. For your cat, these may include certain vaccines and flea control. You may be asked to leave a security deposit. To board at our cat clinic, cats must be currently vaccinated for rhinotracheitis, calici, and panleukopenia; they must be free of fleas or we require a bath; and we like a deposit or credit card imprint similar to what you would provide if you were staying at a hotel. We in turn will guarantee that the cat goes home clean, flea-free, and well cared for.

Meow Wow

There are high-class boarding facilities for cats that offer custom linens, beds, televisions, windows, and exercise facilities. Of course, you pay extra for these luxuries, but you may think it's worth it!

Pet Sitters

You may have a friend, neighbor, or relative that is willing to help care for your cat when you are away from home. If you will only be gone a few days, this may work well for you. If you are going to be gone longer, you need to make sure that your temporary caretaker is going to handle the job.

Things you will want done are:

➤ Feed the animal.

➤ Clean the litterbox.

➤ Check to see that the animal is eating and drinking.

➤ Check for vomiting and diarrhea.

➤ Be sure that the animal is bright and alert.

➤ Give medications if needed.

➤ Take the cat to a veterinarian if health problems arise.

Even though you know someone likes you and is willing to do you a favor, it doesn't mean they care as much as you do about your cat and are willing to be as observant as you might like. If you want to leave your cat at home and feel confident that someone responsible is watching it, you should consider a professional pet sitter. Look for listings in the Yellow Pages or ask your veterinary hospital for suggestions.

Pet sitters can be licensed, bonded, and belong to a national organization. Not only will they provide the services I just listed, pet sitters will bring in mail and newspapers and turn lights off and on to give the appearance that someone is home. If you use a professional pet sitter, ask to see her credentials and get references. You want to be able to trust a stranger coming in and out of your home.

The Big Move

Moving is a stress on all family members, including your cat. If it was up to your cat, it would keep things the way they are; but let's face it, your cat doesn't have a meow in the matter. You can take steps, however, to keep both human and feline stress levels down and help a move go as smoothly as possible.

You might want to confine your cat when the movers come. This can be a hectic and stressful time for everyone, felines included.

Avoid CATastrophe

If you choose to keep your cat at home during a move, put up a sign and alert others as to the cat's presence and whereabouts. Make sure movers know that, for example, the cat *is* in bathroom and the door should not be opened. There is nothing worse than trying to find a cat that has escaped from a house right when you are ready to leave.

Who Are These Strangers?

Many new faces may be present around a house before a move, such as realtors, prospective buyers, and workmen. When movers come in, doors can be left open, and boxes are coming and going. You need to be sure that your cat is kept safely indoors during this hectic time. You don't want the animal to accidentally get let out or get trapped in moving boxes.

Some suggestions for keeping a cat out of the way and preventing it from accidentally getting packed into a box are:

➤ Confine the cat to a room that no one will be using.

➤ Board the cat.

➤ Take the cat to a friend or relative's home.

➤ Buy a collapsible cage.

Getting Used to the New Digs

Each cat will respond to a move differently. Some may be curious and excited, others may stay hidden under a bed. Remember that a cat likes familiarity and will need time to adjust to its new surroundings.

The best way to acclimate a cat to a new home is to confine it to one room when you first get there so that it knows where its food, water, and litterbox are located. When you are settled and have time, let the cat out to explore and supervise its activities. It may only take a few days for a good comfort level to be reached.

Extra care is needed if you move a cat that has been used to going outside. You need to have the cat bond to the new home and not want to go searching for the old one. To do this, you should keep the cat indoors for at least two weeks. Put identification with your new address on the animal, and then start going out with it, supervised, for short periods daily.

You may want to place some familiar items outdoors, such as old lawn furniture or a towel or blanket, so that the cat has something to hone in on. It's also a good idea to check out the neighborhood for new dogs and other dangers your cat could face.

If Your Cat Is Lost

There is a sickening feeling when you come home at the end of a day, call for your cat, and it is nowhere to be found. Cats are very fond of routines, so when a behavior pattern is broken, it should make you concerned. First you should look for the cat in every nook and cranny inside the house. Rattle a bag or shake a can of your cat's favorite treats. Be aware that cats will occasionally escape outside but stay close to home. If the cat isn't found inside, search outside the house next.

Call Out the Search Team

If your cat does not turn up by mealtime, you will want to start an all-out search. Steps to take should include:

1. Posting "Lost Cat" signs in bold letters at intersections near your home.
2. Walking the neighborhood and knocking on doors and passing out your sign.
3. Visiting the local animal shelter.
4. Placing an ad in the local paper.
5. Distributing your sign to local veterinary clinics and pet stores.

Avoid CATastrophe

It is important to personally visit the local animal shelter and not rely on a phone call to look for your cat. Although well-meaning and careful, the employees or volunteers at the shelter may not describe your cat the same way you would. If the shelter only holds cats for five days, be sure to visit at least every four days.

Could There Be Another Explanation?

As much as you may not want to think about it, if your cat does not turn up, it is possible that some misfortune has occurred. This turn of events is even more likely if the animal was not wearing any type of identification. On the other hand, cats without ID can be mistaken for strays and are sometimes taken in by a kind-hearted person. If you live in an area where coyotes are found, they are the most common cause of death in cats that get outside.

It is easy to give up after a few days, but cats do tend to surprise us, so don't lose hope too quickly. Cats can get shut into garages or buildings that they wander into and suddenly show up at home when they are released. Many cats can survive by hunting and eating food at neighbor's homes and come back to your home when they are done with their adventures.

If You Die, What Happens to Your Cat?

Something a cat owner may not want to think about is what would happen to his pet if he were to die. In this day and age estate planning is recommended so you don't have to worry about how your personal matters will be resolved in case of death. If you own a cat, it is a good idea to plan for the animal in your estate.

Can You Count on Your Family?

Not everyone in your family may feel the same way about a pet as you do, but most are willing to take on the responsibility of a cat as long as allergies and logistics make it possible. A cat will grieve its owner, but it should be able to become integrated into a new home. Going to a new home with people that it is familiar with can ease the transition.

I have found that many family members are anxious to provide a home for a relative's cat because it provides a link to that person. When the cat becomes old and dies, another bond is ended, which is sad for all.

A senior citizen may wonder what will happen to her cat if it outlives her.

Check Out Your Will

Today it is common for owners to include their cat in their wills. You might laugh when you first think about it, but it really makes a lot of sense. There is no better way to ensure that a pet is provided for and cared for when the owner is no longer there.

Things to consider when putting a cat into your will or trust:

➤ Will the animal have an assigned guardian?

➤ Will money be set aside for the animal's care?

➤ Do you care what happens to the cat's body when it finally dies?

Worth a Paws

If you live in a state with community property laws, it is better for you to include your wishes for your cat in a living trust than to do so in a will. This measure will avoid probate and allow funds to be immediately available to any heirs, including your cat.

If you don't have someone lined up as a potential guardian for your cat, you may want to discuss the issue with your veterinarian. He may be willing to be a guardian or offer contacts with organizations near your home. In some areas there are "retirement homes" for cats. These homes can be set up as the cat's guardian, and for a pre-set fee, they will guarantee to house and feed the cat for the rest of its life.

Meow Wow

The Bluebell Foundation for Cats in Laguna Beach, California, takes in cats and cares for them for the rest of their lives for a fee of $5,000 per animal. Their facility can house up to 150 cats.

The Least You Need to Know

➤ Plan ahead if you want to take your cat on vacation with you.

➤ Boarding your cat or employing a pet sitter will be necessary if you leave your cat at home.

➤ During a move, cats can become very stressed, so it is a good idea to keep a cat confined.

➤ If your cat is lost, take an active role in finding it by conducting a neighborhood search, putting up flyers, placing an ad in the newspaper, and visiting your local animal shelter.

➤ It is a good idea to plan for your cat's safekeeping in your will.

Chapter 25

Are There Risks to Cat Ownership?

In This Chapter

➤ Human allergies to cats

➤ Why pregnant women shouldn't clean litterboxes

➤ Cat scratch fever—what is it?

Humans have successfully lived with cats for thousands of years, so it always surprises me when a pregnant woman comes into my office and tells me she needs to find a new home for her cat. In these situations, I wonder if her gynecologist has read any medical literature in the last 20 years because cat ownership is probably one of the smallest risks a pregnant woman faces.

Overall, cats are extremely safe pets to own, and they rarely transmit any diseases to humans. You are much more likely to contract a disease from your friends and family members than you are from a cat. There certainly are diseases that cats can transmit to humans, and I've touched on some of these, such as rabies and ringworm, in other parts of the book. I will shed light on some other transmissible diseases here, along with the problem facing many people—cat allergies.

Kitty Ditty

An **allergy** is a reaction to a substance that is not inherently noxious. In an allergic reaction, the immune system makes antibodies and triggers histamine release. This combination produces an inflammatory reaction.

Gesundheit!

It is estimated that 15 to 20 percent of the population may be *allergic* to pets. Humans that are allergic to cats can experience a range of signs from sniffling and sneezing to life-threatening asthma. Many owners know that they have allergies, but they feel that the benefits of cat ownership far outweigh the discomfort of the allergy.

How DO You Know It's the Cat?

If you experience watery eyes, sneezing, sore throat, or congestion every time you are around a cat, chances are that you are allergic to cats. Some people's allergies worsen over time. Others are only sensitive when exposed to a large dose of an allergen. For example, you might be able to tolerate living with one cat but have a terrible time when you go over to a friend's home where there are four.

Allergists can do skin testing to verify the existence of an allergy to cats, but unfortunately, there are no cures for allergies. Avoiding the allergen is the best way to prevent problems.

Less-Allergenic Breeds

Dander is the cat allergen that causes the most problems with people. The dander is flakes of cat skin, not hair. Another allergen is cat saliva. All cats lick and groom themselves to some extent, so this allergen can cover their entire body. All cats have skin and saliva, thus the major allergens are common to all cats.

Some people feel that allergic people better tolerate the breeds with little or no hair than other breeds. Breeds with little hair include Cornish and Devon Rexes, while the Sphynx is a breed with no hair. Longhaired cats may shed hairs with more dander attached, but their hair is no different from that of shorthaired cats. Each cat's chemistry is slightly different, so an allergic person would have to spend time with any prospective pets to see what the reaction would be.

Making Life More Bearable

There are some ways to make life easier for an allergic person to survive life with a cat. If you are allergic, you should:

➤ Wash your hands every time you touch a cat. If you touch your face first, you're asking for trouble.

➤ Do not allow cats in your bedroom. There is nothing worse for an allergic person than to place his face into a pillow full of dander.

➤ Consider using a HEPA filter unit or air purifier to knock allergens out of the air.

➤ Wipe the cat down with a damp rag or use a commercial anti-allergy pet solution daily to weekly, so that loose allergens are removed.

➤ Have the cat professionally groomed and well brushed out on a regular basis. This will limit allergens on top of shedding hairs.

➤ If possible, have just one cat. More cats means more allergens.

This cat's headboard "roost" is fine for the non-allergic owner.

People can work with their allergists to find treatments that help relieve the symptoms of cat allergies. Allergy shots and antihistamines are commonly used. There are a few antihistamines that can be taken regularly without side effects. Research is being conducted today that is looking at other ways the production of antibodies and release of histamine can be stopped in allergic individuals. In the future there may be better options for controlling allergies to cats.

Honey, It's Your Turn to Scoop

Toxoplasma gondii is a protozoan parasite, and protozoa are one-celled organisms. Toxoplasmosis, the disease caused by Toxoplasma organisms, can occur in any human or four-legged animal that ingests one of the infective stages of the protozoa. This organism has a complicated life cycle, which requires that it spend some of its development inside a host. Humans are frequently exposed to Toxoplasma and don't even know it. The biggest threat to humans occurs when a pregnant woman, during her first trimester, becomes infected with the organism. An infection at this time can cause congenital malformations or mental retardation of the fetus.

How Cats Become Infected

Cats become infected with Toxoplasma after they eat raw meat, birds, or mice carrying an infective stage of the organism. Cats shed Toxoplasma oocysts in their feces 3 to 10 days after eating infected tissues. They will shed the oocysts during their first exposure for up to 14 days, and afterward it is unlikely that they will ever shed them again. Within one to four days of being passed in the feces, the oocysts become infectious to other animals and humans. Infective oocysts can live for months in the environment (the litterbox or yard, wherever the cat has defecated). If feces are scooped daily and/or if rubber gloves are worn while scooping, there is little risk of exposure to Toxoplasma from your cat.

Keeping your cat indoors and only feeding commercially prepared cat food will eliminate risk of exposure.

Cats that are infected with Toxoplasma usually do not show any clinical signs and are healthy. A cat that is also infected with FeLV or FIV is more likely to become sick. If a cat develops Toxoplasmosis, the signs of illness can be:

➤ Lethargy

➤ Anorexia

➤ Fever

➤ Diarrhea

➤ Pneumonia

➤ Hepatitis

➤ Uveitis (a type of inflammation of the eye)

➤ Neurological disease

A blood test that measures antibodies to Toxoplasma is used to diagnose the disease in cats. Testing for two different antibodies (Ig G and Ig M) a few weeks apart and finding rising titers is the best method for making an accurate diagnosis.

How Humans Are Infected

Humans can become infected if they touch an oocyst, don't wash their hands, and then touch their mouths. Eating raw meat or drinking unpasteurized dairy products can also expose people to the parasite. Healthy humans who are exposed to Toxoplasma may suffer a brief illness with fever, muscle pain, enlarged lymph nodes, anorexia, and sore throat. People that have compromised immune systems—such as organ transplant recipients or AIDS patients—need to be as careful as pregnant women to prevent infection.

There are many precautions that can be taken to prevent infection:

➤ Wear rubber gloves and wash hands thoroughly after outdoor gardening.

➤ Cover up children's sandboxes when not in use to prevent cats from using them as litterboxes and depositing oocysts.

➤ Empty litterboxes daily so that oocysts will not have the opportunity to develop to the infective stage. Wear rubber gloves for this job or have another family member do it.

➤ Eat only thoroughly cooked meat and wash hands vigorously if you handle raw meat or vegetables.

➤ Consume only pasteurized dairy products.

➤ Have yourself tested for antibodies to *Toxoplasma gondii*. If you are already positive, there is little risk that you will become ill unless your immune system is compromised.

➤ Wash your hands after coming in contact with your cat.

Meow Wow

It is estimated that in some parts of the world, 10 percent of the lamb and 25 percent of the pork are infected with Toxoplasma cysts. Cows and goats can also be infected, so consuming unpasteurized dairy products is not recommended.

For a pregnant woman to become infected through her cat, a series of events must occur. In actuality, it would be extremely rare for a pregnant woman to be directly infected by a cat. If you have an indoor cat that never eats raw meat or gets outside to hunt and eat birds and rodents, you are essentially at no risk. In fact, 30 to 50 percent of women in the world have been previously exposed to Toxoplasma. These women develop immunity, and in these situations there is no risk to a later pregnancy.

Treatment for Toxoplasmosis

There are medications that are effective for treating cats and healthy humans with Toxoplasmosis. Unfortunately, even if an infected pregnant woman receives treatment in her first trimester, birth defects cannot be prevented.

We have reached the 21st century, but many physicians are underinformed about pregnant women and cats. Any woman considering pregnancy should know about Toxoplasmosis; but to hear some doctors talk, if you want to get pregnant, you should get rid of your cat, and this is ridiculous. Millions if not billions of women have been exposed to cats over time and have somehow managed to produce healthy children.

Cat Scratch Fever Really Exists

You may not realize it, but cat scratch disease is a real problem. It is caused by *Bartonella henselae,* which is a common bacteria found worldwide. Infection typically occurs when a kitten breaks the surface of a person's skin through a bite or scratch. Eighty percent of the cases occur in people under the age of 21. People who have compromised immune systems are also at risk for cat scratch disease.

It is possible that at some time in their lives about half of all cats will have an infection with *Bartonella henselae,* and although they appear healthy, they can carry the bacteria for months. Cat scratches commonly occur, but fortunately human cat scratch disease occurs infrequently.

Signs of Cat Scratch Fever

Humans become infected when a kitten or cat scratches or bites them and injects *Bartonella henselae* bacteria into the body. It may take about two weeks, but a lymph node near the initial injury site will then swell, and the surrounding tissues will become red and tender.

Other clinical signs that can be seen in humans are:

➤ Fever

➤ Fatigue

➤ Loss of appetite

➤ Headache

➤ Sore throat

➤ Blurred vision

➤ Joint pain

Diagnosis and Treatment

When clinical signs in humans suggest that cat scratch disease is a possibility, a positive diagnosis is made by:

➤ History of exposure to a cat or kitten

➤ Tests to rule out other causes of swollen lymph nodes

➤ A positive cat scratch disease blood test

In almost all cases, the swollen lymph nodes usually disappear within a few weeks to months, even without treatment. If you have had a previous exposure to cat scratch disease, it is unlikely that the bacteria will ever bother you again. People can take anti-inflammatory medications to help reduce the pain of the swollen lymph nodes.

In some individuals, the lymph nodes become abscessed and need to be surgically drained. In these cases, or when individuals with compromised immune systems are infected, antibiotics are used. People with cat scratch disease are not contagious to others.

This young girl is being cautious as she holds an unfamiliar cat.

If you are concerned about cat scratch disease because of your personal health problems, there is a test that can check your cat's blood for the agent. Because they show no signs of the disease, cats are not routinely treated with antibiotics. To help prevent cat scratch disease:

➤ Be cautious when handling unfamiliar cats.

➤ Keep your cat's toenails trimmed.

➤ Do not allow your cat to bite and scratch during interactive play.

The Joys of Cat Ownership

I included this last chapter as an information resource to help dispel myths surrounding diseases that cats can transmit. Unfortunately, some people are allergic to cats, but aside from this problem, the likelihood of any other health problems arising from cat ownership are extremely low.

Owning a cat will enrich your life and offer far more benefits than risks. Cats are wonderful additions that really do want and need us. Studies show that on average, pet owners live longer than non-pet owners do. I know that after a long day at the office, there is nothing I like better than to cuddle with one of my cats and have it purr in my ear! Cats are super stress relievers. They are curious, mischievous, and very entertaining to watch. They also do a good job of ridding your house of bugs.

Most cats require little care and live long lives. They can easily fit into our busy lives or be constant companions. If you've made it to this part of the book, you have the tools you need to create a happy home for you and your cat.

The Least You Need to Know

➤ People with cat allergies can take some steps to make their lives more comfortable.

➤ Pregnant women need to know about Toxoplasmosis, but there is no need for them to give up their cat.

➤ Cat scratch disease usually causes a temporary inflammation of lymph nodes and resolves without other treatment.

➤ The benefits of cat ownership far outweigh the risks.

Glossary

Abscess   A hole filled with pus and surrounded by infected tissue.

Acute   A disease that begins quickly.

Adulticide   A product that kills adult insects.

Allergens   Foreign substances that cause an allergic response in some animals.

Anaphylaxis   A severe and potentially fatal allergic reaction.

Anemia   Low red blood cell count.

Anorexia   A lack of appetite for food.

Anterior drawer sign   Laxity present in the knee when the anterior cruciate ligament is damaged.

Antibody   Protein produced in the body as a response to contact with another foreign protein.

Antigen   Foreign substance that causes the body to produce an antibody.

Association of American Feed Control Officials (AAFCO)   Organization responsible for creating practical nutritional recommendations for pet food.

Atopy   Inhaled allergy.

Auscultation   To listen to the heart and lungs with a stethoscope.

Benign   Harmless.

Bilateral   On two sides.

Brachycephalic   Flattened facial structure characteristic of Persian cats.

Cancer   Cells that lack a controlled growth pattern.

Cardiomyopathy   Heart muscle disease.

Carnivore   A meat-eating animal.

Castration   Removal of the testicles.

Catnip   A plant in the mint family that has hallucinogenic effects on cats.

Chitin   A protein found in insect skeletons.

Cholagiohepatitis   Inflammation of the bile ducts and liver.

Chronic   A disease that develops slowly or persists for a long time.

Coccidia   A type of protozoal parasite of the gastrointestinal system.

Colostrum   The antibody-rich first milk an animal produces.

Conjunctivitis   Inflammation of the tissue around the eyeball.

Corneal ulcer   Abrasion or scratch on the surface of the eye.

Cryotherapy   A medical procedure that freezes tissues.

Cryptococcus   A type of fungus.

Cytology   Microscopic evaluation of cell structure.

Dermatophytes   A group of fungus capable of causing ringworm.

Dialysis   Process in which a body fluid is removed from the body and cleaned.

Diaphragm   The muscular band that separates the chest and abdominal cavities.

Diastole   Pressure when the heart relaxes.

Dietary indiscretion   Eating something other than food.

Diuresis   Process that causes the body to produce and eliminate more urine.

ECG   An electrocardiogram, which measures the electrical activity of the heart.

Echocardiogram   Evaluates the heart using sound waves.

EEG   An electroencephalogram, a test that measures the electrical activity of the brain.

Elizabethan collar   Protective collar that prevents the animal from licking.

Estrous cycle   The normal four-stage fertility cycle in a female cat.

Foreign body   A substance that is in the wrong place.

Giardia   A type of protozoal parasite of the gastrointestinal system.

Gingivitis   Inflamed gums.

Hepatic lipidosis   A disease of the liver caused by too much fat breakdown.

Hernia   A protrusion of an organ through a tear in a muscle.

Hip dysplasia   Poor conformation of the hip joints.

Holistic   A system of total patient care that considers physical, emotional, social, economic, and spiritual needs.

House-soiling   Inappropriate elimination; in a cat, outside of a litterbox on a horizontal surface.

Hypertension   High blood pressure.

Hyperthyroid   Having an overactive thyroid gland.

Hypoglycemic   Low blood sugar.

Hyposensitize   To decrease an allergic response by injecting antigens.

Idiopathic   Occurring for no known cause.

Incontinence   Loss of control of a body function.

Inguinal   Near the groin.

Interstitial cystitis   Benign inflammatory condition of the bladder.

Jaundice   A yellowish discoloration of tissues due to bile pigments in the blood.

Lethargy   Feeling indifferent or sluggish.

Luxating patella   Kneecap that pops out of joint.

Malignant   A tumor that can invade other tissues and/or spread through the bloodstream.

Mastectomy   Surgical removal of an entire mammary gland.

Maternal immunity   Protective antibodies received from the animal's mother through nursing.

Megacolon   Abnormal widening of the large intestine that causes constipation in cats.

Miliary dermatitis   A crusty, scaly skin condition.

Mutation   A change that occurs within a gene.

Nebulization   A process that creates an aerosol mist.

Neoplasia   Abnormal growth of new tissue.

Neutering   Removing an animal's sex organs.

Nocturnal   Active at night.

Oncologist   A doctor who specializes in treating cancer.

Ovariohysterectomy   Surgical removal of the uterus and ovaries.

Palpation   Using the fingers and hands to examine parts of the body.

Pectus excavatum   Congenital abnormality causing a flattened rib cage.

Pericardial   Having to do with the sac that surrounds the heart.

Peritonitis   Inflammation within the abdominal cavity.

Pheromone   Chemical signals that are present in different animal secretions.

Polydactyl   More than the normal number of toes.

Polyestrus   Able to have multiple estrus cycles throughout the year.

Prostaglandins   Special fatty acids that can act like hormones.

Protozoa   A type of one-celled organism.

Pyometra   Infected, pus-filled uterus.

Radioisotope   An element that gives off radiation.

Renal   Having to do with the kidneys.

Spaying   Surgical removal of the uterus and ovaries.

Spraying   Depositing urine on a vertical surface.

Squamous cell carcinoma   A type of skin cancer.

Subcutaneous   Having to do with the tissue under the skin.

Systole   Pressure when the heart contracts.

Trichobezoars   Hairballs.

Turgor   The normal strength and tension of the skin created by fluid.

Unilateral   On one side.

Urohydropropulsion   A technique for forcing small stones out of the bladder.

Urolith   A stone in the urinary tract.

Uveitis   Inflammation of the iris, choroid, and ciliary body of an eye.

Vascular   Having to do with blood vessels.

Readings and Resources

The Cat Care Clinic

Dr. Wexler-Mitchell's Clinic
The Cat Care Clinic
2638 North Tustin Avenue
Orange, CA 92865
(714) 282-CATS (2287)
www.catcare.com

Books

Allport, Richard. *Heal Your Cat the Natural Way.* New York: Howell Book House, 1997.

Carlson, Delbert G. and James M. Giffin. *The Cat Owner's Home Veterinary Handbook.* New York: Howell Book House, 1995.

Church, Christine. *Housecat: How to Keep Your Indoor Cat Sane and Sound.* New York: Howell Book House, 1998.

Commings, Karen. *Shelter Cats.* New York: Howell Book House, 1998.

Evans, J.M. and Kay White. *The Catlopedia: A Complete Guide to Cat Care.* New York: Howell Book House, 1997.

Fogel, Bruce, D.V.M. *The Cat's Mind: Understanding Your Cat's Behavior.* New York: Howell Book House, 1992.

Foster, Race, D.V.M. and Marty Smith, D.V.M. *The Complete Cat Health Manual.* New York: Howell Book House, 1997.

Hawcroft, Tim, B.V.Sc.(Hons), M.A.C.V.Sc. *First Aid for Cats: The Essential Quick-Reference Guide.* New York: Howell Book House, 1994.

Schwartz, Stefanie. *First Aid for Cats: An Owner's Guide to a Happy Healthy Pet.* New York: Howell Book House, 1998.

Viner, Bradley, M.R.C.V.S. *A-Z of Cat Diseases & Health Problems.* New York: Howell Book House, 1998.

Monthly Magazines About Cats

Cat Fancy
www.catfancy.com

Cats Magazine
www.catsmag.com

Internet Sites with General Information on Cats

Cornell Feline Health Center
College of Veterinary Medicine
Cornell University
Ithaca, NY 14853
(607) 253-3414
http://web.vet.cornell.edu/Public/FHC

American Veterinary Medical Association
1931 North Meachum Road, Suite 100
Schaumburg, IL 60173
(847) 925-8070
www.avma.org/care4pets/default.htm

American Animal Hospital Association
12575 West Bayaud Avenue
Denver, CO 80215
(303) 986-2800
www.healthypet.com

American Association of Feline Practitioners
2701 San Pedro NE, Suite 7
Albuquerque, NM 87110
(505) 888-2424
http://avma.org/aafp

Net Vet:
www.avma.org/netvet/cats.htm
A site with many links for cat care, cat breeds, diseases, and the like.

www.suite101.com/welcmoe.cfm/cats
A site with various links, bulletin boards, and cat articles.

www.thepetchannel.com
A site with health and behavior tips, pet facts, and products.

Internet Sites on Specific Issues

Chronic Renal Failure:
www.best.com/~lynxpt/

Feline Infectious Peritonitis:
www2.dgsys.com/~ermiller/FIP.html

Feline Leukemia Virus:
www2.dgsys.com/~ermiller/FeLV.html

Feline Immunodeficiency Virus:
www.web.vet.cornell.edu/Public/FHC/fiv.htm

Vaccine decisions and sarcomas:
www.avma.org/vafstf/ownbroch.html

Hyperthyroidism:
www.radiocat.com

Cat Rescue and Humane Organizations

Humane Society of the United States
2100 L Street NW
Washington, DC 20037
www.hsus.org

The American Society for the Prevention of Cruelty to Animals (ASPCA)
424 East 92nd Street
New York, NY 10128
(212) 876-7700
www.aspca.org

www.h4ha.org/directory/index.htm
A site listing shelters, humane societies, and rescue groups worldwide.

www.geocities.com/Heartland/Prairie/2461/rescue.html
A site listing cat rescue organizations.

Information on Poisons

National Animal Poison Control Center
(800) 548-2423
$30 per case, credit cards only

Poisonous plant guide:
www.ansci.cornell.edu/plants/plants.html

Index

A

AAFCO (Association of American Feed Control Officials), 14, 287
AAFP (American Association of Feline Practitioners), 102
abscesses, wounds, 254–255, 287
ABVP (American Board of Veterinary Practitioners), 102
acetaminophen (Tylenol), 53
ACL (anterior cruciate ligament) injury, 198–199
acne, feline acne, 171–172
acute diseases, 148
adult cats, 6–7
Advantage (flea control), 73, 262
AFM (Academy of Feline Medicine), 102
aggression, 111, 258–259
    petting-induced, 258–259
aging, 127–140
allergens, 169, 287
allergic dermatitis, fleas and, 73
allergies, 145, 168–170
    atopy, 169–170
    contact allergies, 170–171
    eosinophilic granulomas, 169
    fleas, 170
    food allergies, 170
    human to cat, 280–281
    miliary dermatitis, 168
amputation, 197
anaphylactic reactions to stings, 57–58
anaphylaxis, 287
anemia, 182–184, 287
    cancer and, 132
    FeLV and, 91
    fleas and, 73, 183, 263
    liver disease and, 133
anesthesia, surgery and, 76
anorexia, 50–51, 287
    feline herpesvirus and, 89
    panleukopenia and, 88
    toxoplasmosis and, 282
anti-inflammatory medication, 195
antibodies, 287
antifreeze, 230, 264

antigens, 169, 287
    anti-inflammatory medication, 195
    GAGS, 196
aspirin, 53, 195–196
asthma, 149–150
atopy, 169–170, 287
auscultation (listening to heart), 185, 287

B

bacterial infections
    gastrointestinal, 157
    URIs, 148
bathing, 44–45
bee stings, 176
behavior, 257–261
    illness and, 53–54
birth, 122–124
    discharge after, 123
    examining newborns, 124
    labor, 122–123
    orphan kittens, 124–125
birth control, 121
biting, 26–27, 111
    rabies and, 242
bleeding
    noses, 144
    stopping, 181–182
    urine, 54
blindness, 216
bloating, 54
blood, 54, 181
    anemia, 182–184
    in urine, 224–225
    in stool, 160
    types, 184
blood urea nitrogen (BUN), 131
boarding, 271–272
bones, 193–202
books, 291–292
Bordetella, 93
bowel movements, 57
brachycephalic face (Persians), 199, 287
breast cancer, 210–211
breath, bad, 154
breathing, hernia and, 82

breeding, 119
broken bones, 196–197
brushing teeth, 69–70
brushing/combing, 41–44
    flea combs, 41–42
    hairballs, 43
    longhaired cats, 42–44
    shorthaired cats, 44
bulimia, 157

C

caffeine, 16
calici vaccine, 88–89
cancer, 132, 287
    breast cancer, 210–211
    intestinal, 161
    skin cancer, 177–178
canned food, 14
    urinary problems and, 224
cardiomyopathy, 288
cardiovascular system. See also circulatory system; heart, 179–191
carriers, 5–6, 268–269
carsickness, 57
castration, 288
cat beds, 33
cat scratch fever, 284–285
cat veterinary practices, 102
catnip, 218, 288
cauda equina syndrome, 221
cerebellar hypoplasia, 219
chewing, 108
Cheyletiella, 175
chitin, 288
Chlamydia, 91
    conjunctivitis and, 215
chocolate, 16, 264
cholagiohepatitis, 288
chronic diseases, 148
chronic renal failure, 131
cigarette smoke, 145
circulatory system, 179–191
claws
    grooming, 40
    trimming, bleeding and, 182
cleaning around eyes, 56
cleaning litterbox, 22

coccidia, 72, 288
colds. *See also* URIs (upper respiratory infections), 54
colostrum, 124, 288
conflicts, 253–256
congenital neurological problems, 219–220
congenital heart disease, 184–186
conjunctivitis, 54, 215, 288
  Chlamydia and, 91
  feline herpesvirus and, 89
constipation, 54, 57, 161–162
contact allergies, 170–171
convulsions, 216–218
coolant, 264
corneal sequestrum, 214
corneal ulcers, 214, 288
coronavirus, FIP, 239–240
coughing, 54
  asthma and, 149
creams/ointments, 56
creatinine, 131
cryotherapy, 288
cryptococcus, 288
cryptorchidism, 79–80
crystals, urinary, 228
cuts, cleaning, 56
cystitis, interstitial cystitis, 225
cytology, 177, 288

D–E

deafness, 135
declawing, 75
  alternatives, 77
  anesthesia, 76
  side effects, 78
deformities, bone, 199–202
degenerative joint disease (DJD), 137
dehydration, 17
  panleukopenia and, 88
  vomiting and, 157–158
Demodex, 176
dental care, 69–71
  aching teeth, 154
  bad breath, 154
  gingivitis, 288
  gums, 154–155
  senior cats, 136
dermatophytes, 288
development levels, 107–116
diabetes, 132, 207–209
dialysis, 232, 288
diaphragm, 288
diaphragmatic hernia, 82
diarrhea, 54, 159–161
  FIP and, 239
  panleukopenia and, 88
  toxoplasmosis and, 282

diastole, 288
dilated cardiomyopathy (DCM), heart disease, 187
discipline. *See also* training, 109–112
diseases
  acute, 148
  chronic, 148
  spreading, 87
diuresis, 288
DJD (degenerative joint disease), 194–196
dominance, 110
dry food, 15

ear mites, 174–175
ECG, 285
echocardiogram, 288
EEG, 288
electronic litterboxes, 20–21
elimination
  inappropriate, 22, 259–260
  orphan kittens, 125
Elizabethan collars, 288
emergency care, 55, 103
endocrinology
  diabetes, 207–209
  thyroid, 203–206
  uterine infections, 209
endoscopic biopsy, 160
eosinophilic granulomas, 169
estrous cycle, 114, 115, 288
euthanasia, 138–140
excessive licking, 55
eyes
  conjunctivitis, 215
  corneal sequestrum, 214
  corneal ulcers, 214
  excessive tearing, 216

F

fatty liver disease, 162–163
FECV (Feline Enteric Corona Virus), 92–93, 239–240
feeding orphan kittens, 125
feeding tubes, 164
feline calicivirus, 89
feline herpesvirus, 89
feline hyperesthesia syndrome, 259
Feline Infectious Anemia, 184
feline infectious peritonitis. *See* FIP
Feline Leukemia. *See* FeLV
feline panleukopenia, 243
feline rhinotracheitis, 147
feline rhinotracheitis, calici, and panleukopenia (FRCP), 88–89

Feliway, 29
FeLV (feline leukemia virus), 10, 91–92, 235–237
  gum disease and, 155
  spreading, 78
fever, 51–53, 54
  panleukopenia and, 88
fights, 253–256
  other animals, 255
FIP (Feline Infectious Peritonitis), 92–93, 239–242
first aid kit, 56–58
FIV (Feline Immunodeficiency Virus), 10, 237–239
  gum disease and, 155
  spreading, 78
fixing. *See* neutering; spaying
flea allergies, 170
flea combs, 41–42
fleas, 72–74, 261–263
  anemia and, 183
  control, 262–263
  senior cats, 137
flying, 270–271
foaming mouth, medication and, 60
food bowls, acne and, 172
food. *See also* nutrition allergies, 170
  appetite, 50–51
  canned, 14
  dry food, 15
  kittens, 4
  light diets, 16
  seafood, urinary tract infections and, 15
  toxic items, 16
  urinary tracts and, 15
  variety, 16
foreign body in intestines, 158
foreign objects in nose, 145
fungal infections (URIs), 148–149
FUS (Feline Urologic Syndrome), 224

G–H

gagging, asthma and, 149
gas, 54
gender, personality differences, 249
GI (gastrointestinal tract), 153–165
  bacterial infections, 157
  constipation, 161–162
  IBD (inflammatory bowel disease), 160
  intestinal cancer, 161
  stool characteristics, 159–160

295

viral infections, 157
vomiting, 155–158
giardia, 72, 288
gingivitis, 288
glycosaminoglycans (GAGS),
arthritis and, 196
groomers, 46–48
grooming
brushing teeth, 69–70
brushing/combing, 41–44
claws, 40
growth stages, 112–113
gums (dental care), 154–155

hairballs, 43, 155
coughing up, 156
excessive licking and, 258
handling, 7–9
head shaking, 54
heart, 179–191
diseases, 133
evaluating, 186
leaky valves, 185
heart murmur, 187
heartworm disease, 189–191
heat, 114
heatstroke, 264
cars and, 270
hepatic lipidosis (fatty liver
disease), 162–163, 288
hernias, 82–83, 288
high blood pressure, 189
hip dysplasia, 195, 289
holistic care, 289
holistic veterinarians, 103–104
hooded litterboxes, 20
hookworms, 72
house-soiling, 259–260, 289
human allergies to cats, 280–271
humane organizations, 293
hunting behavior, 27, 109
hydrocephalus, 219
hydrogen peroxide, 172
wounds and, 254
hyperglycemia, diabetes and, 208
hypertension (high blood
pressure), 131, 189, 289
hyperthyroidism, 130, 204–206,
289
hypertrophic cardiomyopathy
(HCM), heart disease, 187–188
hypoglycemic, 289
hyposensitize, 289

I–J

IBD (inflammatory bowel disease),
133, 160
ibuprofen, 53

identification, 251
illness. *See also* disease, 49–61
appetite, 51
behavior and, 53–54
diagnosing, 49–61
failure to respond, 54
FeLV, 10
FIV, 10
irritability, 54
medicine, 58–61
respiratory infections, 10
severity, 55
signs of, 54–55
upset stomach, 56
water, 51
immune system
FeLV and, 236
FIV and, 238
incontinence, 289
indoors *vs.* outdoors, 22–24
inguinal hernias, 82
injuries, 253–255
insect bites, 176
interstitial cystitis (IC), 225, 289
intestinal cancer, 161
intestinal lymphosarcoma, 161
intestinal parasites, 71–72
irritability, illness and, 54
irritants, sneezing and, 145
itching, 55, 168–171

jaundice, 55, 162, 289
liver disease and, 133
joints, 195

K–L

kidney stones, 227
kidneys, 229–233
kitten food vs. adult, 17
kittens
chewing, 108
coming home, 5–6
growth stages, 112–113
milk replacement, 4
newborns, examining, 124
nursing, 108
orphaned, 4, 124–125
overview, 3–6
personality testing, 5
playing, 108–109
safety, 4–5
sexual maturity, 113–116
teething, 26
toys, 5
weaning, 4, 108

labor
difficult, responding to, 123
stages of, 123

lesions, 168
lethargy, 289
asthma and, 150
toxoplasmosis and, 282
licking, excessive, 258
life expectancy, 127–128
limping, 55
liquid medication, 59
litterboxes. *See also* elimination,
inappropriate, 20–22
breaking training, 111,
259–260
dogs and, 11
maintenance, 22
privacy, 19
Toxoplasmosis, 281–284
training, 29–31
types of litter, 21–22
liver, 162–165
liver disease, 133
longhaired cats
grooming, 42
matting, 43–44
lost cats, 275
lower respiratory disorders
asthma, 149–150
pneumonia, 150–151
LSA (intestinal lymphosarcoma),
161
lufenuron (flea control), 263
lung disease, 134
LUTD (Lower Urinary Tract
Disease), 224–226
luxating patella, 289

M–N

mange, Demodex, 176
mastectomy, 289
maternal immunity, 289
mating, 117–119
mats
longhaired cats, 43–44
shorthaired cats, 44
medication, 58–61
anti-anxiety, inappropriate
elimination and, 260
pain-relievers, surgery and, 76
megacolon, 162, 289
Metamucil, 161
miliary dermatitis, 168, 289
milk, replacement, 4, 125
mites
Cheyletiella, 175
Demodex, 176
ear mites, 174–175
scabies, 175
motion sickness, 57
moving, 273–274
multiple cats. *See* social interaction

musculoskeletal system
  arthritis, 193–196
  deformities, 199–202
  hip dysplasia, 195
  polydactyl cats, 200–201
  skull, 200
  soft-tissue injuries, 197–199
mutation, 289

nasal congestion, 55
nasolacrimal duct, eyes, 216
negative attention, 109–112
neoplasia, 132, 289
nervous system, 213–222
neurologic problems, congenital,
  219–220
neurological disease, 134
neutering, 78–80, 289
  personality and, 79
  timing, 113
night time playing, 31–33
night vision, 32
non-core vaccines, 90–94
noses
  bloody, 144
  foreign objects, 145
  sneezing, 144–146
  warm, 51–52
  wiping, 145
nursing, 108
  colostrum, 124

O–P

oils, car, 58
ointments/creams, 56
oncologists, 289
onions, 16
open litterboxes, 20
orphaned kittens, 4, 124–125
outdoors vs. indoors, 22–24
ovariohysterectomy, 81, 121, 289
overweight problems, 16
oxygenation, blood, 180

pain medication, 195
palpation, 289
panleukopenia vaccine, 88–89
paralysis, aortic thrombosis and,
  188
parasites
  fleas, 72–74
  Hemobartonella, anemia and,
    183
  mites, 174–176
  senior cats, 137
  worms, 71–72
parvo virus, 88, 243
pericardial, 290

pericardial-diaphragmatic hernia,
  82
pericardium, 180
perineal urethrotomy (PU), 227
peritonitis, 290
pet sitters, 272–273
petting-induced aggression,
  258–259
pheromones, 290
  scratching and, 29
physical exam, 64–66
pills, 59–60
pinkeye. *See* conjuctivitis
pinworms, 74
placenta, 123
play, 108–109
  biting, 26–27
  multiple cats, 109
pneumonia, 150–151
poison information, 293
poisons, 16
polycystic kidney disease, 231
polydactyl cats, 40, 200–201, 290
polyestrus, 290
pregnancy
  signs of, 119–120
  spaying and, 80–82
  termination, 120–121
pregnant women and toxoplasmosis, 282–283
prostaglandins, 290
protozoa, 290
psyllium, constipation and, 161
PU (perineal urethrotomy), 227
punishment, 30
pyometra, 209, 290

Q–R

queen, 119

rabies, 89–90, 242–243
radioisotope, 290
regurgitation, 157
  dry food and, 15
reinforcing behavior, 110
renal amyloidosis, 231
renal diseases, 229–233
renal failure, 131
reproduction, 117–126
  birth, 122–124
  birth control, 121
  mating, 117–119
  pregnancy, 119–121
rescue organizations, 293
respiratory infection, 10
respiratory system, 143–151
  asthma, 149–150
  URIs (upper respiratory
    infections), 146–149

restrictive cardiomyopathy
  (RCM), heart disease, 187, 188
ringworm, 172–173
  vaccine, 93
roundworms, 72

S

safety, 4-5
  outdoors, 22–23
scabies, 175
scratching, 27–29
scratching posts, 77, 108
seafood, urinary tract infections
  and, 15
seasonal dangers, 263–265
seizures, 55, 216–218
senior cats, 127–140
  arthritis, 137
  cancer, 132
  chronic renal failure, 131
  dental care, 136
  diabetes, 132
  euthanasia, 138–140
  fleas, 137
  heart disease and, 133
  hydration, 135–136
  hypertension, 131
  hyperthyroidism, 130
  IBD (inflammatory bowel
    disease), 133
  kidneys, 231–232
  liver disease, 133
  lung disease, 134
  neurological disease, 134
  nutrition, 136
  parasites, 137
  stroke, 134
sexual maturity, 113–116
shampoos, 45
shorthaired cats, mats, 44
signs of illness, 54–55
skin, 167–178
  acne, 171–172
  allergies, 168–170
  cancer, 177–17
  ear mites, 174–175
  insect bites, 176
  lesions, 168
  ringworm, 172–173
  scabies, 174–175
  spider bites, 176
sleeping, 31–33
slipped disks, 221
sneezing, 55, 144–146
  feline herpesvirus and, 89
social interaction, 247–256
  age and, 249
  conflicts, 253–256
  strays, taking in, 250–252

297

soft-tissue injuries, 197–199
spaying, 80–82, 290
    benefits, 81–82
    timing, 113
specialists, 101–104
spider bites, 176
spina bifida, 219
spinal disorders, 220–222
    cauda equina syndrome, 221
    slipped disks, 221
spine, tail and, 8
sprains, 197–199
spraying, 290
squamous cell carcinoma (SCC),
    177, 290
sterilization, timing, 113
stings, 57–58
stomach. *See also* gastrointesinal
    tract
stones, 227–229
straining to eliminate, 55
strains, 197–199
strays, 250–252
    trespassing cats, 252–253
stress, URIs and, 146
stroke, 134
surgery
    bone deformities, 201
    declawing, 75–78
    hernia, 82–83
    spaying, 80–82
sweating, 65
swelling, 55
systole, 290

T

tail
    broken, 221
    kinks, 199
    spine and, 8
    wagging, 258
tapeworms, 72
    fleas and, 73–74, 263
taurine, 187
tearing, eyes, 216
teeth, 69–71
    aching, 154
    canned food and, 14
teething, 26
testicles, 79–80
testosterone, 78–79
thermometers, 52
thrombus (heart), 188
thyroid, 203–206
timid cats, 9, 112
toenails. *See* claws

topical vaccines, 89
Toxoplasmosis, 281–284
toys, 5
    hunting play, 27
training, 25–35, 109–112
    biting, 26–27
    counters, 34–35
    litterbox, 29–31
    punishment, 30
    reinforcing behavior, 110
    scratching, 27–29
tranquilizers, traveling and, 267
traveling
    boarding, 271–272
    car rides, 269–270
    flying, 270–271
    hotels, 271
    pet sitters, 272–273
    tranquilizers and, 267
trespassing cats, 252–253
trichobezoars, 43, 290
trimming claws, 40
turgor, 290
Tylenol, 53

U–V

umbilical hernia, 82
upset stomach, 56
urethral obstructions, 226–227
urinary problems, 223–233
    diet and, 224, 226
    inability to, 226–227
    renal diseases, 229–233
    stones, 227–229
    straining to urinate, 225
urinary tract
    canned food and, 14
    seafood, 15
urination
    bloody, 54
    hyperthyroidism and, 204
    orphan kittens, 125
    tomcats, 78
URIs (upper respiratory infec-
    tions), 146–149
    bacterial infections, 148
    fungal infections, 148–149
    viral infections, 147
uterine infections, 209
uveitis, 290

vacationing, 267–271
vaccinations, 66–69, 85–94
    core vaccines, 87–90
    disease spread and, 87
    FIP, 241

non-core vaccines, 90–94
    risks of, 86–87
    side effects, 94
    topical vaccines, 89
veterinarians
    cat practices, 102
    checklist for choosing, 99
    education, 95
    emergency medicine, 103–104
    full-service clinic, 97–98
    licensed animal health
        technician, 100
    referrals, 98
    selecting, 95–104
    senior cats, 129–130
    specialists, 101–104
    visiting before selection, 96
viral infections
    gastrointestinal, 157
    URIs, 147
viruses, 235–244
    feline panleukopenia, 243
    FeLV, 235–237
    FIP, 239–242
    FIV, 237–239
    parvo, 243
    rabies, 242–243
    strays and, 251
vision, night, 32
vocalization, excessive, 261
vomiting, 55, 155–158
    FIP and, 239
    liver disease and, 133
    panleukopenia and, 88
    regurgitation, 157
    vaccinations and, 94

W

wagging tails, 258
warm nose, 51–52
water, 17–18
    drinking more than normal, 54
    illness and, 51
watering eyes, 216
weaning kittens, 4, 108
weight, 55
    cancer and, 132
    chronic renal failure and, 132
    FIP and, 239
    hyperthyroidism and, 204
    liver disease and, 133
wheezing, asthma and, 150
whipworms, 72
whiskers, 7
worms, 55, 71–72